Hendrick B. Wright

Historical Sketches of Plymouth

Luzerne co., Penna

Hendrick B. Wright

Historical Sketches of Plymouth
Luzerne co., Penna

ISBN/EAN: 9783337117771

Printed in Europe, USA, Canada, Australia, Japan

Cover: Foto ©Andreas Hilbeck / pixelio.de

More available books at **www.hansebooks.com**

HISTORICAL SKETCHES

OF

PLYMOUTH,

LUZERNE CO., PENNA.

BY HENDRICK B. WRIGHT,

OF WILKES-BARRÉ, PA

With Twenty-Five Photographs of some of the Early Settlers and Present
Residents of the Town of Plymouth; Old Landmarks; Family
Residences; and Places of Special Note.

PHILADELPHIA:

T. B. PETERSON & BROTHERS;

306 CHESTNUT STREET.

DEDICATION.

———•———

To Henderson Gaylord, Esq.,

My Dear Sir:—Three of your name and kindred were members of Captain Samuel Ransom's company, in the Revolutionary War. Another was a lieutenant in Captain Whittlesey's company, and fell in the memorable battle of Wyoming, on the third of July, 1778.

Among the brave men who volunteered under the flag of our country in the recent Rebellion, your son, Asher, occupied as proud a position for courage as the best of them; and was stricken down upon the field, covered with three honorable scars, which he had previously received in the same number of engagements.

A private of his company informed me, since the following sketches were prepared for the press, that

(17)

"Captain Gaylord was ever in front of his men in the heat of action; bidding them 'to follow him.' A braver soldier, or more daring man, never drew sword from scabbard."

As the survivor, therefore, of a family possessing such a record; and having been yourself one of the most successful of our early merchants—a man of exemplary private character, exalted Christian virtues, and liberal charities; to all of which, I have been myself a witness for more than half a century —it affords me much gratification, to DEDICATE to you these sketches, which are designed to preserve, in grateful memory, recollections of the representative men of Old Plymouth, who have reached that goal, towards which we are both rapidly advancing.

VERY SINCERELY YOURS,

THE AUTHOR.

Wilkes-Barré, April 10th, 1873.

CONTENTS.

CHAPTER I.

CHAPTER II.

CHAPTER III.

CHAPTER IV.

(19)

CHAPTER V.

CHAPTER VI.

CHAPTER VII.

CHAPTER VIII.

CHAPTER IX.

CHAPTER X.

CHAPTER XI.

CHAPTER XII.

CHAPTER XIII.

CHAPTER XIV.

CHAPTER XV.

CHAPTER XVI.

CHAPTER XVII.

CHAPTER XVIII.

CHAPTER XIX.

CHAPTER XX.

ILLUSTRATIONS.

(23)

PREFACE.

In a conversation, some months since, with an old Plymouth friend, he remarked :—"that all of the original settlers of the town had gone to their final resting-place, and that but a few of their children remained—and that these were now far advanced in years; that some of the old family names had become extinct; and that some one ought to prepare and write out a few biographical sketches of the most noted and prominent pioneers of the town. Their descendants should be informed of their early trials, sacrifices, and exposures; and what a vast amount of labor they performed, and what hardships they endured, to lay the foundation of all that wealth, which their kindred were now realizing."

I replied, that I thought Mr. Charles Miner had pretty well accomplished this, in his "Hazleton Trav-

ellers." He said, " no ; and if I would refer to Mr.
Miner's book, I would see that he had written of but
some four or five Plymouth families. Mr. Miner
spoke of the representative men, of the old time,
throughout the entire valley. His limits would not,
of course, permit him to go into that detail, which I
am now suggesting."

I said that the publication of a volume containing
such biographical notices, would be attended with
very considerable labor and expense ; that the subject matter of the book would be entirely local, and
of little interest, save to the comparatively small number of people, who were the immediate descendants
of the first settlers of the town, and it would also be
a difficult matter to procure a competent person to
perform it.

He replied, by saying, " that he thought I
was the only person living possessing the necessary
knowledge of the old people of the town—many of
whom were, in their day and generation, men of mark;
some of whom had rendered their country signal
services, while others had been carried into captivity
by the Indians—to write a personal history of their
exploits, sufferings, and perils, and he thought that I

ought to be willing to bestow the labor of doing the work.

"That as to the cost of publishing the work, when written, if the descendants of the old heroes who are now sitting down in comfortable ease and luxury, enjoying the fruits of the large coal properties which they have inherited, and which are the legacies resulting from the toil and hardships, as well as the sagacity of their ancestors, are unwilling to foot the bill, why, you and I will do it for them."

With much warmth and feeling he continued; "it will be, at most, a paltry sum; and the memories of many of these old people are dear to us, and therefore let us put them in history ! There is not a New England town of the population of ours that has not its local history written out and published, and so let us have our history—we have the materials to make it one of interest, and it should be done."

"Therefore," said he, "go at it, and when you have completed it, name my share to be contributed."

Impelled, therefore, by such generous impulses, I could not well decline; and accordingly, soon after this conversation, I commenced writing out some of the personal notices of the representative men of the town, contained in the following pages. But in tracing out the characters of the subjects I had selected, I found they were so intimately blended with the startling and exciting events of the Revolutionary struggle, "the Yankee and Pennamite" dispute, Indian captivities, and border raids, that mere biographical sketches of a few leading men, would not correspond with my own ideas, at least, as to what was due to old Plymouth, and the hardy and intrepid men who had founded the town.

I therefore concluded that instead of drawing a series of personal portraits, I would write up the history of the town. Not a history precisely, either, with its connected chain of events, dates, and chronological tables; but rather outlines and sketches of the principal men, and most noted events; commencing with the settlement of the town, and continuing down to the year 1850; noting the early habits, customs, and amusements of the old settlers; giving memoranda of the early merchants, ministers of the gospel, physicians and schoolmasters; also an account of the shad fisheries, old land-marks, game, and many other matters purely municipal, but still of interest to those who had knowledge upon the subjects directly, or held them, in tradition, from their fathers.

For half of the period of the hundred years of which I write, I have a personal knowledge. Being a native of the town, and a resident in it for a number of years, I had a personal knowledge of, and an intimate acquaintance with, I may say, nearly all the people of the town for more than half a century. From the survivors of the first settlers I received the traditionary characters of their cotemporaries and predecessors. This personal knowledge, therefore, enabled me to collate and prepare materials for the volume which, under other circumstances, would have been attended with much trouble and great research.

Many of the events which I have written out, have been heretofore given to the public by the historical writers of the valley. I have therefore, not in all cases, cited authorities, for the reason that I had the same sources of information, and had become familiar with them long before their publication. The traditionary history of the town was a subject as thoroughly fixed in my mind, as the lessons taught me in the old Academy. As to facts, in some cases,

I differ with the authors who have preceded me and who have written upon the same subject matter. I have done this, however, under the impression that my sources of information were the most reliable.

For instance, the tragedy attending the capture of Pike, Rogers and others, is stated differently by me, compared with previously written accounts of it. I made this change, because I have had repeatedly an extended and minute account of the whole affair from the mouths of both these men. While all the writers agree in the main, they are widely apart as to some of the minor details. This has been mainly produced by the incorrect statements, from time to time made, by Van Campen, and which have been received as truths.

When, therefore, I am in collision with the gentlemen who have gone over the same ground before me as to the verity of any point, I must fall back upon what I regard as my own superior opportunities of information. Nor have I, in such cases, relied wholly upon my own knowledge; but have consulted with aged persons, old residents of the town now living, whose facilities of information were even better than my own; and have accordingly declined to change the thread of published history without their concurrence in opinion with me. But as the changes so made are comparatively few, and do not materially alter former texts, it was probably hardly necessary to have been alluded to at all. Still, those who write should be very exact in their statements, especially on historical matters. It is in this view that I have made allusion to the subject.

To Jameson Harvey and Henderson Gaylord, both aged gentlemen, and old residents of the town, I am under deep obligations for many of the facts and incidents contained in the volume.

To Stewart Pearce, author of the Annals of Luzerne, and Steuben Jenkins, both gentlemen who have devoted much time to the research of those things which concern the early settlement and occupation of the valley by our ancestors, I also tender the expressions of my gratitude. Mr. Pearce is, upon his mother's side, of the family of Captain Lazarus Stewart, whose name occurs honorably in the following pages. Mr. Jenkins is a lineal descendant of Colonel John Jenkins, who headed the first Connecticut immigrant colony that set foot upon the banks of the Susquehanna.

2

Both of these gentlemen have for many years past been very industrious and persevering in hunting out and treasuring up the early antiquities of the valley, and have thus become possessed of a large store of historic matter, from which, at their request and approval, I have made liberal draughts.

The photographic likenesses, and views, were executed and prepared by Mr. William H. Schurch, of Scranton, in this county. It is to be hoped that the clever style, and artistic manner in which they have been produced, may lead to a more general patronage towards him upon the part of the people of the valley.

Wilkes-Barré, April 10th, 1873.

HISTORICAL SKETCHES OF PLYMOUTH.

CHAPTER I.

ITS NAME.—WHEN SETTLED.

I DESIGN to write some of the historical events of Plymouth; give sketches of some of the early settlers, and note down some of the old landmarks. In a few years those who were cotemporaneous with a generation which held the tradition of its early history, will have passed away, as the old monuments and once noted emblems are fast disappearing. For more than fifty years I have had a personal knowledge of the place. It is the town of my nativity; for there, on the twenty-fourth day of April, 1808, I first saw the light of day. The twenty years following, it was my home, and since that time I have lived in close vicinity to it. My father died there, and it had been his residence for more than three-fourths of his long and well-spent life.

I do not therefore hear the name of Plymouth pronounced that it does not remind me of my old home, and bring vividly before me the scenes of my childhood.   There is something inexplicable that clings to the memory connected with the place of our birth.   However humble it may have been, its name has a charm which lingers upon the memory, and which we dwell upon with a keen satisfaction.   And how forcibly will this strike the minds of many who now reside there, engaged in busy and exciting employments, who may chance to read this, whose homes in early life are separated from them by the great ocean !

These reflections carry me back through a long term of years, and bring before me afresh the faces and forms of men, now passed away, who, in their day and generation, were the representative men of the town ; who filled the local offices, who established the public morals, and whose opinion and judgment were the law of the vicinage.   They were a hardy and resolute people, as I first knew them—and they were, many of them, the same men who had erected their residences upon the same places, where the fires had scarcely abated, around which had assembled, in council, the Indian braves and sachems.   These had gathered up their implements of the chase, wound their blankets about their swarthy shoulders, and with their squaws and papooses, turned their faces, and commenced their march toward the setting sun, to give place, under the laws of destiny, to those who were to succeed them.

The conqueror and the vanquished have gone to

their last home ; the Indian to his hunting-ground in the Spirit Land, and the pale face to the white man's Heaven. Who can say that the destination of both is not in the same sphere ?

It is some idea of the appearance and character of some of these early settlers of Plymouth, as I knew them, and as I am informed from other reliable sources, that I would write down—that it may be preserved to their descendants. To a large portion of the people of the present populous town, the subject of which I write may not be of any special interest ; but to that portion of the population whose fathers and grandfathers were among the first settlers of the town, I am quite certain that it will. The labor upon my part will be considerable, but I am willing to bestow it. In my simple and plain narrative of events, and sketches of personal character, I shall make no pretensions to rhetorical style. I will deal with facts in a plain way, and state them as I knew them myself to be, or from the mouths of reliable witnesses, or public records. My object and design being to save from oblivion an outline, if nothing more, of the men of Plymouth a half century ago.

The town fifty years ago, and within my own recollection, was but a small village, compared with its present dimensions—in fact it could hardly be called a village, the residences being so scattered along what is now the great thoroughfare, that it was much more country than town.

The early settlers were principally immigrants from New England. They were a hardy, robust class of adventurers, who came to the western frontier to establish their new homes and erect their religious altars. Firm men, men of decision of character, and who were fully impressed with the conviction that their success depended solely upon their industrious habits ; without means, their strong hands and resolute hearts were their whole stock in trade, and in many cases, their trusty rifle the chief value of their personal effects. Had they not possessed these qualities they would never have incurred the hazard, and toil, and exposure, incident to the wilderness they came to occupy. For the land was not only to be subdued, but the savages were to be expelled. The young adventurer, therefore, thus reasoning at his New England fireside, must needs have had courage as well as indomitable perseverance, or he could never have gathered up sufficient resolution to embark upon his perilous enterprise.

In true Puritan style, and emblematic of their ancestral line, they brought with them the name of their new colony. It was an off-shoot of the "Rock of Plymouth"—hallowed by the first footprints of their fathers, when they stepped from the deck of the "May Flower," upon the shore of a New World.

The refugees of English intolerance had consecrated that rock, and the legacy came down to their children ; and more and more to be revered as time and distance came apace.

The Puritans, under old John Robinson, their pastor and leader, baptized the soil they first landed upon in the New World with the name of Plymouth, after the name of the last place they touched in the Old, previous to their embarkation. Immigrants, in time, carried the name with them to Plymouth, in Litchfield county, Connecticut—and their children brought it to the shores of the Susquehanna.

Our name, therefore, antedates the landing of the Pilgrims, on the twentieth of December, 1620, upon Plymouth Rock. Age has made it venerable, and the stirring incidents connected with its transmission, are subjects that we dwell upon with much satisfaction—and particularly such of us as have had ancestors connected with these incidents.

I have now in my own custody the veritable cane which that stern and unbending old Dissenter from the English Church, brought with him upon the "May Flower," in her voyage to the New World. It has been handed down from generation to generation, with pious and reverential care. It is a family heirloom, inherited by my wife from her father, the late John W. Robinson, Esquire, of Wilkes-Barré, who was a descendant, in direct line, of the founder of the English Dissenter's Church. It is a valuable relic, and considering its age of over two hundred and fifty years, is in a state of perfect preservation, save that the initials, J. R., engraved upon its silver head, have become nearly defaced; but still enough is left of the outline of the letters to indicate their character.

The date of the birth of our Plymouth may be fixed on the twenty-eighth of December, 1768—thus making it over one hundred years of age.

On that day the Susquehanna Company held a meeting at Hartford, Connecticut, to make preliminary arrangements for settling the Wyoming lands. It was then resolved that five townships, each five miles square, should be granted to two hundred settlers; that forty should set out immediately, and the remaining one hundred and sixty in the following spring. The five townships thus decreed to be laid out were named, Plymouth, Kingston, Hanover, Wilkes-Barré, and Pittston. The names of them all were not then assigned, but Plymouth was one of them that was then designated. See *Pearce's "Annals of Luzerne,"* p. 63.

Immediately after this meeting of the Susquehanna Company, immigration commenced; and before the close of the year 1769, the whole of the two hundred had arrived in the valley. Some of them settled at once in Plymouth upon their arrival; but I am unable to ascertain if the whole party, the quota assigned for Plymouth, settled there in that and the previous year. It appears, however, that the Rev. Noah Wadhams, the great grandfather of the present gentlemen of that name, now resident there, was preaching the gospel there in 1772, but three years afterwards.

Plymouth is one of those noted seventeen townships in this part of Pennsylvania, the territory of which was vested in the Susquehanna Company, and known under the name of the "Connecticut Charter." The grant was made on the twentieth of April, 1662, to the Connecticut Colony, by Charles II., in which that monarch recognizes the grant as the same which had been previously made by King James I. in 1620, to the "Plymouth Company." So that we find this name cotemporaneous with the first landing.

The charter for the tract of land named was of peculiar dimensions. It ceded to the company the land between two parallel lines of latitude, in width from the Atlantic to the Pacific ocean.

The geography of the country at that early day was very imperfectly understood. North America was supposed to be a narrow peninsula. When the extremes of the new continent were measured, and the area ascertained, it showed that the boundaries of King Charles' grant to the colony were sixty-nine miles in width, and some four thousand in length!

Within the limits of this grant, and under this title, Plymouth was settled. The length of the Connecticut Charter in years gone by was a by-word; and in old times, when the matter was better understood, and was often the subject of conversation, a person who told a long story was said to have made it as long as the Connecticut Charter. The application of the phrase now would be little understood; but forty years ago, everybody within the Wyoming valley had some knowledge about the length of that ever-memorable charter.

The occupation and settlement of the "Susquehanna Country," as the territory in earlier days was called, were prevented by the hostilities among the Indian tribes, growing out of the French and English war. On the twenty-eighth of December, 1768, as I have already stated, the Susquehanna Company made the first formidable movement towards the occupation of the land claimed under their charter. The reason, probably, of the action of this company at that time, was produced by the settlement of long-standing troubles between the British Government and the Six Nations of Indians, in a treaty at Fort Stanwix, concluded in that year.

This opened the door for immigration, and the company immediately availed themselves of the opportunity. Plymouth was considered as one of the most desirable of the seventeen Yankee towns, on account of the broad sweep of remarkably fertile land which skirted its south-eastern border. It embraced an area of from two to three thousand acres, made up of alluvion, and was without the natural obstructions of forest trees; so that it invited the plough-share of the hardy pioneer, without that preceding toil and labor necessary to prepare ground for cultivation, covered with trees and herbage.

The Shawnee flats were a little *oasis* in the wilderness, ready prepared for cultivation, and was an exceedingly inviting spot to the young New Englander, compared with the rough and stony fields he left behind him.

CHAPTER II.

THE SHAWNEE TRIBE OF INDIANS, AND THE FIRST WHITE MAN.—GRASSHOPPER BATTLE.

THE Shawnee tribe of Indians occupied Plymouth in 1742, when first visited by the white man. The tribe was not numerous. As early as 1608 they had, in league with the Hurons, been engaged in war on the Canadian frontier with the Iroquois, the confederate tribes known as the Six Nations, and defeated, were obliged to leave their hunting-grounds. They wandered south as far as Florida. Their numbers had become decimated, and they were by no means a tribe, considered by their race, as formidable upon the war-path. Becoming there engaged in a war with the Spaniards, who then owned that territory, they migrated west in 1690 to the Wabash; and finally in 1697, upon the Conestoga Indians, who lived near the present city of Lancaster, in this state, becoming security to William Penn for their good behavior, they removed to Pequea creek, below Lancaster.

In 1701 William Penn made a treaty with the tribes upon the Susquehanna, and a portion of the Shawnee tribe located within the present limits of Plymouth, under the order and direction of the Six Nations, whose power and authority was absolute over all the Indian tribes of Pennsylvania, and from whom they demanded and received annual tribute.

When, therefore, Count Zinzendorf, on his Christian mission, visited Plymouth in the autumn of 1742, he found the Shawnees, with their chief, Kakowatchie; and their principal wigwam situate on the west bank of the small stream emptying into the river above the old village, and between the main road and the river, known in the early days of the white settlers as the farm of Noah Wadhams, Esquire, and upon which he lived and died. The Shawnee tribe at this time probably did not number over two hundred braves and warriors. They were subjects of the Six Nations, and completely under their orders and control; in fact a part of their own associates and tribe who had occupied this very ground, were obliged to surrender for the benefit of the fresh immigration from the Delaware, and make a new home upon the Ohio and Allegheny. Because the Shawnees had refused to fight the English, the enemy of the Six Nations, these confederate tribes kept the poor Shawnees almost constantly in motion; and whenever they came within the confederate jurisdiction, they seem to have been dealt with without regard to mercy.

This tribe, however, occupied the present territory of Plymouth at the time of the first imprint of the foot of the white man. It has thus become a proper subject for us to inquire about. There are not enough of them left now to kindle a respectable council fire. The scattering remnant is merged in the names of more numerous and powerful western tribes—and even these in a very, very few years will have disappeared also.

A hundred years ago the decree of the Iroquois, or the Six Nations, was clothed with the elements of power. The messenger who went forth with it was regarded with as much consideration and respect, through the vast country watered by the Susquehanna and its tributaries, as the ambassador, sent out at this day, by any crowned head in Europe to the subjects of his colonies, is treated by them.

But the wheels of progress, or destiny, if the word better defines the idea, have crushed out the rule and sway of the haughty braves and warriors who gave tone and character to the name of these confederate tribes. Their wigwams have disappeared; their hunting-grounds have put on the garbs of civilization, in the shape of towns and hamlets, and cultivated fields. All this may be right. God, in the wisdom of His providence, did not create the red man in vain. The laws of conquest have an indefinable meaning when we come to square them by the Christian impulses of the human heart.

The red man, in this land,

"Was native to the manor born."

Owner, not by discovery, nor that more imperfect title, by conquest, we have no reason to question the theory but that here he was originally created, and this was his proper as well as legal home. How far we may assert the uncharitable, but too often inexorable plea of necessity as a palliation, may be a question of doubt as to his removal and extermination. Civilization has done this, but is that an element of civilization? Statesmen and philosophers may well pause for reflection. It is a knotty problem for solution to determine whether might is right. And when the idea is brought home to us, in robbing us, by force, of that which has cost us a life-time of industry to acquire, we would hardly reconcile our belief to the argument of its legal necessity. I apprehend there is not one of us who would not exclaim against the act as one of oppression and the rankest tyranny.

It is a law of brute force, and not of morality, which sanctions the doctrine of the submission of the weak to the strong. Ages have sanctioned the creed, but does this long usage confirm it as right?

It is said that necessity knows no law. And under this title, the broad acres of the American Continent are now held and occupied.

If the poor Indian were created for the purpose of a temporary occupation of this country, to be succeeded by a higher and more intellectual race, then we may reconcile our ideas to his oppressions and wrongs. But who is endowed with the power of comprehension and knowledge to solve this question? "Man is little lower than the angels," but not high enough in mental stature to grasp this subject, and decide it in conformity with correct principles.

When Alexander the Great was told by the petty thief whom he was about to punish, that he only despoiled individuals of their property, but that the great conqueror robbed and subjected whole countries, it furnished him a new theme for consideration. He discovered in his criminal a mirror that reflected two thieves, one guilty of petty, the other of grand larceny!

And while we profess to be governed by the best and purest principles of moral ethics, we must not conclude that, because our fathers did wrong in the acquisition of property in which we had no participation, we are therefore entirely absolved from all the blame; for we are in the full enjoyment of the fruits. In tracing back, the title of our homestead, it all goes along smoothly enough till we come to that missing link between the *white* and *red* proprietor! If we are keenly sensible at this point, and governed by the true maxims of humanity, we shall begin to conclude "that the partaker is as bad as the thief."

But then we have the soothing consolation that we all stand on precisely the same platform ; that we are not 'only on the side of the majority, as to any question of blame in usurping the whole territory of the country from its original owners ; but that there is not one dissenting voice ! This is a very comfortable view of the subject. The voice of the entire nation cannot be at fault. It is unanimous, therefore it must be right.

This argument before an intelligent judge might be called sophistry ; but then we are relieved from all this trouble, for we are the judges in our own case, and as we conclude so stands the final decision.

But let us return to old Plymouth, and talk about facts, instead of discussing general theories. It is these we must deal with, and let others, if they will, pursue the line of thought I dropped into some dozen paragraphs or so back.

Having given a short sketch of the Shawnee tribe, the people who were in possession before the occupation by a superior race, let us inquire whose was the first *white* foot, that made its imprint upon Shawnee soil ?

This is an inquiry involved in some doubt, but with the traditional evidence we have, connected with the researches upon the subject by Isaac A. Chapman, Charles Miner, and Stewart Pearce, who have all written, and written well, upon the antiquities of the Wyoming Valley, it is to be fairly presumed that

Conrad Weiser was the first white man that visited the Wyoming Valley ; but as to his being the first white man who visited Plymouth, is a question that antiquarians will have to settle between him and Count Nicholas Louis Zinzendorf. As to the time of the appearance of the latter we have correct dates, and there is no room for doubt.

Our local historians agree that Conrad Weiser was "an upright and worthy man." He had resided with the Mohawk Indians from 1716 to 1729, and spoke the language of several tribes. He had made repeated journeys among the Indians north and west : he frequently acted as interpreter, and was often the agent of several of the tribes in their treaties and negotiations,—and Mr. Pearce, whom I regard a very good authority in our early history, concludes that there is no doubt or question but that " he was the first white man who ever trod the soil of Luzerne county."

While this may be the fact, it does not follow that he was the first white man who trod the soil of Plymouth.

We shall see that he was with Zinzendorf in Plymouth in the autumn of 1742, but he did not join the Count for several days after he had been in Plymouth, laboring with the Shawnees on his Christian mission.

As to the time this missionary visited Plymouth there seems to be no doubt ; and the probability is

3

that he was the first white man who put his foot upon Plymouth soil, as we do not learn that Mr. Weiser passed up or down the Susquehanna, on any of the journeys which he performed in his Indian service.

Count Nicholas Louis Zinzendorf, a German of means, a man of great piety, and a leading elder of the Moravian church, came to Bethlehem, Pa., in the year 1741. This town at that time was the principal location of the Moravian brotherhood. During the following year he made up his mind to advance to the Susquehanna, and visit the Indian tribes who lived there. For this purpose he applied to Mr. Weiser, whose reputation was well known as friendly with the Indians, and also understanding the language, to accompany him. His engagements did not immediately permit him; and the Count, in company with John Martin Mack and his wife, set out on their journey in the fall of 1742, and arrived safely on the lands of the Shawnee tribe. And until very recently, when a diary of Mr. Mack turned up, it was supposed that they crossed the mountain by the Warrior Run war-path, from Fort Allen, on the Lehigh, to the Susquehanna, in Hanover township.

It is now well understood that this was not the road they passed over, in their approach to the Susquehanna. Mr. Pearce has placed in my hands an extract from the diary of John Martin Mack, obtained recently by him from the Moravian Society, at

Bethlehem, which gives a general account of the journey of the Count to the Wyoming Valley; Plymouth being the first place where they stopped.

I give the substance of this diary. Zinzendorf went from Bethlehem to Shamokin, Northumberland county; and from thence he went up to the mouth of Loyal Sock creek, now known as Montoursville. The name of the Indian town was Otstenwacken, now in the county of Lycoming. To this place he was accompanied by Mr. Mack and his wife. At this place he preached to the Indians in French. He was entertained by "Madam Montour," a French Canadian woman, who had married Andrew Montour, a half-blood. This woman had great influence at the Indian council-fire. She possessed much shrewdness, and her manners and kind acts made a good impression on the wild men of the forest. From this point, according to the diary, Zinzendorf, in company with Mack and his wife, Andrew Montour, son of the "Madam," as she was styled, with four others whose names are not given, Indians probably, set out upon horseback, by the way of the war-path, to Wyoming Valley, on the head waters of Fishing, Muncy, and Huntington creeks. On the fifth day they reached the Shawnee village, in the plains of "Skehandowanna" (Susquehanna), where they halted at a wigwam of the Shawnee tribe on the banks of a creek, near an Indian burial-ground, and erected their tent. Mack says that the red warriors gathered around

them and brandished their knives in a threatening
and menacing way.

The distance they had made from the mouth of
Loyal Sock creek he puts down at seventy miles,
which is very correctly stated. He speaks of being
opposed by wild beasts, swollen streams of water, and
dense thickets; and that it was five days of hard
labor to accomplish the journey.

He states that they remained with the Shawnees
ten days. Zinzendorf shared what little provisions
he had with the Indians—gave them the buttons off
his shirt, and his silver knee-buckles, and lived principally upon boiled beans during his sojourn with
them. He preached to the Shawnees through his interpreter; told them that the object of his visit was
peace, and to instruct them for the good of their
souls in the spirit land. To all this they listened,
but were incredulous. They could not be persuaded
but that there was some other motive concealed, which
looked to some serious injury to their tribe. And a
secret plan was laid for his assassination.

On one of the evenings of the old man's visit,
some of the Shawnees approached the tent for the
purpose of murdering him, but as they pulled aside
the blanket which covered the opening of his tent,
they saw at that moment an adder pass over his legs,
unnoticed by the holy man, who was deeply involved
in his religious thoughts.

The savage warriors construed this as a direct

intervention of the Great Spirit, and they withdrew, unbending their bows, and sheathing their knives.

The accounts heretofore given of this incident by the local historians, represent the serpent to have been a rattle-snake—nor do any of them give the exact locality.

The diary continues to enumerate several other incidents which, at this remote time, are of exceeding interest. Zinzendorf visited the Mohican village, supposed to have been located at Forty-fort, in the township of Kingston. He preached to the Indians there, and met among them an Indian woman who professed Christianity.

He travelled from one village to another, engaged in his religious instructions, and was joined, after several days in the valley, by Conrad Weiser, and also by three Moravian missionaries, who left Bethlehem on the fifteenth of October. From this date we may infer that Zinzendorf first reached the Shawnee village in the latter part of September. We are not informed by Mr. Mack, the precise length of time the party remained in the valley. Mr. Chapman, however, fixes it at twenty days. He is probably correct, as in a note in his book, p. 22, he speaks of obtaining his information from a companion of Zinzendorf, who afterwards visited Wyoming.

We are informed from the diary that the names of the three Moravian missionaries who joined the

Count were, David Kitschman, Anton Seyffert, and Jacob Kohnn.

Mr. Mack says that on leaving the Shawnee village, near the burial ground (the Noah Wadhams farm), in crossing the creek, which was swollen by recent rains, the horse of Zinzendorf stumbled, and threw his rider into the stream; and that he was rescued by the party from his perilous situation.

The Indians standing upon the bank saw the accident, and in their opinion, here was another miraculous interposition of Manitou. They again expressed themselves as fully satisfied, that the man who had escaped the flood and the venomous reptile must be under the protection of the Great Spirit.

And this is the substance of a journal, written down at the time of the occurrence of the matters contained in it, a hundred and thirty years ago.

It throws new light upon a subject that the local historian did not possess, founded upon an authority that may be considered as authentic.

John Martin Mack, who was also a Moravian missionary, informs us that he was born in Wurtemburg, Germany, on the twelfth of April, 1715; that some time after arriving in this country, he married Jeannette, a daughter of a Mohawk chief. She spoke that language, as well as that of the Delaware and Shawnee tribes.

This knowledge of the Indian tongue of the Shawnee tribe accounts for the presence of Jeannette, in the missionary expedition of Zinzendorf, amidst the perils of his visit to the Susquehanna. She spoke the language of the people who occupied the soil of old Plymouth, before our fathers took possession of that part of the "Skehandowanna plains," now known as the Shawnee flats. It was probably her lips which were the organ of interpretation of the words of the reverend old man, to the stoical and haughty audience that surrounded him. But the language, as well as the tongues and lips of the wild roaming people who gave it articulation, are now alike silent, and will so remain forever.

It would be an interesting fact to know what finally became of this man who was jotting down history over a century ago in old Plymouth, and of Jeannette, his Indian bride, whose voice uttered to the wild warriors of the Shawnee tribe the doctrines of peace and good will. But of their subsequent career we have no record. Zinzendorf returned again to his native land, and died at a ripe old age.

He did not probably live long enough to realize the fact, that to civilize and Christianize the North American red man, was a work not to be accomplished. And probably it is well that it is so; but in either case, it is a question beyond our comprehension, at least.

From the testimony I have thus referred to, and which to my mind is conclusive, I think there can be no doubt but that the first white feet that trod the soil of our township, were those of Nicholas Louis Zinzendorf and John Martin Mack; and also that these were the first heralds there of the doctrines of the Cross, as well as in the other parts of the valley of the Susquehanna. That the first sermon upon the subject of man's redemption, through the mediation of Christ, was preached near the Shawnee burial-ground, within the limits of the township of Plymouth.

We are thus enabled to locate the very spot where these things occurred. And what a study for the artist is here presented? It is to be hoped that some son of Plymouth may yet arise, who shall have the qualifications to place upon canvas, in its true light, the aged missionary and his Indian woman interpreter, his humble tent and his swarthy, sun-burned audience. It is a subject worthy the pencil of the cleverest painter.

The old Indian burial-ground is a spot that was familiar to the early settlers of Plymouth. Its location is near the bank of the little stream I have described, and between the railroad and the main thoroughfare. I have myself, fifty years since, seen the Indian bones turned up by the plough-share, lying in heaps upon the public highway, where they had been cast, taken from the identical place referred to in the journal from which I have quoted. And more than this, for acting under the impulse of revenge, impressed upon my mind in listening to the deeds of horror produced by the tomahawk and scalping-knife, related by the men who had been eye-witnesses of them, I have pounded and pulverized these relics of the departed warriors, and stamped upon them, as if the cruelties their owners had perpetrated could thus be avenged; and my fellow boyish associates and myself have consoled ourselves with the reflection, after an exhibition of this valiant conduct, that if we had not killed an "Ingen," we at least had the profound satisfaction of having had a glorious knock at his dry bones!

What a pity that the "Christian Church" edifice, standing on the opposite side of the way from the site once occupied by Zinzendorf's tent, should not have been located upon it. It is ground consecrated by the acts and deeds of the first man, upon the Susquehanna, who proclaimed "glad tidings of great joy." Though the seeds of faith fell upon savage ears, the noble and self-reliant example of the man is a living model for Christian imitation.

It is agreeable for us, at this remote day, that we are enabled to ascertain definitely the precise locality. And we know it—*the exact place* where the pilgrim missionaries of our religious faith pitched their tent, at the end of their five days' journey in the wilderness; and where their venerable, pious old leader, gave the Indian chiefs of the Shawnee tribe "the buttons from off his shirt, and the silver buckles from his knees," as a peace-offering in the name of the

Lord, amidst the gleams and flashes of their brand-ished scalping-knives, and in the hearing of their piercing war-whoops.

Mr. Chapman, in his history, p. 24, is under the impression that most of the Shawnees had left Ply-mouth before the advance of the white man in 1769; and that at this period the Delawares, who resided on the east side of the Susquehanna, and nearly op-posite, had become proprietors of the Shawnee plains; and the evacuation of the Shawnees is based upon the consequence of their defeat by the Delawares in the memorable Grasshopper battle.

The circumstances which led to this battle, I will briefly relate.   A number of the Delaware squaws, with their children, were gathering wild fruits along the eastern bank of the river, some two miles below their village, which stood on the lower side of the present limits of the city of Wilkes-Barré, where they met with some squaws and their children of the Shaw-nee tribe, who had crossed the river in their canoes for the same purpose.

A child belonging to the Shawnees had taken a large grasshopper, and a quarrel arose among the children for the possession of it, in which their moth-ers soon took part.   The Delaware women contending that the east side of the river was their property, persisted in their right to the grasshopper, and the feminine conflict terminated in the expulsion of the Shawnee squaws over to the west side.   And it is asserted, though I apprehend upon very questionable authority, that some of these women were killed in this engagement.

The expulsion of the Shawnee women irritated and maddened their husbands, and the consequence was a declaration of war on the part of the Shawnees against the Delawares. The Shawnees embarked in their canoes, but were met by the Delawares before they could obtain a foothold upon the east bank of the river ; but still they were able to effect a landing, and a bloody conflict ensued at the great bend of the river, immediately above the present railroad bridge. It is said that nearly half of the Shawnees fell upon the battle-field. They were certainly driven back to their own side of the stream.

As this event took place some thirty years only before the advent of the white settlers, and as the tradition of the battle was then fresh in the memory, and probably pretty well understood by them, it is a little remarkable that they should not have given us the facts of the expulsion of the Shawnees by the Delawares.

The early settlers always spoke of the Indians which they found upon their entry into Plymouth as of the Shawnee tribe. I have heard this often from the lips of Colonel Ransom, Jonah Rogers, and Abraham Pike. The statements of these men were certainly to be relied upon, and they had the means of knowledge upon the subject.

It is a matter of much doubt whether the Grass-hopper battle was a very serious affair. The Shaw-nees and Delawares were generally on very friendly terms, and from the most reliable authority I can find, the greatest number of these two tribes removed to Diahoga (Tioga) some ten years previous to the advance of the white man.

I conclude, therefore, that the Indians who made the greatest incursions upon the early settlers of Ply-mouth, were a remnant of the Shawnees, who were lingering about their old hunting-grounds upon the Shawnee mountain. This is by far the most proba-ble conclusion.

If, as Mr. Chapman writes, the Shawnees were expelled by the Delawares after the Grasshopper battle, it seems strange that ten years after the two tribes should have been travelling together to Dia-hoga, the spot designated for them by the order of their masters, the Six Nations.

A further distinction is drawn by some of our his-torians, that the Shawnees were a more bloodthirsty tribe than the other tribes upon the Susquehanna— the Nanticokes, the Delawares, and the Mohicans; that it was an impelling reason which moved Zinzen-dorf to make the Shawnees, for this cause, the first objects of Christianization. The probability is that the character and temperament of this tribe were not very different from other tribes. The same feeling of bloody revenge for real or supposed injuries, is an element in common with the whole race; and, as a Shawnee man, I feel inclined to stand by *our* tribe, and deny this unjust calumny, which is attempted to be heaped upon their memory.

Though not precisely of the same household, still my young feet trod their paths, and my young eyes witnessed their bones and fortifications; and therefore it would be unmanly, while writing their history, not at the same time to defend their memory against an accusation that "the Shawnee tribe of Indians was the most bloody and revengeful tribe that ever placed foot upon the Skehandowanna plains!"

Having thus disposed of the Shawnee tribe, and the question as to the first white man who visited Plymouth, I will turn my attention to other subjects involved in its first settlement.

CHAPTER III.

THE FIRST SETTLERS.

MOST of the early settlers of the town were men of strong minds: a few of them were eccentric characters, and now and then, one addicted to habits of intemperance; but they were all industrious, and not one of them, as I ever learned, espoused the Tory side of the great question of their day and generation.

They were self-reliant, and this was an imperative necessity, surrounded as they were by cramped means of subsistence, and daily exposure to Indians and their Pennamite enemies.

They were loyal to their Government, and many of them were in the revolutionary war, and some of them served the whole seven years in that protracted issue. As a whole, they were a brave, patriotic, and industrious people, but little acquainted with luxuries, and none more familiar with the severe conflicts of frontier life.

Their hostility to the Indian race was bitter and vindictive. This had arisen from the fact that some of their little society had undergone savage torture and murder; others more fortunate were taken into captivity. One of them, Elisha Harvey, had been sold to an Indian trader, in Canada, for half a barrel of rum.

Even in my day, which did not commence for the period of over twenty years after the cessation of the valley troubles, Colonel Ransom, Abraham Nesbitt, Jonah Rogers, or Abraham Pike would have shot down an Indian, if they had met with him, as unhesitatingly as they would a prowling wolf or panther.

Time did not seem to efface and wear away this embittered feeling. The common subject of conversation, within my own recollection, among these old veterans when they met, was Indian atrocities committed upon themselves, their families, and friends.

The youth of the town therefore grew up under a

deep sense of these wrongs. They fully participated in the emotions produced by the constant rehearsal of Indian butcheries. The sentiment was universal. It was the absorbing topic in the field, the mechanic's shop, the school house, and the pulpit, year in and year out. Probably in no other part of the county did this feeling of Indian hostility exist, to the same degree and extent as in Plymouth.

The old frame Academy, now standing,—and it is to be hoped may be permitted to remain, as one of the few land-marks of the past—was built not far from the year 1816. Jonah Rogers kept school in it. He had been taken a prisoner, when a boy of fourteen, by the Indians. The bloody scene which attended his escape, will be fully noticed hereafter. The old gentleman was in the habit of repeating, almost daily, in open school, his knowledge of Indian tragedies.

He would speak of the number of reeking scalps he had seen strung upon a cord, and dangling from the belt of the red warrior, as a trophy of his prowess; some of them taken from the heads of his own personal friends; how the savages were in the habit of stripping their victims, binding them with thongs to a tree, piercing their naked bodies with sharpened pine knots, and then setting them on fire; and how the poor creatures would writhe in torture, and die the most agonizing of deaths; how they had inhumanly murdered such a man that he knew, pointing to the exact place where it was done, and naming the exact time; of their stealthy habits of lying in ambush and springing like tigers upon their prey; how he could detect them by the smell of their smoked and painted bodies, before they were visible to the eye; and how it would be serving God to remove and exterminate the entire race.

These were some of the lessons we learned in the old man's school, and in a building still standing in our town.   They were a part of the education of the youth, fifty years ago in the township of Plymouth.

The old man was kind and indulgent, and it was not unfrequently that he would resort to these rehearsals as a means of quieting the unruly element of his school; and it worked like a charm, for when he commenced all eyes were fastened upon him, and all ears ajar; nor did their interest in any manner abate from their frequent repetition.   An Indian story would produce instantaneous order.

The effect of these relations upon the mind of children was wonderful; and the moment we were dismissed, how we would collect in groups, and doubling up our little fists, "wish that we were big men, that we could avenge the wrongs that we had heard; and that if we had been big men when these cruelties were perpetrated, the bloody 'Ingens' would have stood but a poor chance for their lives."

And so the children of Jonah Rogers' school reasoned and talked a half century ago.

I repeat these things now, after the long lapse of time, to illustrate the state of popular feeling which then existed in our town, towards the poor Indian, and the feelings of the men who occupied his corn-fields, his hunting-grounds, and the spots whereon he had pitched his wigwams.

We grew into manhood, perfect Indian haters. And to accomplish this was the great lesson of the school.

The early settlers, no doubt, had cause to curse the Indian tribes; but if they had paused in their vehement and rapid conclusions long enough to inquire whether they were not really in the wrong themselves, in driving them from their homes and firesides, they might have made at least some allowance for their atrocities, acting as they did on the defensive! They did not, however, stop to draw the line between civilized and savage life. They seemed to think that brutality was no more to be tolerated in an Indian, than in a civilized white man.

Time, however, has somewhat changed public opinion. As the old people of Plymouth, who were the actors in the wild scenes of border life, have passed away, one after another, the chapter of their sufferings has become more and more indistinct; their exposures and privations less talked of by their children; and the third generation, now in occupation of the homes of their ancestors, seldom, if ever, allude to or mention the trials and incidents of early

4

days. In fact most of them have lost even the traditionary chain of these stirring events. And to remind them of these events, is why I am now writing,
at an advanced age myself, that they may not be
entirely obliterated and lost. The name of Plymouth is dear to me, because it is linked with recollections of the happiest days of my life; and I like to
dwell upon the memory of the brave and generous
people whose hairs were gray, at the remote period
of which I write.

Plain and simple in their habits, they had no idea
of procuring their bread but "by the sweat of their
brow." They lived by hard and continuous labor,
and at a time when labor was not only respectable,
but dignified and inviting. Alas, the change; but
this is not the subject of our inquiry.

I have stated that the white settlement of the
town commenced in 1768, and immediately succeeding the treaty at Fort Stanwix. I am unable, however, to ascertain how many immigrants came in that
and the following year. Forty were assigned to Plymouth: most of that number probably arrived. The
best evidence, in the absence of family traditional
knowledge, is an enrollment of the resident inhabitants of the whole valley, in 1773, made by Colonel
Zebulon Butler, and in his handwriting. This list
comprises the names of two hundred and sixteen settlers. By this list, I am enabled to state with certainty that in that year, and which was not more

than three or four years after the first immigration, the following named persons were residents of Plymouth, *viz. :* Noah Allen, David Whittlesey, Nathaniel Watson, Samuel Marvin, Jabez Roberts, John Baker, Nicholas Manvil, Joseph Gaylord, Isaac Bennet, William Leonard, Jesse Leonard, Nathaniel Goss, Stephen Fuller, Samuel Sweet, John Shaw, Joseph Morse, Daniel Brown, Comfort Goss, James Nesbitt, Aaron Dean, Peter Ayres, Captain Prince Alden, Naniad Coleman, Abel Pierce, Timothy Pierce and Timothy Hopkins.

I am a little surprised that this list does not contain the names of Noah Wadhams, Silas, Elisha, and Benjamin Harvey, Samuel Ransom, James Bidlack, Benedict Satterlee, Caleb Atherton, David Reynolds and Henry Barney. There is an old deed among the valley archives of "Samuel Love of Connecticut to Samuel Ransom, late of Norfolk, Connecticut, now being at Susquehanna," which bears date November fifth, 1773. This is probably for the Plymouth Homestead farm.

Among the same papers is a deed, dated Plymouth, September twenty-ninth, 1773, of Henry Barney to Benedict Satterlee. I think most if not all of these men, were in Plymouth previous to the general enrollment of all the settlers of the valley, in 1773, and it is pretty certain that the Reverend Noah Wadhams preached in Plymouth before this period.

But the persons whom I have last named, if not

in Plymouth in 1773, came immediately afterwards. The persons whose names I have last mentioned were pioneer settlers.

From this period up to the time that Captain Samuel Ransom enlisted what was known as the Second Independent Company, for the Revolutionary service, January first, 1777, there is no list preserved of the early settlers of Plymouth. This was four years after the general enrollment.

On this list I find the names of Mason F. Alden, Charles Gaylord, Ambrose Gaylord, Aziba Williams, Asahel Nash, Ebenezer Roberts, Isaac Benjamin, Benjamin Clark, Gordon Church, Price Cooper, Nathan Church, Daniel Franklin, Ira Sawyer, John Swift, and Thomas Williams, who are not named in the foregoing list, and all of whom, I suppose, to have been Plymouth settlers.

On the list of Captain Durkee's company, First Independent Revolutionary Service, are the names of Jeremiah Coleman, Jesse Coleman, Benjamin Harvey, and Seth Marvin. These were Plymouth men.

From this it would appear that in 1777, the number of men able to bear arms in Plymouth was not far from eighty. There were other persons of course whose names are not included in either of the above lists. There were the Nesbitts, Rogers, Drakes, George P., William and Samuel Ransom, the Barneys, Baldwins, Bennetts, etc. It may be that the number all told exceeded eighty.

There is no further record evidence of the population of the town till 1796. The commissioners' office of this county contains the Plymouth assessment of that year. And it is the first trace of the assessor on file in the county archives, notwithstanding Luzerne had been set off from the county of Northumberland on the twenty-fifth of September, 1786.

As this was after the close of the Revolutionary war, and there was comparative quiet in the valley, it is difficult to understand why there should not be on file, somewhere, a list of taxable inhabitants. The same deficiency in the office at Wilkes-Barré, applies to the other townships of the county.

The assessment list of 1796 shows but ninety-five taxables. But it is not strange by any means that the increase of population advanced so slowly. The Indian troubles had made their mark; the Pennamite war had carried off several; and the Revolutionary war had made sad havoc upon the settlement. All these were fearful obstacles in the way of the increase of population.

If in 1796 we estimate four, in addition to each taxable inhabitant, the whole population of the township, including the territory of Jackson, set off into a municipal jurisdiction in 1844, would be but four hundred and seventy-five souls.

These very facts, which impeded the increase of population, tell us but too plainly of the formidable, and we may add fearful obstructions which were in the path of our pioneer fathers.

Plymouth was never backward in filling its quota of men for the general cause, or raising men for protection against an internal foe. From the time they first put their foot upon the Shawnee plains, down to the passage of the act confirming their title, a period of nearly thirty years, they knew but little of peace and repose. For more than half of this period they were in local broils, Indian invasions, and the Revolutionary struggle. They slept with their arms ready at hand. The rifle was as necessary an implement of husbandry as the sickle. They carried it with them, almost constantly, to the field of their labor during many, many years of suffering, hope, and fear. They had to take turns relieving each other on guard in the night, to ward off the Indian and Pennamite incursions. So that with British, Tories, Indians, and Pennamites, our people had their hands full, and it is really a matter of surprise that they should have had the courage and endurance to fight it out so long and valiantly as they did.

The massacre at the battle of Wyoming alone cost them the lives of not less than thirty of their citizens; the Revolutionary war as many more; and the troubles with the Indians and exposure of a frontier life, and its dangers and wants, an equal number. And these causes probably disposed of at least one-fourth of the people, who were in Plymouth, from

1769 to 1785. It is more probable that my estimate is under than over the mark. These then were not merely troublesome, but they were *trying* times.

I have heard it from the lips of the old people frequently, that death was preferable to the constant alarms and daily exposures that they were obliged to undergo. But they would say, "we had johnny cake, and shad in the spring, and eels in the fall; and here we had pitched our tents, and so we resolved to face all dangers and submit to all perils."

I subjoin the assessment list of 1796. It will be an interesting relic of the names of the men who have now all passed away, but at that time were the active, stirring men of the township:

Samuel Allen, Stephen Allen, David Allen, Elias Allen, William Ayers, Daniel Ayers, John Anderson, Moses Atherton, Isaac Bennet, Benjamin Bennet, Joshua Bennet, Benjamin Barney, Daniel. Barney, Henry Barney, Walter Brown, Jesse Brown, William Baker, Philemon Bidlack, Jared Baldwin, Jude Baldwin, Amos Baldwin, Jonah Bigsley, Peter Chambers, Wiliam Craig, Jeremiah Coleman, Thomas Davenport, Ashael Drake, Rufus Drake, Aaron Dean, Henry Decker, Joseph Dodson, Leonard Dercaus, Joseph Duncan, Jehial Fuller, Peter Grubb, Charles E. Gaylord, Adolph Heath, Elisha Harvey, Samuel Healy, John Heath, Samuel Hart, Josiah Ives, Josiah Ives, Jr., Crocker Jones, Thomas Lameraux, John Lameraux, John Leonard, Joseph Lenaberger, Samuel Marvin, James Marvin, Timothy Meeker, Ira Manvill, Ephraim McCoy, Phineas Nash, Abram Nesbitt, Simon Parks, Samuel Pringle, Michael Pace, David Pace, Nathan Parrish, Oliver Plumley, Jonah Rogers, Joze Rogers, Elisha Rogers, Edon Ruggles, Hezekiah Roberts, Jacob Roberts, Stephen Roberts, David Reynolds, Joseph Reynolds, George P. Ransom, Nathan Rumsey, Michael Scott, Lewis Sweet, Elam Spencer, William Stewart, Jesse Smith, Ichabod Shaw, Palmer Shaw, Benjamin Stookey, John Taylor, John Turner, Abraham Tillbury, Matthias Van Loon, Abraham Van Loon, Nicholas Van Loon, Calvan Wadhams, Noah Wadhams, Moses Wadhams, Ingersol Wadhams, Amariah Watson, Darius Williams, Rufus Williams, and John Wallen. Ninety-five all told. Not one of them now living.

CHAPTER IV.

THE PENNAMITE AND YANKEE WAR.—COMMENCEMENT OF TROUBLES.—CAPTAIN STEWART.—LIEUTENANT JENKINS. — PATTERSON'S ADMINISTRATION. — ARREST AND IMPRISONMENT OF SETTLERS.—BATTLE OF NANTICOKE.

AS the forefathers of our town were almost all of them participators in the serious troubles and difficulties, which grew out of the contest between the Connecticut claimants, under the grant of the Susquehanna Company, and the Proprietary Government of Pennsylvania, as to the questions of ownership of the land, and the civil jurisdiction over it and the people occupying it, there will be occasion to give a condensed statement of the subject generally, and particularly in reference to the part taken in it by the early settlers of Plymouth. And as this township furnished the chief battle-ground during the continuance of this internecine contest, where the parties met in respectable numbers, and in which the almost entire male population of our town took part, it becomes a question of much interest to the descendants of these people.

I have already stated that the territory of the town lies between the two parallel lines of latitude, which were the northern and southern boundaries of the grant to the Susquehanna Company. Under this grant the State of Connecticut not only claimed the ownership of the land, but the jurisdiction over it.

To these pretensions the State of Pennsylvania, at the commencement known as the "Proprietary Government of Pennsylvania," took exception. The proprietors, William Penn and his associates, founded their claim to the same land and jurisdiction under a grant of King Charles II., bearing date the fourth of March, 1681, and nineteen years after the date of his letters patent to the Connecticut Company. I have already stated that the want of knowledge as to the geographical situation of the country produced this blunder. It can be called by no other name; as there was not, undoubtedly, on the part of the British king, a desire to grant a second time any part of his territory, in his colony, which had been previously ceded to others.

Taking, therefore, the dates of these two letters patent, and particularly, as in this case, the precedent occupation by the people of Connecticut, they had the law and equity of the case upon their side. But unfortunately for Connecticut, the State of New York intervened, and thus left a span of over a hundred miles between the western line of the former and the Susquehanna lands. Had not this difficulty been in the way, the final result would in all probability have had a different termination.

The grant to Connecticut bore the oldest date: the people of that State made the first entry. Lawyer or layman, therefore, could not justly decide but in one way, and that in favor of the people claiming under the charter of 1662.

We thus find the Wyoming valley claimed by two separate and distinct parties. Firstly, under corporate grants from the king ; and after the termination of the rebellion, under two separate State sovereignties. The Governors of these issued their paper proclamations, and left the citizens of each to fight out the dispute in a hand to hand conflict ; and at it they went in literally bloody earnest.

The Yankees were ahead of the Pennamites in occupation. As early as 1753, the Susquehanna Company sent out John Jenkins, a surveyor, to make an exploration of the valley, and feel the Indian pulse ; and if favorable, to negotiate friendly relations with them.

His appointment from this company directed him "to repair to the said place" (Wyoming,) "in order to view said tract of land, and to purchase of the natives there inhabiting, their title and interest to said tract of land, and to survey, lay out, and receive proper deeds or conveyances of said land to and for said company."

Under these instructions he commenced the important part of the duty assigned to him, of concluding a purchase of the Indian title ; and his mission would undoubtedly have been attended with success, but for the interference, as we shall notice hereafter, by the Proprietary Government of Pennsylvania: William Penn being under the conviction, and probably honestly so, that the country of the Susquehanna legally belonged to him, under his Royal grant, though of a later date.

Through the representations made to the Susquehanna Company by Mr. Jenkins, on his return, and other reasons which do not become necessary here to state, but by the sanction, however, of the colonial authorities of both Connecticut and Pennsylvania, a Congress of delegates was convened at Albany, in 1754, with the approbation of the Crown, to meet the Iroquois, or the great confederated Six Nations of Indians, and consult together on the subject of their mutual welfare.

At this important council, it appears that the Proprietary Government of Pennsylvania was represented by distinguished men: John Penn, Isaac Norris, Benjamin Franklin and Richard Peters. And it is a marvel why the Proprietary Government, after the consent and approbation of the purchase of the Wyoming lands, by the Susquehanna Company, by such distinguished agents, should ever have made the effort to annul the solemn act of the Albany Congress! For at this very Congress, and as Mr. Miner states, "under the eye of the Pennsylvania Delegation, a treaty with the Indians, the acknowledged proprietors of the territory, was executed, dated July eleventh, 1754, and a purchase of land made." See *Miner's Hist.*, p. 68.

A deed was executed, signed by eighteen chiefs and sachems of the Six Nations, of the Wyoming lands, to the Susquehanna Company. The purchase money, "two thousand pounds current money of New York," was counted out in silver, "and carried by the Indians in a blanket into an orchard, and there divided among them." It is a little singular that the word MINES is mentioned in this ancient deed.

The Connecticut charter, therefore, based on a Royal grant, and a subsequent purchase of the Indian claim, would seem to establish an indisputable and unqualified title. Such, however, as the bloody sequel which follows shows, does not appear to have been so considered by the Proprietary Government of Pennsylvania.

In January following, the Pennsylvania authorities made an appeal to Governor Johnson of New York to use his influence with the Six Nations to nullify and cancel the deed made on the eleventh of July previous. This course was persisted in, until at a council, at Fort Stanwix, on the fifth of November, 1768, a conveyance of the same lands was made by the Iroquois to the Pennsylvania proprietors. At this time then, the local strife that had smouldered from 1754, broke out into a blazing, consuming fire.

In 1755, the Susquehanna Company again sent

Mr. Jenkins with a corps of surveyors to locate lands on the Susquehanna. Among these was Ezekiel Hyde, a well known name in the valley for years succeeding. Some surveys were made, and the party returned to Connecticut.

Some seven years elapsed before an effort was again made to establish a settlement in the valley. This delay was undoubtedly produced by the troubles and difficulties growing out of the English and French war, which terminated in 1763. The people, however, interested in, and claiming under, the Susquehanna Company, from the fact of the attempt being made by the Pennsylvania proprietors to destroy and annul the deed of the Iroquois, executed at Albany in 1754, came to the conclusion that their occupation must necessarily be one of conquest.

The Indian atmosphere was murky; dark clouds hung over the beautiful valley and the noble river meandering through as fertile soil as the husbandman ever cultivated,—as delightful a spot as ever the eye of red or white man looked upon. There was a prize worth a noble effort. The Yankee was fully persuaded as to the equity of his claim and the legality of his title, and why should he hesitate? It is true the Indian hand lay upon it, but he held against the solemn obligations of a treaty, and beside this it was weak. A powerful competitor had crossed the "big water in his big canoe," and he was strong.

There was but one avenue now open to occupation, and that was conquest. The treaty had been violated; the deed of purchase had been annulled. The man who had been reared amid New England rocks and upon her sterile soil, had manly development; he could endure hunger and fatigue; he possessed ambition and courage; these were about the only legacy inherited from his proud and independent ancestors. They had furnished him a precedent, in the way of adventure, remarkable for its boldness and daring. They had crossed a tempestuous and unknown sea in mid-winter, and planted the standard of religious toleration upon a savage and inclement coast. The fame of this achievement had been the first lesson of his infancy. For him to shrink, therefore, from the obstacles which lay in his road to the Susquehanna, and the difficulties which awaited him there, would be unworthy of his ancestral name. In money and this world's goods he was poor; but the self-denying, self-sacrificing and indomitable courage of his Puritan father led him on. That same blood which coursed through the veins of the bold Dissenter of the English Church, galloped in the veins of his offspring. If that one could muster resolution to abandon home and country upon the score of religious dogmas,—this one could enter the wilderness and maintain his home there against fearful opposition.

In 1762, the year preceding the treaty of peace between England and France, the Susquehanna Company sent out Mr. Jenkins again, in company with

Isaac Tripp, Benjamin Follet, William Buck and a hundred and fifteen other adventurers, to take possession of their lands here, and by force if necessary.

They commenced the erection of log houses at the mouth of Mill Creek, a mile above the site of Wilkes-Barré. They cleared some land and sowed it with grain ; but we learn of no effort to reconcile the Indians.

In the autumn of this year they returned to Connecticut. In the following spring they came back, and remained till the month of October, when they were expelled and driven from their improvements by the Indians. Some of them were cruelly butchered.

This was a check upon their enterprise. Those of them, however, who had seen the valley, became fascinated with the inducements it held out to them. They saw a plain of good and fertile land, twenty miles in extent, and an average of five in width. It was virgin soil: the plough-share had never entered the glebe. The climate was salubrious ; and when they compared this land with the rock-bound hills of their Connecticut homes, they regarded it as the land of promise, and one " flowing with milk and honey."

All these things they painted in glowing colors on their return ; but some of their brethren they left behind them, who had been murdered by the Indians. This was a drawback to their hopes and expectations, yet they coveted the land, though beset with dangers.

In hope and fear a half dozen more years passed away. The treaty at Fort Stanwix had been completed; the French and English war ended, and they supposed the Indian races had become more reconciled; and they began to prepare for another expedition to the Susquehanna country.

In 1768–9 the Connecticut people came back with a determination to remain. They had resolved to stand by their possessions; but upon their arrival in the valley, they found them in the occupation of Stewart, Ogden, Jennings and others, who had reached the valley a few days in advance of them, and had raised the flag of the Proprietary Government.

Here was a dilemma; this was an incident upon which they had made no calculation.

What was to be done? There were two alternatives only: either to retrace their steps to Connecticut, or stand their ground. They chose the latter.

And here began that long and bitter conflict between the Connecticut and Pennsylvania men, known as the "Yankee and Pennamite War," which never became finally settled till the passage of the compromise law of 1799, by the Legislature of Pennsylvania. Sometimes attended by bloodshed, sometimes reprisals only, but always a bitter and vindictive feud. The jails of the adjoining counties of Northampton and Northumberland were often filled with Wyoming prisoners, sent there by the authorities of Pennsylvania for trespassing on the disputed

5

lands. And thus a series of murders, arsons, battles, sieges, arrests and angry personal disputes, continued for more than a fourth of a century.

I have said that Ogden and his party occupied the Yankee buildings and improvements at the mouth of Mill Creek. They also erected a block house, the first military fortification in the valley. This looked too formidable for an attack, and the Yankee immigrants crossed the Susquehanna and erected a block house ; and in compliment to the number of men to whom the territory of Kingston was set off, they called it "Forty Fort."

After thus securing themselves, they concluded, upon consultation, to attack Ogden and his party in his stronghold. They crossed the river, and invested his fortification. In the name of Connecticut they demanded a surrender. Ogden hoisted a white flag and demanded a parley. The Yankees sent a committee to the fort, as they supposed, to agree upon terms of capitulation and surrender, when they were arrested by the sheriff of the county of Northampton, who was concealed in the fort, with his warrant of arrest in his pocket. The committee being seized, the party outside surrendered, and the whole number were marched over the Blue Mountain to the Easton jail.

This quiet and unresisting surrender was an evidence certainly, that these Connecticut men were a law-abiding and peace-loving people. A few years later we shall find that they were not so submissive to the Proprietary civil authorities.

They were soon released, however, upon giving bail for their appearance, when they returned to their land of promise.

As there were a hundred and sixty behind, of the two hundred raised by the Susquehanna Company, these came on soon after the return of the Easton prisoners, and erected a fortification on the southern extremity of the Wilkes-Barré river common. This, in honor of their captain, they christened Fort Durkee.

Within less than two years after the first real occupation of the valley by white men, the Yankees had two fortifications—Forty Fort and Fort Durkee; and the Pennamites, Fort Ogden.

A pretty good display, for mutual attack and defense, considering the Indian tribes that both of them had to contend with. As was to be supposed, Ogden could not withstand the forces occupying the two fortifications, and in 1770 they expelled him.

This act aroused the Proprietary Government, and they sent back Ogden with additional men, who erected Fort Wyoming, on the common, near the terminus of Northampton street, and some sixty rods above Fort Durkee.

This enabled the Pennamites to retake Fort Ogden at Mill Creek. During this year the parties, being pretty equally divided as to numbers, carried on a succession of storms and sieges, arrests and imprisonments; sometimes attended with the death of a man or two, and the wounding of several, without any decided advantage upon either side.

Of the party who came out to the valley in 1768–69 there was a son of John Jenkins, known in the subsequent history of the valley as Lieutenant, and afterwards as Colonel John Jenkins. This young man, then in his nineteenth year, became one of the prominent and leading spirits of the valley in the long and continuous chain of tragic events, which occurred during the quarter of a century succeeding the first settlement of it.

And although Lieutenant Jenkins does not come within the exact sphere to which I have limited my sketches, I will not pass over him in silence. I shall have occasion to use his Diary hereafter, and a brother of his belonged to the Plymouth colony. His father having been the leading man in immigration, and Provisional Judge of the new settlement up to the time the town of Westmoreland was established by the State of Connecticut, and made a part of the county of Litchfield, and a long period subsequently; also a prominent person among the pioneers: president of that town meeting of the people of Westmoreland, held on the first of August, 1775, approving of the acts of Congress which preceded the Declaration of Independence, and also of the meeting held on the eighth of August following, when the feeble colony endorsed the measures of Congress "in opposing ye late measures adopted by Parliament to enslave America;" in 1776 a member of the Colonial Assembly from Westmoreland; at the meeting of the people, over which Colonel Zebulon Butler presided, convened at Wilkes-Barré on the twenty-fourth of August, 1776, when it was resolved to proceed at once to the erection of forts for the common defense, "without fee or reward from ye town," and immediately after this meeting joined with his neighbors, in the erection of Fort Jenkins, in the upper end of the valley : all of which furnished young Jenkins with a motive for the entry into that field, which afterwards became one of danger, toil, and exposure.

In October, 1776, he enlisted in Captain Solomon Strong's company of United States troops, Twenty-fourth Regiment Connecticut Militia, as First Lieutenant. In the year 1777 he was taken prisoner and sent to Fort Niagara, where he was treated, after the fashion of all the Continental soldiers, with great severity—brutality is the better word. In 1778 he made his escape, and after many exposures and great suffering, he made his way to his family, in Westmoreland. On the day of the Wyoming battle, he was assigned by Colonel Butler to take charge of Forty Fort. After the terrible disasters of that day of gloom and horrors, we find him among the fugitives in their desolate march through the wilderness. He accompanied Colonel Hartley in his march from the

west branch of the Susquehanna, through the Indian
country to Tioga Point, and participated in all the
engagements in that expedition with the Indians and
Tories. He was detailed to the command of the
company, charged with the burial of the slain on the
Wyoming battle-field. This was accomplished on the
twenty-second of October, 1778. General Washington
summoned him to his headquarters in the early part
of the year 1779, for the purpose of procuring information, preparatory to the march of the expedition
under General Sullivan, as to the condition and state
of affairs along the line of that anticipated military
movement. He returned from headquarters, and met
Sullivan at Wilkes-Barré, and was appointed by that
general as his guide, up the Susquehanna, and through
the Indian country. He participated in the skirm-
ishes and battles of that expedition. He was also at
the siege of York Town, and in the trenches, under
Baron Steuben, at the surrender of that place.

This man passed an eventful life, and may be
classed among the prominent leading men of the valley. The Diary of local events, which he kept, has
been of great benefit to the historians of the valley.
The data are written in plain and intelligible language,
and so far as corroborating circumstances are left to
us, they are remarkable for their truthfulness. He
began with the occupation of the valley, and he survived its perils and afflictions. Always taking an active part, and ever at the post of honor and of dan-

ger. He lived to realize the fruits of his early hardships, and died, at his residence, *upon* the Wyoming battle-ground, on the nineteenth of March, 1827, in his seventy-sixth year.

I have in a manner digressed from the line of local township history, in giving this short notice of one of the prominent men of the valley ; but as he headed that colonial band who forced their way through the wilderness—through the Indian border bristling with spear heads—exposed to hunger and the severest suffering and privations, I felt that I could not pass the old veteran by, in silence.

But the chances are that the Yankees would have been driven out of the valley by force, had they not been joined by Captain Lazarus Stewart, and his company of forty others, known as the Paxton Rangers. This new ally produced a kind of equilibrium of power, and saved the Connecticut men from probable defeat and expulsion.

These men came from the county of Lancaster, Pennsylvania, to join the Connecticut standard. They were a brave and gallant set of men, fearing no danger, and able to sustain great fatigue and exposure. The late Judge Matthias Hollenback, the head of the family of that name in this county, was one of these Paxton Rangers. The Susquehanna Company gave them the township of Hanover, as a consideration for their services to the Yankee cause.

Captain Lazarus Stewart was a bold, chivalrous

soldier.   I cannot pass the opportunity without saying a word or two about this remarkable man.

He commanded a company at Braddock's defeat, in
the French and English war.   He was engaged to be
married to a Lancaster girl, on his return from the
war.   In his absence, the home of the father of this
young lady was burned by Indians, and the whole
family butchered : her head was severed from her
body, and planted upon a pole, and raised above the
smouldering ruins.

Captain Stewart on his return from the disasters
of Braddock's field, was in time to see the slaughtered remains of this family, and of his affianced
bride.   The smoke of the building had not yet subsided on his arrival.   The scene lashed his mind into
a state of fury.   Seized with a paroxysm of frenzy,
and impelled by a deep sense of revenge, he swore
eternal enmity toward the whole Indian race.   Brood-
ing over the terrible wrongs he had received, he
became more and more embittered against the Indian
tribes.   He firmly resolved that between him and
them, there should be no peace.   He pursued and
slew them whenever the opportunity was presented.
He was unceasing in his energy, and unrelenting in
his purpose.   This conduct the Proprietary Government could not sanction.   It was the policy of the
government to have peace with the Indian tribes if
possible.   The course of Captain Stewart was prohib-
ited by law, and the consequences were that the Pro-

prietary Government ordered his arrest and trial.
This he would not submit to. He turned his eye to
the Wyoming valley, and his mind to the making of
a league with the Connecticut settlers.

The views and opinions of these people ran in the
same channel with his own. They hated the Indians and so did he. They were in opposition to the
Proprietary Government, and the curbing of his revenge by that government, had placed him in that
position also.

The Wyoming valley was therefore the spot of
all others for him; and the hardy pioneers of New
England, fighting under the rights of first grant and
first occupation, in deadly hostility to the jurisdiction
of Pennsylvania, were the people whose sympathies
were in perfect accord with his own.

Here then was a new field for operations. He
made up his mind to enter it. He made common
cause with the Wyoming settlers. At the head of
his brave and intrepid band he came, and surrounded
by his new allies, he threw down the gage of battle,
and with them and their fortunes he pledged the
service of his life.

And true to them and their cause he faithfully
remained. Wherever was the post of danger, there
was Captain Stewart. He was one of the leading
spirits of the Connecticut men amidst all their conflicts, even up to his death upon the Wyoming battle-ground, where he fell at the head of his company,
in the foremost rank.

For the particular biography of this remarkable person, I refer the reader to the "*Annals of Luzerne*," written by one of his kinsmen, Stewart Pearce, Esq. They are well worthy a perusal. I have glanced only at the picture, which is there very cleverly drawn.

The Yankees being joined by such an auxiliary as Captain Lazarus Stewart, and who by his military prowess and daring had infused into the rank and file of the company under his command all the spirit and enthusiasm of their leader, were rejoiced at this piece of good fortune. It gave them new hope, it nerved them with new energy.

A new spirit seemed to prevail, and the capture of a fort upon an assault for that purpose, under the charge of Stewart and his Paxton boys, as they were termed, was always a matter of almost absolute certainty.

Thus, at the very commencement of the actual settlement of the lands upon the Susquehanna, we find two hostile flags displayed, each as the index of a separate power. And while the continued struggle upon the side of both belligerents was pretended to be classed under a civil régime, and as a means only of adjusting civil wrongs, there were all the paraphernalia and outward demonstrations of war—fortifications, arms, munitions, drills, parades, and all the demonstrations and martial appearances which surround the camp. And to complete the picture, there was the most vindictive and burning hate in the hearts of the opposing factions. The Yankee hated the Pennamite, and the Pennamite hated the Yankee. There was not the least particle of love between them, to incur the risk of loss.

The capturing and recapturing of forts, the taking of prisoners, robbery and murder, all passed under the name of civil proceedings. The sheriff of Northampton would have a hundred armed deputies to execute a warrant, and Sheriff Cook, of Northumberland, was surrounded by Colonel Plunket and seven hundred militia, to make an arrest of a few persons charged with a breach of the peace!

This was the way in which the Proprietary Government conducted its civil administration!

And in the selection of agents by it, men were appointed who seemed to pay no regard to the ordinary feelings of humanity. A fellow, by the name of Alexander Patterson, who was sent to Wilkes-Barré as a civil ruler, seemed to relish the persecutions he heaped upon his prisoners, to a degree that astonishes the mind of a civilized man; and he gloried in the opportunity for the exercise of his vindictive feelings toward the Yankee population. He regarded them as outlaws, and no punishment was too severe to inflict upon them. Some of the acts of brutality of this *civil magistrate*, upon Plymouth men, I shall allude to hereafter.

But it is not within the line I have shaped out to

go into a general account of the circumstances and incidents of this Pennamite and Yankee war, save so far as it may have a particular bearing upon the people of Plymouth.

To those who would wish to understand the subject in its lengthy details, I must refer them to our local historians—Chapman, Miner, Pearce, Peck and Stone. The three first named, speak more particularly of this conflict than the two latter.

The chief scenes of these feuds were upon the east side of the river, and in the vicinity of the forts at and near Wilkes-Barré—though the last grand demonstration came off at the battle of Nanticoke, which was upon Plymouth soil.

The people of Plymouth had a small fort or stockade upon "Garrison Hill," which had been erected by the early settlers, in 1776, as their first movement of defensive operations, on the declaration of war, by the United States against Great Britain. This spot is at the turn of the flat road, and some seventy rods from the main travelled road through the town, and not far from the location of the old "swing gate."

It was years ago, and within my recollection, the field where we went in search of Indian curiosities—arrow-heads, pipes, stone hatchets, pots, etc., and sometimes we would find leaden bullets and pieces of broken muskets, which were the evidences of civilization.

This stockade never became necessary for the exercise of its military properties, in the Revolutionary or Pennamite troubles. It was important, however, as an Indian defense.

But the people of Plymouth, composing at least one-fifth of the whole population of the valley, had their full share of the troubles, as well as the responsibilities of the border war. Several of our people were killed, many of them imprisoned and cruelly treated—for it was the Plymouth man who received no quarter, if he was so unfortunate as to fall into the enemy's hands.

As the Shawnee tribe before them had been the especial objects of persecution by their masters, the Iroquois, so their misfortunes seemed to have fallen on their successors, as to the spirit of malevolence ; and whenever one of them fell into the clutches of Esquire Patterson, or Captains Christie and Shrawder, he was certain to feel the pangs of their malice.

These people had been of the first Connecticut importation—"The Forty Thieves," as Patterson denounced them, and as such he treated them.

Mr. Miner, in his history of Wyoming, informs us that Patterson, in his capacity as Justice of the Peace, visited the Shawnee settlement with an armed force, and under some legal pretext, arrested eleven respectable citizens and sent them under guard to the fort at Wilkes-Barré.

"Among the prisoners was Major Prince Alden,

sixty-five years old, feeble from age and suffering from disease. Compassion yielded nothing to attenuate his sufferings. Captain James Bidlack was also arrested. He was between sixty and seventy. His son of the same name had fallen, as previously recorded, at the head of his company in the Indian battle; another son, Benjamin, had served in the army through the Revolutionary war. Mr. Bidlack himself had been taken by the savages and suffered a tedious captivity in Canada. All this availed him nothing. Benjamin Harvey, who had been a prisoner to the Indians, was also arrested. Samuel Ransom, son of Captain Ransom, who had fallen in the massacre, was most rudely treated on being arrested. 'Ah, ha!' cried Patterson, 'you are the jockey we wanted; away with him to the guard-house, with old Harvey, another damned rascal!'

"Eleven in all were taken and driven to the fort, where they were confined in a room with a mud floor, on the thirty-first of October, wet and comfortless, with no food and little fire, which as they were sitting round, Captain Christie came in, ordered them to lie down on the ground, and bade the guard to blow out the brains of any one who should attempt to rise. Even the staff of the aged Mr. Alden was taken from him."

The object of these acts of brutality upon the part of Patterson, it is supposed, was to enable him in their absence, to drive their families from their houses and their homes, and put some of his minions in their places. Another motive may have been to punish old Mr. Harvey for an act it appears he had committed, which consisted in being sent as an agent by some of his people to Connecticut, to ascertain the names of the two hundred, who came out under the auspices of the Susquehanna Company.

I insert an extract of a letter from Captain Shrawder, who backed legal precepts with a military company, and was at that time stationed at Wilkes-Barré. This letter bears date, Wyoming, March thirtieth, 1783. " On Monday Colonel Butler arrived here, and the day following he and several of the principal inhabitants were over the river to Shawnee; but whether on private (as they would fain make me believe) or public business, I cannot tell. On Thursday they had a town meeting here, when they agreed, according to Captain Spalding's information to me, to send Mr. Harvey to a certain place in Connecticut for a copy of records, to see what time the first settlers came here, and who they were; accordingly Mr. Harvey set off yesterday morning."

This little piece of service, therefore, of Mr. Harvey, was by no means palatable to Patterson and Shrawder, and was a thing to be jotted down and remembered some day on the general summing up of charges against the "damned rascal," as Patterson pleased to designate him.

The jail calendar at Easton contains the names,

among others, of Gideon Church, Abram Pike,
Thomas Heath, Prince Alden, Justin Gaylord, Abraham Nesbitt, and Benjamin Bidlack. But this was
but one importation. The calendars of that and the
Sunbury jail, in Northumberland, if all produced,
would run into scores. And for what offence? The
cultivation and claim of land to which they had the
first grant and the first occupation. And this was
defined and punished as a crime, in the terrible days
of which we are writing.

The people of our town had, in common with
their New England friends, done everything in their
power to aid the Colonial struggle in the effort for
liberty. At least two men out of three were in the
Revolutionary service, including the terrible slaughter
at Wyoming, and still this great tax, paid with half
their substance, and sealed on Revolutionary battle-
fields with the heart's blood of scores of them, availed
them nothing, after the surrender of Cornwallis' sword
to Washington. The occupation of land they had
settled upon was a sufficient cause, upon the part of
the Proprietary Government, to harrass the remnant
of them, saved from slaughter, with every imaginable
device.

When peace came, most of the soldiers of the nation who had survived the seven-years' conflict, were
at rest. Not so with the people of Plymouth and the
Wyoming valley at large. The foreign foe had suffered his defeat, returned to his home, and yielded

to the fortunes of war; and the people generally who had achieved the victory were at rest. But the Wyoming soldier, on returning to his fireside after a seven-years' siege, and when he should have been released from further exposure and excitement, could not lay down his arms; for though war had relieved nearly the whole country, it still showed its glowering features at the threshold of his home.

He had survived Brandywine and Germantown, to meet as vindictive a foe, on his return, as he had faced upon those fields. This was cruelly hard, but so it seemed to have been noted down in the book of his destiny.

As the battle of Nanticoke was contested on Plymouth soil, and as every able-bodied man and boy in the township were engaged in it, there will be a propriety in giving the full details of it. At least one third of the Yankee force was made up of its citizens.

In the month of December, 1775, the Proprietary Government sent an armed force of some five hundred men, under the command of Colonel William Plunket, to destroy the Yankee settlement at Muncy, on the west branch of the Susquehanna. This settlement embraced the two townships of Charleston and Judea, which were within the limits of the charter of the Susquehanna Company, though settled some years after the Wyoming valley. The number being small, and not having the necessary means of defense, they were obliged to surrender at discretion.

6

One man was killed by Plunket's command, a few wounded, and, as was usual in such cases, the leading men were conveyed to the Sunbury Jail.

Flushed with this easy victory over the defenseless people of Charleston and Judea, the Proprietary Government resolved upon sending Colonel Plunket to Wyoming, to remove the Yankees from that place.

So they commenced making preparation for the campaign, by the addition of two hundred more Northumberland militia, collecting the necessary supplies and boats for their transportation.

Any property in those times which belonged to a Wyoming Yankee, was the proper subject of plunder by the Proprietary Government, through its agents. It required two boats to carry their supplies, ammunition, and a field-piece. It seems they were determined on this occasion to add artillery to their small arms. It would have a more imposing appearance.

They had little difficulty in procuring their ships of war. They were at hand. A boat of Benjamin Harvey, Jr., had been seized a few days before at Fort Augusta, and the cargo confiscated, upon the ground that he was a traitor to the government. One of his neighbors had been treated in the same way. Here then were the two boats for the expedition. And what was better, Mr. Harvey was impressed in the service, to pilot the boats up the Susquehanna, with the glorious privilege, on arriving at Nanticoke, of shooting at, or being shot by, his family and friends. But there was no release from his position. There is no apology available against vindictive force. He submitted.

But there was another necessary wanting. When the Proprietary Government made war, it was done under the authority of a civil process. To meet this emergency, a warrant was sworn out to arrest some Yankee settler for treason. Against whom it was directed in this case, we have not the record to show. The blanks in these warrants were generally filled up with the names of John Franklin, Zebulon Butler, Lazarus Stewart or one of the Harveys. But this was of little importance. The warrant of arrest was obtained, and put in the hands of Sheriff Cook, of the county of Northumberland, for execution, in the name and on behalf of the Proprietary Government of Pennsylvania.

The two hundred additional men were mustered into the service of the sheriff's posse, which now numbered from six to seven hundred strong. Ammunition and supplies were stored in the two ships of war, the cannon mounted, and in the early part of December, the soldiery commenced their march to Wyoming, upon the main road skirting the west side of the river; and the flotilla, with Benjamin Harvey, Jr., as pilot, weighed anchor upon the head-waters of the Susquehanna. With colors flying and martial instruments sending out notes of the slogan, or some other tune in character, the whole force commenced their movement toward the enemy's country.

On the twentieth of December, Colonel Plunket, at the head of his invading army,—to carry out the civil process in the hands of Sheriff Cook,—arrived at the mouth of Nescopeck creek, something like twenty miles below Nanticoke. On this very day Congress, probably having been informed of the onslaught upon the poor settlers of Charleston and Judea, and the preparation by the Pennsylvania authorities, prompted by the chivalrous acts of the colonel in that campaign, for the subjugation, if not the expulsion of the Yankees on the north branch of the Susquehanna, passed a very important resolution.

Its substance is, that in the opinion of Congress, the contending parties on the Susquehanna should cease all hostilities, and avoid every appearance of force ; that all property taken should be immediately restored to the original owners ; that there should be no interruption caused by either party in the passing and repassing of persons behaving peaceably, through the disputed territory; that those who had been seized and kept in custody ought to be immediately released, that they might go to their respective homes; and recommending peace and quiet until a legal decision could be had on the dispute, or until Congress should take further orders.

It is probable that, in those days of mail facilities, Colonel Plunket and Sheriff Cook did not receive this resolution of Congress till after the battle of Nanticoke, which was fought on the twenty-fourth and twenty-fifth. It is possible, however, that the knowledge of this may have had something to do with their precipitate retreat; and it is fair to presume that their Yankee reception, the floating ice in the river, and the severe cold weather which came on every northern blast, had much more to do with it. Railroads and telegraph wires had not then made their appearance.

There was but little ice in the Susquehanna, when the expedition left Fort Augusta. This obstruction, however, increased as they ascended the river. The fact of making but thirty miles in three or four days is evidence that they had pretty serious obstacles in the way.

The people of the valley had received information of the fitting out of the expedition, before the march had been commenced from Sunbury. They therefore had but little time for preparation. And as there had been a respite from any serious collisions for a year or two previous, they were not in a condition to meet successfully so large an opposing force. The whole valley could not muster, including old and young, seven hundred men.

Under the direction, however, of Colonel Zebulon Butler, they commenced operations with a right good will. Impressed with the idea that they were to fight on their own territory, and in defense of their civil rights, their homes and their children, they mustered men and boys some three hundred. A small force compared with the little army of Colonel Plunket; but for the deficiency in rank and file, they made up in resolution and courage. Those who could not be provided with guns were supplied with long poles with scythes fastened upon the ends—a formidable weapon in a hand to hand encounter; and as the soldiers marched along they jokingly named their unique weapons, "the end of time."

On the night of the twenty-third of December, Colonel Butler encamped with his command near the mouth of Harvey's creek. From this position he sent Major John Garret, with a flag, down the river some two or three miles to meet the advancing column, and inquire of Colonel Plunket as to the meaning of this hostile approach and military display? Major Garret was informed that it was altogether a peaceable demonstration, for no purpose but to aid the sheriff of Northumberland county in executing a warrant for the arrest of several persons at Wyoming, for the violation of the laws of the Proprietary Government, and that it was to be hoped there would be no resistance to such a reasonable and proper request!

And this was the mode and manner, at that time, in this part of Pennsylvania, of executing civil process! Major Garret knew well, from the military force before him, that this declaration was a most infamous lie.

So on his return, he reported that the enemy outnumbered their own forces more than two to one. "The conflict will be a sharp one, boys," said he. "I for one am ready to die, if it need be, for my country."

Early on the morning of the twenty-fourth, Colonel Butler retired up the river about a mile from the place, where he had bivouacked on the night of the twenty-third, to a point of natural defense on the Harvey farm. This natural defense consists of a line of elevated rocks, extending from the base of the mountain, in a south-easterly direction, almost to the bank of the river, a distance probably of half a mile. The road crossed this ledge through a gorge in the rocky promontory, at a short distance from the river. The ground was covered with forest trees. Here he took his stand ; his men finishing an addition to the breast-work, which they had partially constructed on their way down. The outline of this natural barricade may be easily traced by the eye. On the south-west line of it are the entrances to a coal mine which is now in operation.

Colonel Butler, on leaving his camp in the morning, had detailed Ensign Mason Fitch Alden, with eighteen men, to remain there as a corps of observation, with orders to report as to any movement of the enemy.

He also detached Captain Lazarus Stewart, with twenty men, with orders to cross the river to the east side, and take position a short distance above the Nanticoke falls, on the Lee farm, to repel any attempt that might be made, on the part of the enemy, to effect a landing on that side of the stream.

Having thus disposed of the details of his plan of arrangement, and which were done with profound military skill, he put his men in position behind his rock barricade, and awaited the approach of the enemy. He was thus guarded at all points, and his position was one that was almost impregnable against a force, such as was about to advance upon it.

On the same morning, December twenty-fourth, Colonel Plunket reached the ground occupied by Alden, about eleven o'clock. Alden slowly retiring out of the reach of gunshot, was followed by the enemy up to the barricades.

Colonel Plunket marched up with much display, his drums beating and music pealing from his instruments. Observing the strong position before him, he halted at a respectable distance, exclaiming, "My God! what a breast-work."

Mr. Miner, in his history of this battle, and whose text I have mainly relied on, says that John Carey, who was in the action, told him, in speaking of the conduct of Colonel Butler throughout the affair, "I loved the man; he was an honor to the human species."

The taking of life was not the object or design of these defensive operations. As the Yankees were in a safe position, Colonel Butler ordered his entire line to fire a volley of blank cartridges, thinking that this would give the enemy the idea, by the report, that their force corresponded with the formidable character of their breast-work.

The device answered the purpose; the enemy's line was thrown into confusion. Without firing a gun they retreated out of range of the fire at the breast-work.

Colonel Plunket, supposing that the barricade could not be stormed without great loss, commenced another movement. Placing a reconnoitring force into a boat, he directed them to cross the river, with a view of ascertaining the practicability of entering the valley, on the east side. The passage of this boat and crew was watched by both parties with much anxiety. The Yankees, however, had some knowledge as to the result of the adventure, which the Pennamites did not.

As a kind of shield, Benjamin Harvey, Jr., was put upon this boat. As the crew were approaching the shore, Capt. Stewart with his guard of twenty men gave them a volley. As there were no blank cartridges about this part of the affair, there was some mischief done; two or three were wounded, and probably the whole crew would have been killed if Harvey had not called out to them to desist, as they might kill some of their friends. Recognizing him, Captain Stewart discontinued his fire.

The crew plying their oars, and coming within the draught of the rapids below, passed through them in a moment.

And thus ended the operations of the twenty-fourth. Colonel Plunket withdrew to the camp which Colonel Butler had left in the morning, and remained there over night.

The result of a military consultation that night, it is to be presumed, held between him and Sheriff Cook, was to divide the attacking column in the morning—the right of his line to storm the breast-works of the Yankees, and the left to outflank their right. This was a matter which seemed more feasible in theory, than it afterwards proved to be when tested. And if Colonel Plunket had understood the ground as well as Colonel Butler did, he might have changed his plan of attack.

I have already stated that this natural defense of rocky ledges was nearly a half mile in length, striking the base of a very steep hill on the west terminus, and reaching nearly to the bank of the river on the east. A flanking movement, therefore, on the settlers' right, was opposed by a steep hill, and by the river on the left. This then was impracticable. And as for storming or scaling the breast-work, that was a serious affair when met squarely in the face.

With this plan of operations in view, Colonel Plunket marched out of camp, on Christmas morning, to give battle. Concealing his men with branches

and loose rocks, he advanced upon the fortifications.
The fire now became general along the whole line.
Guarded at all points, Colonel Butler had provided
for the movement on his right, by detaching a force
to guard his flank, at the base of the mountain.

The conflict lasted most of the day. The flanking party was repulsed at every attempt, to storm or
scale the fortifications.

It has never been known what number were
killed or wounded in this battle. Probably as many
as a dozen were slain on both sides, and maybe three
times that number wounded. A son of Surveyor-
General Lukens was killed, on the side of the enemy,
and I have been informed by those who were in the
battle, that there were three or four others, and several wounded.

Four days after the battle, December twenty-
ninth, the records show that the people of Westmoreland were in town meeting, and among other things
they,

" *Voted*—Titus Hinman and Perin Ross be appointed to collect the charity of the people for the
support of the widow Baker, the widow Franklin,
and the widow Ensign."

Baker and Franklin were Plymouth men.

Mr. Miner gives it as his opinion, and he had
been very industrious in the collection of facts in the
compilation of his history, and most of his knowledge derived from the actors in the affair—"that

probably six or eight were killed, and three times that number wounded," on the side of the settlers.

Towards the close of the day, Colonel Plunket, finding Colonel Butler's position too strong to be carried, withdrew from the field, and immediately commenced his retreat on the west side of the river.

He was pursued by Captain Stewart on the east side of the river some miles, but without any damaging results.

And thus ended the battle of Nanticoke. The design of the invasion, in mid winter, though with very formidable numbers for those days, was an evidence if not of folly, at least a want of military skill and precaution. The battle itself was the most formidable, and concentrated more force, and was attended with more bloodshed, than any one other conflict between the Connecticut and Pennsylvania people. And as the field of action was upon Plymouth soil, that township being more in immediate danger, it is probable that on that memorable day, there was not one of her citizens, capable of bearing arms, that was not engaged in it.

An incident or two connected with the battle of Nanticoke, must be mentioned for the first time in history. It is related by William Jameson, who was in the engagement, that he and old Benjamin Harvey (father of the Benjamin impressed in the boat service of Colonel Plunket) occupied a position together behind one of the rock breast-works. Mr. Harvey was an aged man, and grandfather of Jameson Harvey, Esq., late of Plymouth. He fought with a musket, and as the old hero would drive down the bullet with his ramrod, he would "pray the Lord to direct it to the hearts of the bloody Pennamites;" and whenever he would fire through the loop-hole, he would exclaim, "there, damn you, take that!" He thus loaded with a prayer and discharged with a curse !

I learn on traditionary authority, that on the first day of the battle, when Colonel Butler ordered the first round of blank cartridges to be fired, he noticed the bark, limbs, and twigs falling on his left where the Plymouth men were stationed. He turned to a subaltern, remarking, "that there was no more use in attempting to restrain those fellows, (the Shawnees) than wild Arabs ; that they would shoot a Pennamite if they knew they were to die for it the next minute, and by refraining, they could save their life."

More than fifty years ago, I remember seeing a large flat rock, set up on edge between two trees, near the natural breast-work, upon this battle-field. It stood between two chestnuts, and as the trees grew, it became firmly imbedded between them. This was pointed out to me by my father as "one of the barricades of the early settlers of the valley, in a battle that had been fought on that ground many years before." I saw it often in after years. It is not there now.

Progress has removed this old landmark, an in-

dex of early border warfare, a monument in commemoration of brave and fearless men, and around
which clung the dearest recollections of the past.

Why was it done?

Progress did the work, and so progress drilled
holes into the great boulder, detached from the
precipice, on the brow of the hill above and near the
entrance to the Grand Tunnel, and put in blasts of
powder and rent it into pieces. This huge rock,
some ten feet in height, with an even surface of
some twenty feet in diameter, was a precious relic of
the past : it was the threshing-floor of old Benjamin
Harvey, before the dawn of Independence. It remained there quietly in its bed as late as 1840. Progress itched for its destruction, and it is gone!

The next movement of this modern Sirocco will
be the tearing away of the old Academy. Vandal-
ism is unloosed.

Progress, unrestrained by sound and discriminating judgment, is a more ferocious monster than the
beast of seven heads and ten horns of the Apoca-
lypse, which arose out of the sea, the fearful type of
the great enemy of man, and which so troubled the
visions of St. John!

His greedy and capacious maw can contain everything : Yankee fortifications, rock threshing-floors,
public commons, dedicated under the solemnities of
law as places for the recreation of toiling men and
their little ones; the Column Vendome, the Palace

of the Tuilleries, and will yet swallow up the Pyr-
amids !

Progress will soon turn his great glaring eye-balls
upon the old Academy, which in its day, has sent out
some of the very best business and professional men
of this Commonwealth. You who doubt, look to the
substantial business men and merchants of Plymouth during the last thirty years, and call to mind
the stirring appeals and nervous forensic declama-
tions of Harrison Wright.

It is a subject of regret that, of the numerous
members of the Harvey family, many of them being
conspicuous men in the early settlement of Plymouth,
no likeness is to be had of any one of the earlier immigrants.

I insert the photograpic likeness of Mr. Jameson
Harvey, now well advanced in years; but who is of
the third generation of the family, since their settlement in the town. The same farm that his grandfather resided upon, this gentleman occupied as his
home till within the last three years, when he removed to Wilkes-Barré, where he now resides. The
land is underlaid with coal, and has become very valuable.

CHAPTER V.

THE battle of Nanticoke was upon the eve of the Revolution. The intervening time was but from Christmas to July. Local strifes were to be laid aside. The great and momentous question of a nation's liberty, was at hand. The cry "to arms!" resounded throughout the land. The issue was between Liberty and Despotism. The people of Plymouth were undivided on this issue; their enemies were not. Our town furnished more soldiers than its quota.

For the present we pass over the ensuing seven years of toil and exposure, of misery and bloodshed, and come down to the close of the rebellion, to see how our veterans were rewarded for their sacrifices and their valor.

Articles of peace, in which the Independence of the United States of America was recognized, were signed and exchanged on the twentieth day of November, 1782. The soldiers of Plymouth who had survived the terrible encounter returned to their

(110)

homes in the winter of 1782–83. They laid aside their implements of war, and took up those of the husbandman. During the summer they prepared their ground and sowed their grain, but they were not allowed to gather their harvest.

They would do to fight on the battle-fields for liberty, but not to reap the harvest their hands had prepared. The children of the men who perished from the inclemency of the winter at Valley Forge, or who fell at the Wyoming Massacre, could plant the seeds, but not gather the crop.

On the thirteenth and fourteenth of March, 1784, occurred the memorable ice flood in the Susquehanna. The elements seemed to have joined the common enemy of the poor settlers. It is said that misfortunes never come singly.

I copy the account of the flood and its disasters from Mr. Chapman:

"After a winter of unusual severity, about the middle of March the weather became suddenly warm, and on the thirteenth and fourteenth rain fell in torrents, melting the deep snows throughout all the hills and valleys, in the upper regions watered by the Susquehanna. The following day the ice in the river began to break up, and the streams rose with great rapidity. The ice first gave way at the different rapids, and floating down in great masses, lodged against the frozen surface of the more gentle parts of the river, where it remained firm. In this manner

7

several large dams were formed, which caused such an accumulation of water that the river overflowed all its banks, and one general inundation overspread the extensive plains of Wyoming. The inhabitants took refuge, and saw their property exposed to the fury of the waters.

"At length the upper dam gave way; huge masses of ice were scattered in every direction. The deluge bore down upon the dams below, which successively yielded to the insupportable burden, and the whole went off with the noise of contending storms. Houses, barns, stacks of hay and grain were swept off in the general destruction, to be seen no more. The plain on which the village of Wilkes-Barré is built, was covered with heaps of ice, which continued. a great portion of the following summer."

A graphic and well-drawn picture, truly. Those who have witnessed the breaking up of the huge ice fields of the Susquehanna, caused by a sudden thaw, will recognize the force and power of the description from the pen of Mr. Chapman.

There has been no flood approximating to its character since, in the Susquehanna. The one known as "St. Patrick's Flood," of 1865, approaches the nearest to it. So called because of its occurrence on the seventeenth and eighteenth of March, the former being the birth-day of that saint.

It was regarded as proper for the subject of record. The court of the county at August session 1865, caused the following entry to be made on the minutes : "The flood of the seventeenth and eighteenth of March, 1865, known as "St. Patrick's Flood," was 24 7-10ths feet above low-water mark in the Susquehanna, and it is the general opinion that it was four feet higher than the "Pumpkin Flood" of October, 1786."

From the most reliable information I can gather, the flood of 1784 was from five to six feet higher than the one of 1865. It may therefore be styled the king of the floods of the Susquehanna. The river probably rose thirty-three feet above its ordinary low-water mark. A fearful and terrible deluge was the result.

The people of our town were not aware of these sudden and great rises which occasionally occurred in the Susquehanna, and therefore did not exercise proper precaution in the selection of the sites for their new homes. There were eight or nine dwellings on "Garrison Hill" in 1784. No one in these days would think of erecting buildings upon that level. All of those dwellings with their sheds and out-houses were swept off, in that memorable flood. Rev. Benjamin Bidlack was carried away in the house he occupied. After a perilous voyage of a night, plunging about amidst ice bergs and floating débris, expecting every moment to be engulphed, he finally found a safe harbor at the lower end of the Shawnee Flats.

Mr. Asa Jackson, of Abraham's Plains, was drowned. There were no lives lost in Plymouth, but the destruction of property there, as well as throughout the valley, was immense.

Before the calamities of the flood had subsided, the people of Plymouth and the whole valley were subjected to a new horror.

Alexander Patterson, the civil magistrate of Wilkes-Barré, conceived that the time had come to exterminate the Yankee race in Wyoming. Devoid of the common impulses of the human heart, and impelled by the most wicked designs, he commenced the work of driving a helpless people, now composed principally of old men, boys, women and children, from the few homes that the angry waters had spared them.

John Franklin, whose brother was a Plymouth man, and had been killed at the battle of Nanticoke, informs us in his journal, "that the soldiers (Christie's and Shrawder's companies, stationed in the Wilkes-Barré garrison, and the body guard of Patterson), were set to work removing the fences from the enclosures of the inhabitants, laying fields of grain open to be devoured, fencing up the highways, and between the houses of the settlers and their wells of water; that they were not permitted to procure water from their wells, or travel their usual highways. The greater part of the people were in the most distressed situation, numbers having had their houses swept off by the uncommon overflowing of the Susquehanna, in the month of March preceding; numbers were without shelter and in a starving condition. They were not suffered to cut a stick of timber, or make any shelters for their families. They were forbid to draw their nets to fish; their nets were taken from them by the officers of the garrison. The settlers were often dragged out of their beds in the night season by ruffians, and beat in a cruel manner. Complaints were made to the justices, as well as to the commanding officers of the garrison, but to no purpose, and were equally callous to every feeling of humanity."

What a picture is here presented of the condition of our people. The elements and the wrath of man seemed to have been in accord. The evil passions of the human heart had culminated. The worst of passions were unloosed, and mercy no longer had an existence in the heart of Patterson, and the minions whom he had in his train. He unleashed his hounds and they eagerly scented, and savagely pursued, their prey. The grievances portrayed by Franklin, were but the prelude of the tragedy which followed.

On the thirteenth and fourteenth of May, just sixty days after the horrors of the flood, the two companies of soldiers, under the order of Patterson, were marched out, with fixed bayonets, for the purpose of expelling the whole Yankee population of the valley.

The settlers were weak now; the battle-fields of

the revolution had decimated their number. The Goddess of Liberty smiled complacently upon the people of most of the land, but her face was veiled upon the plains of the Susquehanna.

The day of their tribulation had usurped the day of their jubilee. Rejoicings and thanksgivings were the songs elsewhere, but here was the land of mourning. The woman who had become widowed, and the child who had become orphaned, by the ravages of war, had none to lean upon. The old man who had given his sons to his country in the hour of need, hobbled upon his crutches as his only support now.

The battles and the floods had joined hands; these had erected the scaffold, and Patterson now appeared as the common hangman.

His orders were to expel the people; "to take no excuse; to give no quarter; to burn the houses of those who were refractory or disobeyed orders."

Not more unrelenting and revengeful were the decrees of Pharaoh, issued against the children of Israel. The same evil spirit actuated the minds of both. The Egyptian king gave his fugitives the choice of the road they should travel; Patterson's orders were that the Wyoming people should travel the roads where there were no bridges, and where the wilderness had not yet received the kindly imprint of the foot of the pioneer.

The poor settlers begged that they might go up or down the river, as in this way they could use boats. Their horses and wagons had been carried away by the floods. Patterson said no. They then besought him to permit them to take the road by Stroudsburg, to Easton, on the Delaware. The monster said no. These roads had bridges over the streams and wagons could pass over them, and therefore the exodus could not move upon them.

The road to Lackawaxen was the road to Connecticut, that the refugees must travel upon, and no other, and upon that they must take up their line of march at once, without food, without clothing, without the means of transportation, without hope. Sixty miles of a howling wilderness lay before them, and there was no land of promise beyond. The road they were compelled to travel had not been repaired, or used during the seven years of the Revolution; it was almost impassable, even for persons on foot. The streams were swollen with rains, the bridges were decayed and gone, there was no inn by the wayside, and no shelter to screen the helpless creatures from winds and storms.

Mr. Miner, in his history, p. 345, says: "About five hundred men, women and children, with scarce provisions to sustain life, plodding their weary way, mostly on foot, the road being impassable for wagons; mothers carrying their infants, and wading streams up to their arm-pits, and at night slept on the naked earth, the heavens their canopy, with scarce clothing to cover them. A Mr. Gardner, and John Jenkins, (who had been a representative to the Connecticut Assembly, and who was chairman of the town meeting which had in 1775 adopted the noble resolutions in favor of liberty,) both aged men and lame, sought their weary way on crutches. Little children, tired with travelling, crying to their mothers for bread, which they had not to give them, sank from exhaustion into stillness and slumber, while others could only shed tears of compassion and sorrow, till in sleep, they forgot their griefs and cares. Several of the unhappy sufferers died in the wilderness, others were taken sick from excessive fatigue, and expired soon after reaching the settlement. A widow with a numerous family of children, whose husband had been slain in the war, endured inexpressible hardships. One child died and she buried it as she could, behind a hemlock log, probably to be disinterred from its shallow covering and be devoured by wolves."

One of the exiles, Elisha Harding, Esq., gives a very spirited account of this terrible journey through the wilderness, which I cannot omit. He says:

"It was a solemn scene; parents, their children crying from hunger; aged men on their crutches; all urged forward by an armed force at our heels."

In seven days they made their journey of sixty miles. They had reached the Delaware; they were in a civilized land. Some of them went up and some of them went down that river, seeking shelter where they could, and living as they could.

Mr. Harding says he took the road, east, in the direction of Connecticut, but when he reached the summit of the Shongum Mountain, he turned back, as did the Israelites of old, to survey the land he had left. But hear him in his own language : " I looked back with this thought—'Shall I abandon Wyoming forever ? ' The reply was ' No, oh, no ! There lie your murdered brothers and friends. Dear to me art thou, though a land of affliction.' Every way looked gloomy except towards Wyoming. Poor, ragged and distressed as I was, I had youth and health, and felt that my heart was whole. So I turned back to defend or die."

The news of the brutal conduct which caused these sufferings spread wide and far. The sympathy of the whole country was aroused. The entire people of the State of Pennsylvania, except the few land-speculators who had title rights in Wyoming, became excited, and demanded that these people should be restored to their possessions. The Proprietary Government had become a Sovereign State. An order was issued on the thirteenth of June, directing the companies of Christie and Shrawder to be forthwith discharged. These soldiers immediately left the valley. ·

A month of exile thus passed, and the settlers of the Susquehanna were stragglers and outcasts, wandering upon the shores of the Delaware; but the people of New Jersey and of Pennsylvania who lived in that region, were hospitable and kind to the wretched and forlorn objects, who appealed to them for charity.

The Pennsylvania authorities not only directed the soldiers stationed here to be discharged, but they also ordered the sheriff of Northumberland—the present territory of Luzerne at that time being a part of it—to repair to Wyoming, invite the settlers back again, and reinstate them in their possessions. Sheriff Antis accordingly came into the valley about the middle of June. He sent messengers to the Delaware to inform the settlers; in the name of the State, that they might return to Wyoming. This was of course glad tidings to them, and they commenced their march back again, and in a week or ten days afterwards, most of them had arrived. They halted on the summit of the Wilkes-Barré mountain, and erected a fort there, called "Fort Lillo-pe."

There were reasons, of which they were informed, why they did not at once descend into the valley below.

After the discharge of the soldiers of Christie and Shrawder, Patterson immediately — setting the orders and decrees of the State authority at defiance, — commenced enrolling those of the Pennsylvania claimants who were here ; persons also who had taken the side of Great Britain in the war, tories, and all the disaffected characters whom he could seduce, either by threats or promises, and took possession of the garrison. Under this state of affairs, the authority of the sheriff amounted to nothing.

Patterson sent a flag up to the fort on the mountain, to give the people an invitation to come on. They having heard from their runners that their houses and farms were in the possession of the tories and Pennamite claimants, were afraid of Patterson. They knew the man and the perfidy of his heart.

Upon consultation, however, it was agreed to send a committee and see how matters stood; but the Plymouth people were excluded from this piece of work. It would not do for the Franklins, the Bidlacks, the Harveys, the Gaylords, nor the Nesbitts, to go on such a mission. These were marked men.

The committee came, but this monster in human shape, disregarding all rules of honor and the sacred character of a flag of truce, immediately caused the committee to be arrested; and two of them, Captain Jabez Fish, of Wilkes-Barré, and John Gore, of Kingston, were cruelly beaten with iron ramrods.

This information reaching the people at their mountain fortification, they unanimously resolved to brave every thing, and, if needs be, die in the cause. Their committee, invited under a flag of truce, had been shamefully and cruelly beaten with iron rods; and they made up their minds, old and young, women and children, to take up the line of advance, preferring death to the terrible state of suspense and suffering to which they were exposed.

They had reached the mountain on the thirtieth of May, and in accordance with the resolve, I have stated, they boldly commenced their advance into the valley on the third of July. And the same night, without molestation, they took up their quarters in Kingston, on Abraham's (now Tuttle's) creek. Patterson having satiated his venom by beating their committee with iron rods, considered this, we are to suppose, as a sufficient vent to his malice and revenge, and laid no further obstacles in the way of their march.

And thus, after nearly two months of great suffering, want and destitution, the settlers were again in the valley of blood—if not within their own houses, spared by flood, or the occupation of their enemy.

The next thought was to gather such of their crops as still remained upon the ground. For this purpose, as well as for measures, we may say not of retaliation, but purely self-preservation, a company of thirty young men associated themselves together, their first object being to gather the crops. Armed with the rifles and muskets which were left, and taking their farming implements, they started to gather the crops upon the Shawnee flats. On the western slope of Rosshill they were met by a band of Patterson's men, who immediately gave them battle. The young settlers did the best they could, but lost in the skirmish two very promising young men, Elisha Garret and Chester Pierce, one of whom was a Plymouth man. Patterson's men had two wounded and left on the field, Wilhelmus Van Gordon and

Henry Brink; another one of them returned to the garrison, his broken arm swinging in his sleeve: three or four others were wounded.

This new trouble put an end to the gathering of the crops on Shawnee flats, the seeds of which had been sown by the men who had returned the previous year from the Continental battle-fields! There was no peace.

The wanton slaughter of those two young men produced among the settlers, in camp at Abraham's creek, the keenest anguish, and the bitterest feeling of revenge. How could it be otherwise? Under a flag of truce Patterson had decoyed some of their old men into his clutches to gratify the black malevolence of his heart, beating them in a cruel and barbarous manner. He had slain some of the young men who were going to gather the crops to save the lives of starving women and children.

These settlers were mortal; they were subject to the like feelings and moved by the like passions of their race. They were now driven to a stage of desperation. A general rally of the settlers was the result. Forty-two effective men and twenty old men mustered under John Franklin, marched to Shawnee for the purpose of exterminating the tories who had taken possession of their lands, under the permission of Patterson, while they were in miserable exile upon the Delaware.

Here they found the interlopers, Brink and Van

Gordon, wounded a day or two before upon Rosshill. These men were helpless: they spared them. Such would not have been the fate of two of their own men, under like circumstances, falling into the hands of Patterson.

Captain Franklin cleaned Shawnee thoroughly of the tory element, save the two men wounded. They, however, never found that locality a very agreeable residence, and I do not find the names of either upon any of the enrollments or assessment lists from that time down. The probability is that when they recovered from the wounds received upon Rosshill, they left the town. In fact there can be but little question of that! Plymouth had an un-wholesome atmosphere for tories to breathe. Too many revolutionary heroes lived there to make it healthy in this particular.

After disposing of Shawnee, Captain Franklin crossed the river at Nanticoke, and removed all persons between there and Wilkes-Barré who had squatted down upon Yankee possessions. Driving them before him, they took shelter in the garrison occupied by Patterson and his men at Wilkes-Barré. He invested the block-house and demanded a surrender.

So war was inaugurated anew; and it seemed that the Connecticut settlers were farther from the dawn of peace than ever. Christie's and Shrawder's companies, on retiring from the valley, had left a hundred and thirty stand of arms, and large quantities of ammunition. The block-house had four cannon; the ancient four-pounder of the days of Stewart, and three left by Sullivan in his expedition through the valley. With these means of defense in the hands of four hundred men, what could Franklin do with the handful of old men and boys under his command? The attempt at the investment of the fort was desperation.

Patterson's men made a sortie from the garrison, drove off the besiegers, and applied the brand to twenty-three buildings in Wilkes-Barré, which were consumed. These were of course the dwellings of Connecticut people. And Patterson no doubt relished exceedingly the assault upon his fortifications, as a pretext to burn out his helpless and impoverished enemy. Captain Franklin retired with his people to Mill Creek; took possession of the only flouring mill in the settlement, kept it running day and night, till his friends were bountifully supplied with meal. Their wants were few, and a few pounds of flour was a blessed affair in their limited view of the necessaries of life.

But the stakes I have set to define the limits of a local inquiry, will not permit me to proceed further with this Yankee and Pennamite war. I have culled from the controversy such incidents of it as had an immediate bearing upon our town. To do this intelligibly, I was forced into a statement of the leading measures which necessarily involved our people.

It will be sufficient to say that the beating of Fish and Gore with iron ramrods, and the slaughter of Garret and Pierce upon Rosshill, swung back the gate of war upon its creaking hinges; and scenes of murder, reprisals, and imprisonments were of very frequent occurrence for the ten following years.

During the same year, 1784, thirty of the settlers were sent in irons to the Easton jail; forty-six others were bound with chains and cords and confined in barns and stables in Wilkes-Barré; forty-two of these were sent to the Northumberland jail, in both of which places they remained a long time in captivity. Thus we find sixty-six of the settlers at one time in prison.

And during the confinement of fathers and sons, what shall be said of the wives and helpless children? Ah! this is a question that cannot be answered. The cloud of suffering has passed away, and so have the miserable objects of pity which it covered.

Patterson, as civil magistrate, was succeeded by Armstrong; but the change did not much improve, if any, the iron rule of these petty tyrants. They looked at but one side of the question, and the coloring of that was crimson. Extermination of the Susquehanna claimants was the grand absorbing theme. All minor questions, involving humanity, charity, and even justice, were merged in the one grand idea of extermination.

The people of our town came in for their full share. Of the sixty-two in irons in the jails of Easton and Sunbury, one-fourth at least were people of Plymouth.

The rich alluvial lands of Wyoming were a prize. To hold them cost our people blood, carnage, starvation, and many of them death. There is no record of the number of slaughtered men during this long-continued struggle. It ran up to hundreds. Almost every family contributed to the hecatomb.

Under Timothy Pickering, a man of New England birth but Pennsylvania proclivities, matters assumed a somewhat more peaceable character. In his administration there were some grains of clemency; though in the end he was obliged to leave the scene.

Matters never became finally settled till the passage of the compromising law of 1799. By this law the Connecticut man triumphed. But the flag of his victory waved also over the graves of his slaughtered relatives and friends. Its fruits were bitter; but their descendants were enriched by the toils, privations, and exposures of their ancestors.

Are they fully sensible of it? Do they ever pass these exciting and bloody turmoils in review? Do they look back to those fearful days, and nights, and weeks and months, and years of the severe past? Some of them may; but I fear that the greater majority do not realize who placed the rounds in the

8

ladder of their elevation in wealth, nor stop to estimate the cost of them.

I am by no means speaking in the way of cen-
sure; but if there be a Plymouth man who is to-day
in comfortable circumstances in life, whose wants are
all within the range of his means of gratification,—
and I know there are many such,—let these reminiscences of the past which I have grouped together and
placed before him, be a reminder of the dark days
which have preceded him.

My mother, now in her ninety-sixth year, a Connecticut woman, informs me that during these early
times, though not in the valley till 1790, she passed
through the wilderness between here and Connecticut
no less than eight or ten times. The little party
made up for the journey, would go on horseback,
carrying their own provisions and provender for their
horses, encamping frequently at night in the open air.
Sometimes the journey was made in consequence of
the turbulence of the times, sometimes for the purpose of friendly visits to New England friends.

W-h-e-w!! Young ladies of Plymouth, what
would you think now of mounting a horse on top of a
canvas bag, with oats in one end, and pork and beans
in the other, with a journey of two hundred and
fifty miles before you, and half the way a howling
wilderness, the sky for your canopy by night, and the
music of wild beasts your lullaby?

Well, well, probably if the emergency arose, you

would have equal courage to meet the occasion—and certainly I shall not pass judgment upon you, till you have made the trial—and may the time never come to require the test.

CHAPTER VI.

PENNAMITE WAR.—LEGISLATION.—DECREE AT TREN-
TON. — CONFIRMING ACT. — COMPROMISE ACT. —
PEACE.—JOHN FRANKLIN.

THE paper proclamations of the State of Connecticut, like the Pope's bull to the comet, amounted to nothing. And yet we find that these early settlers of Wyoming were paying large sums of money for that period. The assessment of 1776 was £16,996 13s—a large amount of money for the times. The assessment made in 1780, and the first one after the slaughter at the Wyoming battle, was £2,358. It is not probable that much of this money found its way into the Connecticut treasury, but one fact is very clearly shown, that the settlers were by no means a bill of expense to that State.

The troops raised here for the revolutionary struggle were credited to that State by the Continental establishment. The people here mustered into the Colonial army more than twenty to one over the home department compared with the population.

Two representatives were annually elected from Wyoming to the Connecticut Assembly from the year 1774 to 1782 inclusive. Commencing with Zebulon Butler and Timothy Smith, and ending with Obadiah Gore and Jonathan Fitch.

During these nine years the claims of the people of Wyoming for losses, and the expenses for the erection of fortifications for their defense, made through their representatives, generally ended in tabling the resolves offered.

The government of Connecticut never seemed to have exhibited that disposition to aid and defend her Colonial establishment, in its dark hours and troubles, that the necessities of the case demanded.

Litchfield county, Connecticut, is situate on the extreme western line of the State; the town of Westmoreland, in that county, borders upon the line of New York. This being the nearest to the Yankee settlement on the Susquehanna, the "seventeen towns," as they were called, were made a part of the town of Westmoreland, of the State of Connecticut. So they remained till the year 1776; when the territory was set off into a separate municipal existence, under the name of the county of Westmoreland.

It was a strange state of things, under our present view, this representation in the Connecticut Legislature from *the town of Westmoreland, in the county of Litchfield, State of Connecticut, in the Commonwealth of Pennsylvania !*

Congress finally, at the instance of the State of Pennsylvania, with the concurrence of the State of Connecticut, intervened the federal authority to adjust the Susquehanna troubles.

This body adopted a resolution, naming commissioners, who met at Trenton, New Jersey, in November, 1782. The commissioners, after a protracted session of forty-one days, during which the agents and attorneys on both sides discussed at length the subject of the troubles, decided, on the thirtieth of December, 1782, that the *State* of Connecticut had no right to the land in controversy, and that the jurisdiction and pre-emption of all lands of right belonged to Pennsylvania.

To this decree, as it has always been called, the two contending States, as well as the settlers, assented.

It was supposed now upon all sides that the troubles had found a peaceful as well as final end. Not so, however. Those who claimed title, under the Proprietary Government, of the land paid for by the Connecticut settlers to the Susquehanna company, and in pursuance of which they had taken possession, asserted that such title had been decided in their favor by the decree at Trenton. That the commissioners not only decided the question of jurisdiction and title to the land between the two States, but also between individual claimants.

The question of individual rights, it was supposed, was neither submitted to nor decided by that tribunal. And the probability is that this was the view taken previous to the decree by both of these State authorities.

Jurisdiction became a fixed fact; the title to land not occupied or claimed by purchase was also conceded to be determined; not so with land owned and occupied by the settlers under the Susquehanna company.

The people of the valley having reason to fear that the State authorities might claim that personal rights had been decided by the Commissioners at Trenton, presented their petition to the General Assembly of Pennsylvania. This paper is written in strong language, and is supposed to have emanated from the pen of John Franklin. The composition could not be improved in these days. The following is an extract, which I copy from Chapman's history:

"WYOMING, January 18, 1783.

" The Honorable Congress established a court; both sides were cited and appeared; the cause was heard for more than forty days, and the ground stated in which each asserted their right of jurisdiction. On which the court finally adjudged in favor of Pennsylvania, by which the jurisdiction of the disputed territory on which your memorialists live is adjudged yours. By this adjudication we are under your jurisdiction and protection. We are subjects and free citizens of the State of Pennsylvania, and have now to look up to your honors as our fathers, guardians and protectors—entitled to every tender regard and respect, as to justice, equity, liberty and protection.

"It is impossible that the magnanimity of a powerful and opulent State will ever condescend to distress an innocent and brave people, that have unsuccessfully struggled against the ills of fortune. We care not under what State we live, if we live protected and happy. We will serve you, we will promote your interests, we will fight your battles ; but in mercy, goodness, wisdom, justice, and every great and generous principle, leave us our possessions, the dearest pledge of our brothers, children and fathers, which their hands have cultivated, and their blood, spilt in the cause of their country, enriched."

It will be observed that this memorial, couched in strong and respectful language, does not yield the question of their title. And the old veterans were in the right. The law was with them.

Franklin set out for Annapolis on the second of May of the following year, where Congress was in session, carrying with him a petition of like import for the consideration of that body. I quote from his venerable and almost obliterate diary, lying on the table before me :

"May 2d, 1784, I set out for Annapolis with a petition to Congress, setting forth our situation, and praying to be made quiet in our possessions; went in a canoe.

"Monday, 3d, went to Middletown.

"Tuesday, 4th, left my canoe at Conawago Falls, and travelled by land twelve miles below Little York.

"Wednesday, 5th, went within six miles of Baltimore.

"Thursday, 6th, went on board a schooner at Baltimore.

"Friday morning, the 7th, arrived at Annapolis, and put up at Mr. Brenner's. I found Esquire Sherman and General Wadsworth; gave my petition to Esquire Sherman, which was laid before Congress, and referred to a committee that had been appointed upon a motion for suspending the loy * * * (oblit.).

"The 10th, wrote a letter to His Excellency, the Governor of Connecticut, in which I gave an account of the proceedings of the State of Pennsylvania towards us, from the decree of Trenton to this time. Sent it by Mr. Gilmore.

"Wednesday, 19th, left Annapolis and set off for Sunbury. I got no business completed in Congress.

"On Tuesday, 25th, I arrived at Sunbury; the Court of Quarter Sessions being held; met Mr. Mason and Ransom, and a number of others; they informed me that on the 12th the troops at Wyoming and Patterson's party disarmed the Connecticut settlers."

The Commissioners of Trenton had no power over personal rights. They had power over jurisdiction and title to land not appropriated. The question of pre-emption they decided. This was proper; and this applied to lands not located or claimed. Preemption means the exclusive first right to buy. The Connecticut settler had bought his land, paid for it, and located upon it. It became a personal vested right, and so he regarded it ; and he was justified in holding on, and he did hold on, and he held on to some purpose.

The response to the memorial by the General Assembly of the State was the appointment of three Commissioners to visit Wyoming, "to examine the state of the country, to act as magistrates, and to recommend what measures the government should adopt in relation to the settlers."

These Commissioners, entirely under the influence of the Pennsylvania claimants, after visiting the valley and making what they deemed a general inquiry and examination, reported to the State government: "That reasonable compensation, in land, should be made to the families of those who had fallen in arms against the common enemy, and to such other settlers as had a proper Connecticut title, and did actually reside on the land at the time of the decree at Trenton; provided they immediately relinquish all claim to the soil they now inhabit, and enter into contract to deliver up full and quiet possession of their present tenures to the rightful owners, under Pennsylvania, by the first of April next."

And here was the cause of the terrible prelude to those successive acts of inhumanity the following year, and which instigated persecutions, and imprisonments, and bloodshed, and murder, in quick succession, overspreading the entire valley, and which continued for years.

First came the civil magistrate, Patterson, with his two armed companies under Christie and Shrawder, with instructions "to march to Wyoming, and take every proper measure for maintaining the post there, and for PROTECTING the settlement. I underscore the word protecting. The original order contained no such ear-mark.

These gentlemen were on the ground within a month after the report of the Commissioners. Under the sanctity of the law, and for the *protection* of the settlement, those acts of brutality on the part of Patterson were inflicted which I have already mentioned, some of them being extracts from Franklin's diary.

Strange protection was that in robbing the poor settlers of their fishing-nets; tearing down their fences, burning their buildings, and driving five hundred helpless old men, women and children at the point of the bayonet through a howling wilderness, some of whom died by the wayside of starvation and exposure! Protection indeed; the protection the wolf extends to the lamb, the falcon to the sparrow.

From the moment the civil magistrate, Patterson, and his two companies of armed soldiers arrived, the settler realized his position. He made an effort to accept the new situation, but this was in vain, unless he surrendered his home and his fields, and abandoned the valley.

I have had it from the mouth of old Mr. Abraham Nesbitt, who lived many years and died on the spot where Mr. Love's house now stands, that the insolence of these soldiers was intolerable; and that they did no act of indecency or impropriety shocking to civilization, that even elicited a reprimand from Patterson when informed of it.

They were instructed to treat a Yankee with any kind of abuse; and such conduct was the cause of praise and approbation upon the part of their commander.

The Legislature of the State began to understand that a whole community of people, now numbering—men, women and children—two or three thousand, ought not to be annihilated, and particularly when the public sentiment was running strongly in their favor throughout the commonwealth; that the decree at Trenton might not bear the construction, that private rights were involved in, and had been decided by, the Commissioners under the resolve of Congress.

Some of the wiser heads, and with more humanity in thought and action, did not relish the remark which Patterson had made in a communication to the Executive Council on the twenty-ninth of April, two or three weeks after the disastrous ice flood, and some two weeks before the inhuman creature expelled so large a number from the valley, burning their homes and destroying their crops, "that it must not be construed into a want of zeal or love for the Commonwealth, if he should, through dire necessity, be obliged to do *some things* not strictly consonant with the letter of the law."

When the news of the terrible suffering of the poor settlers came, in hot speed, from thousands of disinterested people residing along both sides of the Delaware, for fifty miles in extent, the legislator began to know what he meant by "*some things*" done under a sense of "dire necessity, and not consonant with the letter of the law."

Humanity screeched out from one end of the broad Commonwealth to the other, and the echo was taken up, and it went from hill top to hill top throughout the whole land. A great wrong had been perpetrated, and justice demanded redress.

As time moved on public sentiment underwent change—so that the Assembly of the State, which convened in 1787, was prepared for an effort to accommodate affairs in Wyoming, that peace might reign and the flowing of blood cease.

During this year the people of the seventeen townships concluded to propose to the Legislature a plan for the adjustment of difficulties.

The townships known and designated as the "seventeen," were Salem, Newport, Hanover, Wilkes-Barré, Pittston, Kingston, Northmoreland, Braintrim, Plymouth, Bedford, Exeter, Huntington, Providence, Putnam, Springfield, Claverack and Ulster. The four latter being within the present territory of Bradford and Susquehanna counties.

The substance of this proposition, embraced in a memorial to the Legislature, and read in that body in March, 1787, was, that if the Commonwealth would grant them the land within the "seventeen" townships, and on which settlements had been commenced previous to the decree of Trenton, in 1782, they would, on their part, relinquish all claim to any other lands within the Susquehanna purchase. Coupled with this proposition was another condition, that the Pennsylvania claimants who held conflicting warrants and surveys within the townships, should relinquish their title to them, and the money paid be refunded to them by the State. I may add that these warrants and surveys were generally in the hands of land jobbers and speculators, and had not been reduced to residence and occupation.

The Legislature, on the twenty-eighth of March, 1787, accepted this proposition, and passed an enactment generally known as the confirming law.

It was hailed pretty generally as a pacific measure,

and really seemed to be a pretty fair adjustment.
But the trouble still in the way, was that the settlers outside of the " 17 " towns, and claiming by the
same title as those within, were not recognized under the liberal provisions of the confirming act.

It was as a kind of moderator under this law, for
the purpose of quieting matters, with the commissions
of the court offices in his pocket, that brought Timothy Pickering into the valley.

The great majority of the Connecticut people resided within the " 17 " townships—but still a considerable number did not, and that made a determined
opposition to the confirming law. They contended
that they were as worthy of protection as their brethren, whose farms happened to be within these townships. Such undoubtedly was the fact, and the error
was that the enactment did not include them. It
was possibly an oversight, and in many instances these
people were under the impression that they were
within the certified township lines, and were only un-
deceived by an actual survey upon the ground.

The people of Plymouth had no cause to com-
plain of the law, and did not, save that their sympathies were with their Connecticut friends, who may
be called outsiders. There may have been exceptions.

For the first time now the Connecticut people presented a divided front, and the feelings of acrimony
and ill-will extended very generally among them.

The Pennsylvania claimants taking advantage of this family quarrel, and Timothy Pickering having been taken a prisoner from his home by a party of turbulent settlers, to be held as a hostage for the exchange of John Franklin, who was at the time a prisoner in Philadelphia upon a charge of treason for opposing the confirming law, the Legislature suspended the law in the way of a menace. But this did not have the desired effect, and the consequence was the repeal of the law soon afterwards.

Chaos was once more the *order* of the day, and the question again rested upon the award of the Trenton Commissioners. But the same discord did not prevail. Luzerne county was now established; the majority of the people within it were Connecticut settlers; the new constitution of the State was more liberal than the Proprietary establishment, under the Penns : they now elected their own members to the Legislature, as well as the county and township officers. They had the matter therefore pretty much in their own hands.

And although nearly ten years passed before a definite compromise, bloodshed, imprisonments, and reprisals had ceased. The conflict assumed more of a political complexion, and the elections were not unfrequently conducted in a most boisterous and turbulent manner.

But the settlers would elect their assemblymen, and they therefore had a friend at court.

Finally, in 1799, and nearly thirty years after the commencement of the troubles growing out of this Pennamite and Yankee difficulty, the whole question was arranged in the passage by the Legislature of the "Compromise Law."

Under the terms of this enactment, commissioners were appointed to cause a survey to be made of all the lands claimed by the Connecticut settlers within the seventeen townships previous to the decree of Trenton, in which titles had been granted to them, according to the rules and regulations among them. They were to classify and value these lands, and give certificates to the owners, upon the presentation of which, to the secretary of the land-office, on the payment of a small sum as purchase-money, a patent was granted by the State. The purchase-money to be paid was for the first class, $2.00 an acre; for the second, $1.20; for the third, 50 cents; and eight and one fourth cents for the fourth class.

The lands of the Pennsylvania claimants were also to be ascertained and valued, and where they came in conflict with the claim of the Connecticut man, they were required to relinquish their title to the State and receive from the Treasury, in full compensation for land of the first class, $5.00 an acre, $3.00 for the second, $1.50 for the third, and twenty-five cents for the fourth.

As soon as forty thousand acres should thus be released to the State by the Pennsylvania claimants, and the Connecticut claimants, who owned an equal quantity, should bind themselves to submit to the law, to the satisfaction of the commissioners, then the act was to take effect.

This, then, provided for the settlers within the "17" townships : and the minority outside, as is the usual case with minorities, had to fight their battle in the best way they could; but as none of these were residents of Plymouth, it is not my purpose to examine the subject further.

And so ended the Pennamite and Yankee controversy. Both sides accepted the terms of the act of 1799, and it still quietly reposes upon the statute book, not obsolete from age precisely, but in a measure a dead letter, for all the troubles it was designed to heal have been long since disposed of, and the actors in the busy scenes connected with them have passed from the stage.

As many as forty years ago, when I came to the Luzerne bar, it was rare that a case came into the court that required to be decided under the provisions of the law of 1799.

The Yankee surveys, and particularly those on the east side of the river, were strangely located. They commenced upon the bank of the stream, and extended to the top of the mountain. They were some forty rods wide, and in some cases five miles long. The mountain end frequently at an elevation of fifteen hundred feet above the other on the plain.

9

They thus had all varieties of soil, and almost of climate.

The Yankee idea, as they expressed it, was a "streak of fat and a streak of lean" in each lot.

Nathan Beach, of Salem, and whom I knew well, and for whom I procured a pension for Revolutionary services as long ago as 1832, told me that the settlers' price for one of these lots was a horse, saddle and bridle. The young Yankee, therefore, who could become owner of these, could, on his arrival here from Connecticut, exchange them for a lot. Some of these same lots are worth to-day one hundred thousand dollars.

The Plymouth surveys were on a smaller scale. The house and meadow lots, as they are termed in the certificates, vary from ten to twenty acres. This land being regarded remarkably valuable, was subdivided into small slices. The most of Kingston, in the days of the Wyoming battle, was a pine plain.

I can remember myself when that part of it above the village of Troy, or Wyoming, was mostly covered with pitch pines.—Shawnee flat was a prairie when the white man took possession of it.

I cannot conclude the sad story of the Wyoming troubles, growing out of the conflict between the Pennsylvania and Connecticut jurisdiction, without a biographical sketch of one of the great and acknowledged leaders of the Connecticut settlers. The man of probably the largest intellect and most persevering energy.

JOHN FRANKLIN was this personage. And it is a matter of much satisfaction to me that I am able to classify this distinguished character among the first settlers of Plymouth. It is true that he remained there less than a year before removing to Huntington township, where he made his permanent abode.

Mr. Jameson Harvey, now an aged man, informs me that Franklin and his father were very intimate friends; that Franklin never passed his father's house, in travelling to and from Wilkes-Barré, then the principal rendezvous of the Connecticut people, without stopping, and generally arranged his journey so as to stay over night; that he has very often heard him, among other narratives of his adventures, speak of his immigration, and where he first settled.

Mr. Harvey represents him as a tall, muscular, well-built man, with wonderful developments of physical power. He leaned slightly forward in his walk, but moved with a firm step.

Mr. Charles Miner makes him six feet in height; Mr. Harvey, six feet four inches. From the accounts of both, he seems to have been a man of Herculean frame, and possessing strong muscles and sinews. This we may readily understand when we learn that it required the united strength of four men to hold and bind him with cords when arrested for treason (?) and sent off to the Philadelphia prison. All of the early settlers, from whom I have gathered information, in years gone by, represent him as a "tall, square-shouldered man," and endowed with great physical power.

He was a native of Canaan, Litchfield county, Connecticut. He came with his wife and children to Plymouth in 1774. He had brothers who either immigrated with him, or about the same time, to the valley. One of them, as already stated, fell at the battle of Nanticoke the year after. Some of the family settled in Hanover at a very early day. I am unable to ascertain if Roswell, Jr. and Arnold Franklin were brothers to John. The probability is that they were not.

Roswell and Arnold were taken prisoners by the Indians, in Hanover, in September, 1781. The spring following the wife and four children of Roswell were also carried off by them into captivity. The wife of Roswell was murdered by the Indians in an attempt to rescue the prisoners.

In the spring of 1775 John Franklin entered, solitary and alone, the wilderness; and upon the banks of Huntington creek, in the territory now embraced within the township of that name, made his "pitch." Having circumscribed the limits of his claim by notching and blazing the bark of trees, he knocked up some turf with the pole of his axe, and these were the formalities appropriating the forest: this was his warrant of entry.

No white man had preceded him in this vicinity. He was the first; and the unmolested choice of the virgin soil, that had never been turned up by the plough-share, or impressed by the white man's foot, was spread out before him, and here he made his selection and dedicated his future home. His faithful dog, the only witness to this act of possession, and his rifle, leaning against a tree hard-by, the only battery of his defense.

The man who had the courage and personal bravery to do all this, possessed the qualifications to fill the places of trust that were in years afterwards conferred upon him.

During the summer of that year he chopped over and cleared off some three or four acres, sowed it with grain, erected his log hut, and was now ready for the introduction of his wife and little children to their home in the woods.

His nearest neighbor was at the Susquehanna river, a distance of some seven or eight miles. "In that year he came up to take a round in Plunket's battle," and returned to his wild home again when it was over; a little variety in his life, the incidents of that affair, compared with the peace and quiet which reigned amid the forest about his new home.

And thus we find the resolute man engaged, whose capacious intellect, in succeeding years, dispelled the sophistry concealed in the Trenton decree, and whose untiring energy and iron will gave cast and coloring to the almost helpless Yankee cause.

The same, too, whose persuasive language and

solid arguments before the legislative body, in after years, gave legal form to the conclusions of his own well-balanced and discriminating mind. The man of the people ; the man for the people. The tall and stately form, whether at the head of his company, driving the Tories before him out of Plymouth ; taking his oath of revenge against his persecutors upon the rifle, all stained with the heart's blood of his friend; bound in chains as a traitor, for serving his people but too well; at the head of his company, under Sullivan, exterminating the enemy who had covered the Wyoming battle-field with his slaughtered relatives and friends, or pleading the case of his afflicted associates, ever loomed up, and was the object of love, affection, and the profoundest veneration by the Connecticut settlers of Wyoming.

In the following spring of 1776, he installed his wife and children in the primitive home he had prepared for them. Even at this time his was the only family in the township. He resided there up to the time of his arrest and imprisonment at Philadelphia. Sometime after his release he moved to Bradford county, but still within the "17" towns, where he spent the remainder of his life, and died in 1831, at the advanced age of eighty-two years. Some of his children remained in Huntington, and members of the family still reside there.

His wife died within two or three years after his settlement in Huntington. I make the following extract from Mr. Miner's history. He says: "Not long after his removal to Wyoming, his wife died, leaving three small children, one an infant of a week old. Having no person to take care of them, he determined to place them in charge of his kind friends in Canaan. Harnessing a horse to a little cart, he put in the three children, tied a cow by the horns to follow, and drove on, having a cup in which, as occasion required, he milked and fed the babe. Thus he travelled the rough way, more than two hundred miles, in safety, exhibiting all the patience and tenderness that might be expected from a mother."

There cannot be much doubt but that this man, and more particularly after the first ten years of his residence here, was the leading, controlling spirit of the Yankee people.

No one questioned his bravery; no one doubted his integrity and honesty; while they all relied on his sound and well-balanced judgment. It is true that he differed with some of them as to the propriety of accepting the confirming law of 1787, but while there was this difference, the view that John Franklin took of the question was the one which ultimately prevailed. To it the opinions of statesmen, of jurists, and of laymen, were forced to give place.

Upon that question there was ground for an honest difference of opinion. At a meeting, in which an angry debate occurred, held in Wilkes-Barré, on the propriety of acquiescing in this law, Judge Hollenback struck a blow at his head with a loaded whip, which he had at the time in his hand. Great confusion ensued, and came near ending in an open fight. But this did by no means put down the old hero; it only added new converts to his side. The judge, who was a passionate man, and easily excited, afterwards made ample apologies.

Franklin was on his voyage, in his canoe, to meet Congress at Annapolis, when Patterson expelled the Connecticut people from the valley in 1784. I have stated that after the return of these people they encamped in Kingston, upon Abraham's creek. Here they immediately erected four large log tenements, for the double purpose of occupation and defense.

Armstrong, who had succeeded Patterson,—and in this exchange matters were not very much improved, —made an attack upon these houses with an armed force. They were gallantly defended, and the besieging party compelled to retreat. An intimate friend, however, of Franklin, William Jackson, was seriously wounded. Seeing his comrade in what he supposed a dying condition, Franklin, then captain, as he had been promoted to the command of the fortification, seized the rifle from the hands of Jackson, covered with the blood from his wounds, and summoning his companions around him in the log hut, with his eyes elevated to heaven, and his right hand upon his heart, solemnly took upon himself an oath—

"That he would never lay down his arms until

*death should arrest his hand, or Patterson and
Armstrong be expelled from Wyoming; the people
restored to their rights of possession; and a legal
trial guaranteed to every citizen by the Constitution,
by justice, and by law."*

This scene, when we reflect upon the tall figure
of the excited and angry man; the nature of his
oath; the terrible cause of provocation; the group of
ragged, famished men about him; the silence, save
only the voice of imprecation; the visages of sorrow,
hope, fear and revenge variously reflected from the
audience ; makes our blood tingle and thrill through
our veins.

We being thus impressed, after a long lapse of
time, at the rehearsal only, what must have been the
impulses and feelings of those who were actors in the
drama ?

In this transaction we read the heart of Franklin,
and learn the brave and determined character of the
man. His position was established now among his
associates ; he had fully defined his status. The effect of the oath upon the bloody rifle had brought
out a full development; he saw in himself, and so did
his men, his future position—the leader of the cause.
His nine previous years of training had culminated.
He stood before them the head of the line.

Not long after this, "at a parade in Shawnee,"
Captain Franklin was unanimously elected colonel
of the regiment. By common consent he was now

their chosen and revered chief, and upon him were
centred all the affection and confidence that the
soldiers of the Revolution had ever reposed in Washington.

Henceforward he was their agent, their chief man-
ager, their representative, their advocate, and their
bosom companion. And probably no man ever became so familiar with his associates, and yet at the
same time retained their respect. He could let himself down, but his dignity of character was sustained
in the exalted qualities of his heart.

Mr. Miner thinks "that he could make no pretensions to eloquence; yet he rarely failed to command attention, even from the learned and accomplished; earnest, often vehement, and his whole soul
seemed to be in the matter he discussed."

I don't want to take issue with Charles Miner. I
have a great regard for his opinions. I honor and
revere his memory. But I think in the above para-
graph he has pretty well defined oratory.

What is eloquence? The utterance of strong
emotion; the power of persuasion; elevated, forcible
thought; well chosen language, and an impassioned
manner. Most of these qualities Colonel Franklin
possessed, and to a large degree.

The language of his memorial to the legislature,
which we have already recorded, and his oath upon
the bloody rifle, are specimens of the highest order of
eloquence. It cannot, of course, be said that he can

be measured by the standard of men like Burke or Clay, whose choice language, lofty tones, refined sentences, an impassioned delivery, furnish models of their kind for the world; but it can be said of Franklin, as of Paul before Felix, that when he spoke there was silence, and men trembled.

The few specimens left us of his legislative efforts show a thorough comprehension of his subject, and a bold, fearless course of argument. No tropes, no figures, but great solidity of matter and concentration of thought. They may be classed as solid and common-sense productions.

He possessed but the rude elements of education, and lacked a want of the knowledge of the proper grammatical construction of sentences. What the schools had not supplied, God Almighty had.

The general features of the compromising law of 1799, and which were the panacea of Wyoming troubles, were mostly the result of his labors. He was a member of the general assembly of that year, and he made his mark. For these services he was continued a representative for the four succeeding ones, ending in 1803.

The members for the county for the three preceding years, were Ebenezer Bowman and Roswell Wells, both men of very respectable standing at the Luzerne bar; Mr. Wells, particularly, had a very good reputation as an orator. They both failed, however, in effecting a compromise of the Wyoming struggle.

This work was reserved for Colonel Franklin, and he accomplished the task.

It was the crowning act of his life. He lived not only to see peace restored, as the result of his own labor, but he had the proud and triumphant satisfaction of seeing it established upon his own basis; and upon a theory, too, for which he had at one time contended, against the opinions of eminent lawyers and many of the Connecticut settlers, among whom were several who had been leaders at an earlier day. The effect of the decree at Trenton as decisive of title to lands thus became abrogated, and the principles of that same confirming law, for opposition to which he had undergone an imprisonment of six months in the Philadelphia jail, were also abandoned.

Colonel Franklin triumphed, and the flag of the Connecticut settlers, which had long trailed in the dust, went to the head of the staff.

The acts of his treason found ample and full justification with the legislative power of the State—and so his crimes became virtues.

At this period the Legislative body met at Lancaster. There were no public stage coaches; the condition of the roads forbade their use, the members were accustomed to go and return on horseback; they could not travel either, for the same reason, in private carriages, and if they could, they were generally too poor to own them.

It was the custom of Franklin to walk with the

bridle rein over his arm, his horse following after, with a huge portmanteau on his back, filled with his clothes, books, and papers. The people along the road became accustomed to the tall, athletic figure known as the man who travelled "a foot on horseback;" and as they could easily recognize him at a distance, would exclaim, "there comes Franklin, the great Yankee hero!"

After the conclusion of his services in the assembly, he retired from public life. But his home was always the resort of the old settlers; many of them would make him annual visits. He had a wonderful memory, and treasured up all the incidents, adventures, and anecdotes of the eventful times in the valley, in most of which he had participated, and even up to the close of his checkered life, delighted to dwell upon them in his conversations.

And when he gave his last breath, there died the head and front of the Yankee column. But he had lead it to victory, and his heart had been cheered with the shouts of triumph.

CHAPTER VII.

REVOLUTIONARY WAR.—PATRIOTISM.—CAPTAIN DUR-
KEE'S AND CAPTAIN RANSOM'S COMPANIES.—GAR-
RISON HILL.—OUR MEN UNDER FIRE.—WASHING-
TON'S OPINION OF THEM.—BATTLE OF WYOMING.—
MR. WASHBURN'S STATEMENT.

IT has been stated that the enrolment of the settlers of Wyoming, in the handwriting of Colonel
Zebulon Butler, in 1773, contained but two hundred
and sixteen names. They are called settlers: it was
probably the number of men who were capable of
bearing arms.

The whole effective force of the valley was probably assembled on the reception of the news of Plunket's advance, in December, 1775. This was an exciting occasion, which affected every one of the Connecticut settlers, and it is to be presumed they were all
out. All the local authorities fix the number in that
battle at about three hundred.

On the Declaration of Independence, the fourth
of July following, the whole fighting force of the valley did not exceed four hundred men. Mr. Miner
estimates the entire population at that time at twenty-five hundred. He is probably not far out of the
way. (156)

Congress had declared war; the tocsin of rebellion had been sounded, and Wyoming was expected to do her duty. She responded nobly. On the twenty-fourth of August, 1776, "at a town meeting legally warned and held in Westmoreland, Wilkes-Barré district, Colonel Butler was chosen moderator for ye work of ye day."

."Voted, as the opinion of this meeting, that it now becomes necessary for the inhabitants of this town to erect suitable forts, as a defense against our common enemy."

Sites were accordingly fixed on in Pittston, Hanover, Plymouth, and Wilkes-Barré. Forty Fort, in Kingston, was to be repaired and enlarged.

The meeting closed after adopting the following vote: " That we do recommend it to the people to proceed, forthwith, in building said forts, without either fee or reward from ye town."

From the fourth of July to the fourth of August, thirty days, and the people of Westmoreland were in council, and ready to begin the campaign at their own expense.

The people of old Plymouth at once commenced operations, and erected their fort upon " Garrison Hill." And they piled up with their strong hands, and with willing hearts, the walls of their fortress, *"without any fee or reward from ye town."*

Their heart was in the sacred cause of liberty. Our people were but carrying out those imperishable principles which had driven their ancestors from London to Leyden;· from Leyden to Plymouth Rock; to Plymouth in Connecticut, and thence to Plymouth on the shores of the Susquehanna. The first generations endured persecution, imprisonment, and death for *religious* liberty: their children in the vast wilds of Pennsylvania, with the same blood coursing in their veins, the same haughty and independent carriage, were now building up the breast-works of *civil* liberty. And they went at it in earnest : the metal was in them. The old Puritan blood boiled; and to a man they rallied around the tri-colored flag.

Captain Samuel Ransom hauled the first log of the garrison, and old Benjamin Harvey planted the first flag upon the turret ! An effigy of George III. was hung up by the neck, and Yankee Doodle, upon the drum and fife, concluded the ceremonies of installation.

Men of Plymouth, is there to-day one of twenty amongst you that can point out the spot where this exciting scene occurred? No Fourth of July sun should hereafter be permitted to send his morning rays over the town without gilding the tri-colors, flung to the breeze, from a flag-staff on Garrison Hill. See to this !

Congress being informed of the exposed condition of the valley to predatory Indian tribes, and its location being comparatively nearer to the Canadian frontier, passed a resolution on the twenty-third of

August, and the day only preceding the town meeting in Westmoreland, directing—

"Two companies on the Continental establishment to be raised in the town of Westmoreland, *and stationed in proper places for the defense of the inhabitants of said town and parts adjacent,* till further order of Congress; the commanding officers of the said two companies to be immediately appointed by Congress."

This resolve, however, was coupled with a strange and inexplicable condition, and which was within four months afterwards made available, certainly against every principle of justice. The only plea that can be put in by way of extenuation is that of necessity. This, it is said, knows no law.

This condition was, "that the said troops be enlisted to serve during the war, unless sooner discharged by Congress;" and further, "that they be liable to serve *in any part* of the United States."

On the twenty-sixth of August Congress appointed Robert Durkee, of Wilkes-Barré, and Samuel Ransom, of Plymouth, captains for the companies to be raised, and also their respective subalterns.

It was mutually agreed between the two commissioned officers, that Captain Durkee should take the east side of the river for the enlistment of his company, and Captain Ransom the west.

They immediately commenced mustering men, and notwithstanding the severe terms prescribed by Con-

gress, within sixty days they each had their complement of eighty-four men.   This rapid enlistment of
so large a proportion of the people was, undoubtedly,
effected under the impression that the companies
*" were to be stationed in proper places for the defense
of the inhabitants."*   Upon no other principle can it
be possibly accounted for, as we shall see that this
included nearly half of the population of the valley
capable of bearing arms.   And had there been the
least prospect or intimation that they were to be
transferred to the general service, leaving their friends
and families to be slaughtered, as did afterwards occur,
they would never have put themselves willingly into
such a position.   Nor did the cause justify such a sacrifice.

They relied upon the clause of the resolution that
their location was to be within the valley and for
" the defense of the inhabitants."   In this view, however, they were sorely, and as it turned out, *fatally*
disappointed.

On the twelfth of December following, Congress
resolved : "That the two companies raised in the
town of Westmoreland, be ordered to join Washington *with all possible expedition."*

Before two months elapsed they were under his
immediate command.   And thus the people of the
valley were in that helpless and exposed condition
which soon after invited the northern invasion of
British, Indians, and Tories, which deluged the val-

ley with blood, leaving its red marks upon almost every hearth-stone in Westmoreland.

Previous to the raising of the companies of Captains Durkee and Ransom, Wisner and Strong, two recruiting officers had enlisted for the service thirty men. Adding these to the two companies of Durkee and Ransom, and we find that of the four hundred fighting men of the valley, one hundred and ninety-eight are enrolled in the Colonial service. And this all transpires within six months after the Declaration of Independence. Had the authorities of the new government, throughout the limits of the States, mustered a corresponding complement of men, Washington would have had an army of a hundred and fifty thousand, in the place of forty thousand.

No spot of ground of the same extent, and containing the same number of people, made anything like such a contribution. One half of the whole population of the valley, capable of bearing arms, are in the short period of six months transferred from their exposed homes upon a savage frontier to the national camp. It remains for history to justify the action of Congress in thus exposing the people of this valley to the scene of horror which resulted from this proceeding. Humanity and justice are now groping in the dark for a solution of the question. A satisfactory reason will never be attained, and the pursuit may as well be abandoned. The resolution of Congress, holding out the pretext that these two compa-

nies were *"to be placed for the defense of the inhabitants,"* was a trap; the unsuspecting settlers took the
bait, and murder, rapine, and the extermination of
almost a whole community of people, were the consequence.   But the error, upon the part of the citizens·
in volunteering, had been committed, and there was
no remedy to cure it.   The national arm had been
strengthened; but the stout hand that could firmly
resist the combined predatory bands of savage, British and Tory invaders, was paralyzed.   The defenseless homes were thus made the inviting lure of a
relentless and terrible foe.

And in this hour of trial, in these days of gloom,
and amid these clouds of despondency, what was the
position of Connecticut?   Ah! she was but a foster
mother at best.   She stood aloof in action and saw
her child divided by the sword.

The two companies of troops raised in her town
of Westmoreland, two hundred miles from her border,
and far from the hearing of the wails of women and
children, in a strictly *business way*, were entered to
her credit, as a part of the quota of the military force
which Congress exacted of her.   She should have
sent to the frontier two hundred armed men for the
support and protection of the people of her town
of Westmoreland.   In this there would have been
justice and reason.   Connecticut always acted in a
penurious and selfish manner with her people of
this valley.   She refused aid and assistance to-

wards compensating the poor settlers in their losses in the Plunket invasion. John Jenkens and Solomon Strong, who were the representatives of Westmoreland the year succeeding the Nanticoke battle, prepared a bill and urged it upon the consideration of the Assembly, but it was laid upon the table, and there suffered to sleep. A like application was made after the ice-flood, which destroyed an immense amount of property, but it shared the same fate as the Plunket bill. And within my own recollection, when we were all making a strong effort to erect a monument upon the Wyoming battle-field, in commemoration of the brave men whose bones still repose there, a committee, with Charles Miner at the head, visited the legislature of that State, humbly asking the bestowal of a mite for that noble purpose; but they failed to get a farthing. Ever ready to avail herself of the people of Westmoreland, to fill up the military requisition, but always turning a deaf ear to the petition for alms, education, defenses, and memorial columns.

A hundred years have now elapsed since she claimed jurisdiction over the valley, and we can afford to talk out, and talk plainly.

How stands the Revolutionary record of our old town of Plymouth? What response had her sons to make to Captain Samuel Ransom, when his drum beat for recruits? The roll of the Second Independent Company was immediately filled up, and nearly one-half of the eighty-four men were residents of the town.

It would be a subject of gratification at this remote day to know where Captain Ransom had his headquarters. It was undoubtedly at Forty Fort or Garrison Hill. As he was a resident of the town, then occupying the same site where now stands the old red house, fast falling to ruins, and so long the residence of his son, the late Colonel George P. Ransom in after years, that Garrison Hill was the rendezvous of his recruits. But this is conjecture merely, as much more of our early history might be, if permitted to rest much longer without the efforts to collect and save the fragments.

It is pretty difficult to ascertain a majority of the names of the men which made up Captain Ransom's roll, and who were Plymouth people.

The following I think were: Caleb Atherton, Mason F. Alden, Isaac Benjamin, Oliver Bennett, Benjamin Clark, Nathan Church, Pierce Cooper, Daniel Franklin, Charles Gaylord, Ambrose Gaylord, Timothy Hopkins, Benjamin Harvey, Asahel Nash, Ebenezer Roberts, George P. Ransom, Samuel Sawyer, Asa Sawyer, John Swift, Thomas Williams and Aziba Williams. To these twenty we may add the names of Jeremiah Coleman, Jesse Coleman, Nathaniel Evans, Samuel Tubbs, and James Gould—total, in the two companies, twenty-five men. The name of Benjamin Harvey appears upon the roll of Captain

Durkee; but Mr. James Harvey, his grandson, informs me this is a mistake, that he was a member of Captain Ransom's company.

The roll, as we now have it, contains but fifty-five names. If we give Plymouth the credit of one-third of the full complement of eighty-four men, then it would appear that the town furnished not less than thirty-five men in the two companies in the Revolutionary establishment.

The name of Benjamin Bidlack does not appear on either of the rolls, when it is a fact that he served throughout the whole seven years of the war. It does not appear either from any records how many of the men were from Plymouth, enlisted by Wisner and Strong, who recruited previously in the valley.

If we put down the whole number at forty, we should probably fail to do justice to the early settlers of the town.

There is one undeniable, positive fact, however, which does not admit of dispute or cavil, and that is, that the people of the town came boldly up to the work, and that they have left behind them a record worthy of the imitation of their descendants, if occasion shall ever require, and one which will never cause them to blush.

And another fact is also positive, that each and every one of them went through the terrible ordeal of those days with honor and credit, and that they are well entitled to our gratitude and respect: to our gratitude for the rich legacy they bequeathed to us, in the kind of government we enjoy; to our respect, for the deeds of daring and bravery they exhibited.

Our men, under Durkee and Ransom, were stationed between the British and American lines, near Morristown, N. J. The first time they were under fire was on the twentieth of January, 1777, at the battle of Millstone, " as gallant and successful an action," says Miner, " considering the number engaged, as was fought during the war." They were attached to a command under General Dickinson, which numbered about four hundred men ; they made a raid upon a foraging party of British troops of about the same number. The affair resulted in a complete success. They nobly repulsed the enemy ; he fled in confusion, leaving to the victors some fifty wagons loaded with flour and provisions, and over a hundred horses. Each man shared in the booty—the prize-money of each amounting to several dollars. Captain Ransom sent home a wagon to Plymouth as a trophy. Porter, one of Ransom's men, was killed in this action by a cannon-ball.

General Washington, in giving a report of this affair to Congress, uses the following complimentary language :

" This action happened near Somerset Court House, on Millstone river. General Dickinson's behavior reflects the highest honor on him; for though his troops were all raw, he led them through the river, middle deep, and gave the enemy so severe a charge, that although supported by three field-pieces, they gave way and left their convoy."

It will be borne in mind that half of this force of Dickinson was composed of Wyoming men, and probably not less than forty of these were from old Plymouth. Raw and undisciplined, yet true to their colors, under the first fire, and receiving the compliment of their great chief in a written report of the battle.

How often have I listened to the details of the affair at Millstone, from the lips of our old friend, Colonel George P. Ransom, who was in his father's company, and in that engagement!

We next hear of the two Independent companies in the battles of Brandywine, Germantown, Bound Brook and Mud Fort. The battles of Brandywine and Germantown were severely fought contests; the two companies were merged in large masses, and we cannot follow them through these engagements. They had stood fire at Millstone, and they undoubtedly maintained their courage afterwards.

At the terrible bombardment of Mud Fort, Lieutenant Spalding, of Ransom's company, was in command of a detachment. As the raking fire of the British artillery made sad havoc with the slender breast-works, and the balls came whizzing through in all directions, one of his soldiers threw himself upon the ground, exclaiming, "nobody can stand this!"

"Get up, my good fellow," said Spalding coolly, "I should hate to have to run you through; you can stand it if I can;" and the man, springing to his feet, returned to his duty.

Constant Mathewson, one of Ransom's men, was killed in this engagement, and several were wounded. The two Sawyers, Plymouth men, died soon after with camp disease; also Spencer, and one of the Gaylords. Others died whose names are not given. Benjamin Harvey was frozen to death at Valley Forge— so that we find Captain Ransom's company, in October, 1777, reduced to sixty-two men.

The following spring dark and ominous clouds began to overshadow the valley. The Indians began to show themselves on the outskirts, committing murder and carrying off prisoners. The tories, heretofore silent, began to throw out hints of an approaching storm. "Coming events cast their shadows before."

The demon of carnage and battle was preparing for his grand banquet, which was to be displayed on the approaching third of July. The entire population became restive and excited; the runners who were sent out brought back chilling information, and a general alarm throughout the valley was created. This state of things reached Washington's camp, at Morristown, where the two Independent companies were stationed. Those of them who had left their unguarded and unprotected wives and children at home became excited and furious. All the commissioned officers but two resigned; and these, with some twenty or thirty men (with or without permission does not appear), left the camp and sped to Wyoming.

It is probable that the authorities in the camp, knowing the desperate condition of the families of the men, winked at their departure. The single men remained, and on the twenty-fourth of June, 1778, the two companies were united in one, and Lieutenant Spalding, of Ransom's company, was appointed captain.

As this was but ten days preceding the massacre, it is probable that was about the time that the men left the camp. They had waited to the last moment: human endurance could be delayed no longer. Their love and affection for their families, their fear for their safety, their knowledge of the terrible foe that was hovering over them, were reasons which could brook no restraint. They came; but alas, poor fellows! they came to sodden the field of carnage with their blood. Their bones, now gathered together in one common receptacle, repose at the base of the humble and unpretending monument which their children in after years erected, to point out the spot, to strangers, where their fathers were slain.

It was not my design in giving Historical Sketches of Plymouth, to write an account of the details of the battle of Wyoming. I find, however, that there were so many of our town's people engaged in it, that my outline would be imperfect did I not give at least a condensed view of the engagement. Connected as our people were with this battle, and so many of them having fallen on that eventful day, my sketches would not be complete were I not to include in them an account of it.

While, therefore, this will lengthen out the chain of local events necessarily, still they are so intimately blended with our township history that it is proper to speak of them.

In the latter part of June the people of the valley were fully apprised of the approach of the enemy. The Indian vanguard, descending both sides of the Susquehanna, commenced gathering their crop of scalps for the British market. The price of the article varied : this was graded in amount, beginning with the scalp of the robust and able-bodied man, and so down to the child of two years. They were all assorted, and labeled, and baled as the Indians pack their peltry, and in this way delivered over to the officers of the Crown entrusted with this *branch of the British service !*

In their descent upon the valley they murdered and scalped all before them, sparing neither age, nor sex, nor condition.

On the thirtieth of June, the British Colonel Butler, at the head of some four hundred provincials and tories and about seven hundred Indians, took up his position on the mountain bordering the north-eastern part of the township of Kingston. Here the British, tory and savage commander made his point of observation. He soon ascertained that his tory allies, the Wintermoots, Van Gorders, Von Alsteens, and Secords, who had visited him the year before, in the "Lake country," had made a true and faithful exposition of the helpless condition of the people of the valley. It was an easy prey.

To meet this invading force now became the great and momentous question upon the part of the people of Wyoming. And when we take into consideration that the whole possible available force of the valley did not amount to one-third of the number invading it, we may well be amazed that an effort should even have been made to resist it. But retreat would have been death, and to meet the foe would only add the pangs of torture which were to follow. The poor chances of success overbalanced these: a firm stand was the only alternative.

A council was convened, and resistance to the last determined upon. Plymouth, ever ready to respond, gave every man and boy that could bear arms. Captain Samuel Ransom, now at home, having resigned his commission in the army to stand or fall with his friends and neighbors, went into the Plymouth company as a private in the ranks. The people of the town assembled, had elected Asaph Whittlesey captain. The rank and file of this company, the remnant of the people, after the drain made upon them to fill up the muster-roll of the Second Independent company of United States troops, numbered *forty-four*; too many for the slaughter that was depending.

The roll of this company was not preserved. Probably it perished in the pocket of the dead orderly upon the battle-field. The only way left to us to ascertain who were on it after the lapse of ninety-three years, is to copy the names of our dead from the marble slab of the monument erected upon the ground where they fell.

The following are believed to have been Plymouth men; their names are enrolled upon the monumental tablet: their memory should be upon the hearts of the people of Plymouth in all time to come.

Samuel Ransom, Asaph Whittlesey, Aaron Gaylord, Amos Bullock, John Brown, Thomas Brown, Thomas Fuller, Stephen Fuller, Silas Harvey, James Hopkins, Nathaniel Howard, Nicholas Manville, Job Marshall, John Pierce, Silas Parke, Conrad Davenport, Elias Roberts, Timothy Ross, —— Reynolds, James Shaw, Joseph Shaw, Abram Shaw, John Williams, Elihu Williams, Jr., Rufus Williams, Aziba Williams and William Woodring. These are supposed to be twenty-seven of the forty-four. As to the remaining seventeen, those who knew them have passed away, and their names, as well as the fate of some of them, are lost to history.

Of the little band of forty-four of our town's people whom Captain Asaph Whittlesey led to the field on the third of July, 1778, probably twenty of the number did not survive the disasters of the day.

Captain Whittlesey occupied and owned the present Calvin Wadhams homestead. The little stream running through the premises, and emptying into the river near the Nottingham coal shaft, still bears his name.

The united force of the valley amounted to from three to four hundred men, and most of them were enrolled into four companies.

1st. Captain Dethick Hewit's company, composed of forty men, regulars, just recruited for the general service.

2d. Captain Asaph Whittlesey's company, Plymouth, forty-four men.

3d. Captain Lazarus Stewart's company, Hanover, forty men.

4th. Captain James Bidlack's company, lower Wilkes-Barré, thirty-eight men.

5th. Captain Rezin Geer's company, upper Wilkes-Barré, thirty men.

6th. Captain Aholiab Buck's company, Kingston, forty-four men.

The companies of Plymouth and Kingston, each forty-four, were the largest companies in the little army. All told make two hundred and thirty-six men. There were others who volunteered for the occasion, not enumerated in either of the company rolls, the whole constituting a body of some four hundred men.

The historians of the valley fix the number at about three hundred, but the probability is that it approached nearer to four hundred. As there was a general excitement and alarm, the people rushed to the common headquarters, and there was not that attention to enrollment and classification by companies that there would have been in a state of quiet. The enemy was upon the border, and it was not known what moment he would advance. So that confusion was the element which ruled the situation.

The names of one hundred and sixty-four persons are preserved to us of the slain. There can hardly be a doubt but there were nearly three hundred. Franklin's account in his journal of the event says "that near three hundred brave men fell a sacrifice to Indian barbarity." He was on the spot the evening of the day of the battle, and probably his journal is as correct an account as is left us of the actual number slaughtered.

But the exact number of our people who went forth to battle upon that eventful occasion will never be known.

On the twelfth of December, 1837, I carefully wrote down the narrative given me by Samuel Finch, one of the survivors of the battle. The old gentleman was, at the time of my interview with him, in his eighty-first year. His mind was unimpaired, and his memory about details, so far as I had previously learned from others who had escaped from the general slaughter, was very correct.

This old veteran, in 1837, was a resident of Tioga county, in this State. He was on a visit, at the time I speak of, to Mr. George M. Hollenback, of Wilkes-Barré, who brought him to my office, with the request that I would write down his account of the battle. Mr. Hollenback's father, the late Judge Hollenback of this city, and Mr. Finch, made their escape from the field together. Hollenback was in Captain Durkee's company. The captain was seriously wounded in his thigh and could not walk. Hollenback, being much attached to him, carried him some distance from the field on his shoulders; but being pressed closely by Indian pursuers, Captain Durkee "prayed him to abandon him to his fate, as they would both lose their lives in any further effort to save him." Reluctantly, Hollenback laid him upon the ground, with his prayer of "God Almighty protect you, captain," and sped on towards the river in company with Finch. They had gone, however, but a few rods before they heard the crash of the tomahawk in poor Durkee's brain. Hollenback was an expert swimmer. He plunged into the river—having disposed of the most of his clothing as he ran—and putting a guinea in his mouth—about his only fortune—amidst the discharge of Indian bullets, safely reached the western shore. Finch being unable

11

to swim, concealed himself in some drift-wood near the shore, but was, on the following morning, discovered, taken back to Queen Esther's rock, and among the orgies there practised, was ordered to run the gauntlet, which he safely accomplished, escaping twenty-four blows directed at him by twenty-four tomahawks, in the hands of the same number of savages, standing in parallel lines some ten feet apart! His escape from this terrible ordeal "he attributed to the fact that it was a common pastime among the earlier settlers of those days to practise running the gauntlet, not knowing but the time might come when their skill thus acquired might be of ser- . vice to them, and in my case it most certainly was."

Mr. Finch further stated, "that along with the other prisoners he commenced the march toward the Canadian frontier, but on the journey made his escape, and found his way back to his friends in Wyoming."

But my design in referring to this narrative, written down from the mouth of the witness thirty-five years ago, is to throw light, if possible, upon that long-disputed and never-to-be-settled point, touching the number of our people who fought the battle of Wyoming.

Samuel Finch states, " that he, with another soldier, was stationed at the gateway of Forty Fort by Colonel Butler to count the men as they passed out to battle; and that, including the regulars and militia, there were FOUR HUNDRED AND EIGHTY-FOUR MEN."

If this information be correct, then the number is larger than that mentioned by any of the numerous persons who have heretofore written upon this subject.

My written memoranda is in the exact language of the witness; nor am I aware that there is any reason why the account thus given by him should not be entitled to credit and belief. He could certainly have had no motive to state a falsehood.

Mr. Finch further stated, "that he was the messenger sent to Colonel Dorrance, at the extreme left of the line, with the order to 'fall back,' which, through mistake, was accepted as an order to retreat."

The memorable field upon which the Wyoming battle, or more generally and appropriately known as the field of the Wyoming massacre, was fought, is situated upon the west bank of the Susquehanna, and a half mile north-east of the granite monument erected, commemorative of the event, in the "old certified" township of Kingston. The base of the mountain being the northern, and a break or elevation in the plain, midway between the mountain and river, the southern boundary. At the foot of this divide, in the plain, one portion being some twenty feet higher than the other, is a morass, which at the date of which we speak, was covered by a thick growth of underbrush. At the base of the mountain was also a much wider morass than the one named, covered densely with scrub oaks and a thick net-work of undergrowth, very difficult of access. From this jungle came forth the Seneca chief and his savage braves. The distance between the southern boundary of the upper plain and the thicket at the foot of the mountain is about a half mile. This space was mostly covered with a sparsely growth of native pines, there being a cleared field of some two acres on the extreme right of the American line.

Upon the brow of the little hill was located the Tory fortification, known as Fort Wintermoot. When this fort was first erected, it was considered as belonging to friendly people; in a few years it passed as one of neutrality. On the morning of the battle, however, the British flag floated over it.

The lower plain was also sparsely covered with pines, and it was across this ground that a large number of the fugitives, after the defeat, made an effort to reach the river.

Such I believe to be a pretty correct description of the ground upon which was fought the short but decisive and disastrous battle of Wyoming, in the afternoon of the third day of July, 1778.

On the second day of July, the day preceding the battle, Colonel John Butler, the commander of the British, Tory and Indian army of invasion, removed his camp from the mountain, in the immediate vicinity, entered the valley, and established his chief depot at the Wintermoot fort. The Wintermoot family occupied the fort at the time, and by previous arrangement, had made all the necessary preparations for the reception of their distinguished guest.

The day before this, Colonel Zebulon Butler had made a reconnoissance in force, of the upper end of the valley, to inquire into the circumstances of the murder of the Harding family, and others, perpetrated by the Indians who were attached to the command of the British leader, as well as to gather what information he could of the position and numbers of the enemy.

The day that the British Butler established himself at Wintermoot, he sent a deputation of three men to Forty Fort, under a white flag, who demanded a surrender of that fort, together with all the other stockades and military defenses of the valley, munitions of war, public property, as well as all men in arms, in opposition to his majesty the King of Great Britain.

This demand of course was refused. On the morning of the third of July, a like deputation was sent, which ended in a like result. A demand of surrender had thus been made and refused. The next step was the casting down and the acceptance of the red gauntlet of battle. Which, if not done with all formulas of civilized warfare, was understood well by the offensive and defensive parties.

From the thirtieth of June to the morning of the fatal third day of July, the entire effective force of the whole valley, including men of seventy years of age and boys of fourteen, had been gathered together, and mostly enrolled and organized into companies, for the purpose of meeting the approaching foe; as to the actual numbers of which, the people of the valley entertained but a vague and indefinite knowledge.

The women and children had been placed in the different fortifications of the valley, on both sides of the river, for safety and protection. The greater number, however, had been quartered in Forty Fort, that being the most capacious as well as the strongest garrison. Its enclosure contained an area of about a half acre of ground, surrounded by a stockade, the sharpened timbers firmly set in the earth, and of sufficient height and strength to afford an available defence, except against siege artillery, which neither of the belligerents possessed.

Here assembled on the morning of the disastrous day, in council, for the last time, the little band of bold and daring men who were soon to meet in deadly conflict with more than three times their own number, to decide the momentous issue, whether they would fall with their faces or backs to the foe. To meet them was death; to retreat was death; and death therefore tainted the atmosphere which the people of the little garrison inhaled. But they were nevertheless firm and resolute, and they had made up their minds that if they must die, they "would die with harness on their backs."

Colonel Zebulon Butler, a commander of one of

the regiments of the Continental army, being at his home in Wilkes-Barré on a furlough, had been, by common consent, invested with the command in chief of this little army. His staff consisted of Colonel Nathan Denison, Lieutenant-Colonel George Dorrance, and Major John Garret. To this he added Captain Samuel Ransom and Captain Robert Durkee, men of military skill, and upon whose judgment he placed great consideration and reliance.

The first question to be disposed of on that day, which terminated amid the darkest gloom and the the most heart-rending sorrow, was to decide upon the proposition of the British commander to surrender! Upon this question there was not a dissenting voice. A conflict was inevitable, so they took up the gage of battle defiantly thrown at their feet by the leader of a force more than thrice their own number; a fact which he knew, but which they did not. And if they had, it would not have changed their conduct.

The next point to be determined was, whether they should immediately give battle, or remain within the fortification and stand a siege, with the expectation of the arrival of reinforcements. This gave rise to a division of opinion.

Colonel Butler and his staff took the ground that there should be delay, for a short time at least, because there was reason to hope that Captain Spalding, with his Continental company, was on his way to Westmoreland; that Captain John Franklin, with a company from Huntington and Salem, was also on his way to join them; that there should be time for the general panic throughout the valley to subside; that coolness, resulting from discipline, as well as valor, were elements necessary for success.

To these arguments were interposed the objection, that the enemy had now been three days in the valley; they were fast carrying on their work of conquest and murder; that this fact would be likely to create instead of suppress panic; that two forts had already surrendered; that all the craft in the river above Forty Fort were in the possession of the enemy, thus affording him an opportunity to cross to the east side, which would compel the abandonment of the only really stronghold they had for retreat in case of disaster; that they could not rely upon keeping their men together when most of them were within gun-shot sound of their helpless and unprotected families; and finally, if death was to be their doom, there were enough of them to suffer the penalty. These arguments were decisive of the matter. The last one reminds us of the speech of Henry V. before the battle of Agincourt:

> "If we are mark'd to die, we are enough
> To do our country loss: and if to live,
> The fewer men, the greater share of honor."

It is not for us to say, after the lapse of nearly a hundred years, without those means of knowledge which existed on that occasion, whether the decision

they arrived at was judicious and prudent, or otherwise.   The men who made it had to assume the fearful consequences that followed.   If an error was committed, the motive which prompted it cannot be questioned.   It is true that Captain Spalding was between
the Pocono and the Blue Mountain, within two days'
march of Wilkes-Barré, with a company of sixty men
or more, and that Captain Franklin, with thirty-five
men, was within eight hours' march of the camp.   But
it is no more than reasonable to suppose, as circumstances afterwards transpired, that if Spalding and
Franklin had been present, that there would have
been contributed an additional hundred to the slaughtered hecatomb in reserve.

The decision of the council of war to adopt immediate offensive action may possibly have been premature.   From the limited knowledge, however, of the
circumstances which is left to us at this remote period
of time, we cannot help concluding that the decision
was right.

The men who made it were not aware of the nu-
merical strength of their enemy; and the sequel, as developed afterwards upon the field, is pretty conclusive
that a hundred men more could not have saved the
day.   The fair presumption is, that a hundred more
would have fallen had they been in the engagement.
Three or four to one are fearful odds in an open
field, and where the strategy of war cannot be made
available.

Two o'clock in the afternoon had arrived; the solemn decision to fight in the open field had been made; the minority had cheerfully yielded their opinions to the majority, and the little army of four hundred men marched out of the fort in battle array.

Colonel Butler detailed Captains Durkee and Ransom, and Lieutenants Ross and Wells, for the purpose of making a reconnoissance of the ground, and to establish the locality of the line of battle. These men had been under fire upon continental battle-fields, and were, therefore, properly selected for the purpose with which they were entrusted. They went, but they never returned from the field they surveyed.

Upon the ground they designated, Colonel Butler formed his line. The two posts of honor were assigned to Captain Durkee, who was put at the extreme right, and our townsman, Captain Whittlesey, upon the extreme left. Durkee was protected as to any flank movement by the morass; Whittlesey by the mountain and dense thicket at its base, which the savages however could penetrate.

Colonel Butler, with Major Garret, took the command of the right wing; Colonel Denison, supported by Colonel Dorrance, the left. Durkee was placed with Bidlack, and Ransom with Whittlesey. This was the order of battle at three o'clock in the afternoon of the third of July, 1778.

All this preparation had undoubtedly reached the ears of the British, Tory and Indian commander, for at about the same time he had formed his line a short distance below Fort Wintermoot. Divesting himself of his plumes and martial tawdry, with a black handkerchief bound about his head, he took the command of his left wing, composed of regulars and provincial troops. He placed his right wing, composed of Indians and Tories, under the command of Gucingeracton, a Seneca chief, supported, *probably*, by Captain Caldwell, of Johnson's Royal Greens. The fact as to the presence of Johnson is somewhat obscure, but as Caldwell was his next in rank, the better opinion seems to favor the idea that he commanded the Royal Greens on this occasion.

Both parties, therefore, being within a half mile of each other, and in battle array, it required but the signal gun for the commencement of the conflict.

Colonel Butler made a short address before he displayed his column. He said: "Men, yonder is the enemy. The fate of the Hardings tells us what we have to expect if defeated. We come out to fight not only for liberty, but for life itself; and, what is dearer, to preserve our homes from conflagration, our women and children from the tomahawk. Stand firm the first shock, and the Indians will give way. Every man to his duty."

As Denison was filing his column off to the left, he again repeated: " Be firm, everything depends on resisting the first shock."

Our line began the advance, and at the same time

the flames and smoke were seen to ascend from Fort Wintermoot. The motive for this has never been disclosed; but as the burning embers were afterwards used as a means of torturing wounded and disabled prisoners of war, we may suppose that the savage-hearted man, who that day. led his Indian and Tory bands, prepared his rack in advance for the torture of his victims.

Colonel Zebulon Butler ordered his men to fire throughout the whole line, and to keep up the volley as they advanced. The fire was rapid as well as steady the whole length of his line. The British advancing at the same time, the discharge of musketry became continuous.

There being fewer natural obstacles on the right, Colonel Zebulon Butler made rapid advances, and drove the left wing of his adversary before him: he not only compelled him to yield his ground, but also created confusion in his ranks. The British line could not withstand the regular and steady fire to which it was exposed. Following up their advantages, the British Butler's left wing was now more than a quarter of a mile in the rear of the point of attack, and very close upon the burning fortification; everything looked favorable upon the right, but, alas ! not so on the left.

Colonel Denison had to meet a concealed foe. The morass literally swarmed with savages, and while our people were partially upon a plain, they became the objects of deliberate aim from the concealed savage warriors. In a few moments they had picked out Colonel Dorrance, Captains Ransom and Whittlesey, and who, like brave men as they were, fell in the front ranks. The Indians becoming encouraged at their success in the fall of these officers, with a tremendous yell, which was taken up and repeated from band to band through the morass, darted upon the company of Whittlesey by a flank movement which of course threw it into confusion. Colonel Denison did what any prudent soldier would have done under the circumstances. He made the effort to place Whittlesey's company with its front to the enemy, which had just turned his flank. To do this it was necessary that they should fall back, and such was his order; but we must bear in mind when this order was given probably half of his company had fallen, and that each survivor, in this hand-to-hand fight, had to contend with a half dozen infuriated savages against him. Orders under such circumstances could amount to nothing. The left wing was overpowered; it had not the strength nor the numbers to resist the enemy it had to contend with.

Seven hundred of these excited and wild savages let loose upon the left wing, which probably did not exceed two hundred men all told, was a fearful obstacle ; and therefore whether the order were retreat or fall back, it could not have changed the result. The line was too feeble to withstand the avalanche; it did not waver, it was crushed. Nothing short of a miracle could have resisted the overpowering weight thrown upon it.

Most of our local historians, from Chapman down, taking up the oft-repeated version of this feature of the Wyoming battle, impute the failure upon our part to the misunderstanding of the order to fall back for one of 'retreat.

There is no doubt whatever but what many men who escaped death upon that field were under this impression. Suppose the left wing had understood the order to fall back, would it have been possible for them to have faced successfully an enemy of such superior force? Where would they have made their base? They were surrounded on all sides, in front, and rear, and flank.

It is time that public opinion should decide this question, and that the facts should be properly understood.

The rout upon the left became general. The success which Butler had achieved on the right amounted to nothing amidst the disasters which had taken place on his left. Amid desperation and hope he rode between the two lines, appealing to his men, whom he called his children, "to stand their ground." It was the last act remaining for him to do as a brave man; but superior numbers had accomplished its work, and thus within half an hour after the commencement of the battle, the whole line was in full retreat, each flying for his life, and seeking the most available refuge from his bloodthirsty pursuers.

The scenes of brutality and murder which followed the disastrous defeat at the Wyoming battle, thank God! have but few parallels. The sickening, abhorrent and disgusting details of which, though done within an enlightened age, perhaps ought not to be repeated to an enlightened people. The part played by the wild and savage Indian does not so much shock the senses, because he was cradled in blood and educated in the belief that he was serving the Great Spirit in taking vengeance in the most cruel manner upon his real or imaginary enemies. But what have we to say in defence of the memory of the man, born and educated within the pale of civilization, and placed in command as a reward of merit, probably, of a regiment of British infantry?

. And can we wonder either that a British King, whose sense of humanity, as exhibited in his conduct towards his American subjects, was of the most cruel kind, should have stood aghast and refused the honor of knighthood to Colonel John Butler until he cleared up the charges against him of brutal conduct at the battle of Wyoming. It was too much for George III., by no means a monarch of nice and discriminating virtues, to swallow the dose.

And how grateful it is to reflect that British gold could not purchase from our old settlers of this valley a certificate palliating the monstrous conduct when eagerly sought for by his entreaties! They were poor, but they were honest. Gold *did not* buy them.

The principal avenue of retreat from the battle-ground was in the direction of the river. The flank movement made by the savages cut off the means of escape by the road leading to the fort. Some few escaped in that direction, but the main body of the fugitives sought the river, the enemy in full pursuit. Scores of them were shot down, or wounded and carried back to Queen Esther's rock for the bloody carnival which was to come off there. Twenty-seven mutilated and disfigured bodies were afterwards found at that place, and so disfigured by wounds and gashes as not to be recognized.

The Tory animosity and hate, if they did not exceed the savage disposition, came almost up to it. Upon Monocasy Island, in the immediate vicinity of the battle-ground, where many of the poor creatures sought refuge, a beast in human shape, by the name of Pensil, deliberately shot down a brother who was upon his knees before him supplicating for his life. With the imprecation that "he was a d—d rebel," he blew out his brains. There were instances where other Tories invited back their fleeing enemy, under the promise that their lives should be saved, but in every case where they returned under such promises, they were mercilessly butchered. Captain James Bidlack, with others, who were wounded, were thrown by the Indians and Tories into the flames of Fort

Wintermoot, and held down by pitchforks till the burning embers consumed their bodies. Deeds of cruelty inflicted in the civil family feuds between the houses of York and Lancaster are dwarfed in their comparison with those of the Wyoming massacre, and perpetrated, too, under the eye, if not by the order of the British commander, a man who had the benefits and advantages of civilization. But the progress in moral reform of three hundred years had extended no kindly influences over him.

The battle did not exceed half an hour in duration, so that from four o'clock until the dawn of the next day, the horrid creatures carried on their fearful orgies. The atmosphere for miles around was polluted with the stench of burning human bodies. "All night long," says Pearce, "there was a revel in blood and in the fumes of burning human flesh. Not until the morning light did they cease their demoniac orgies for want of victims. The sun never shed his rays on a bloodier field. Spectators standing upon the opposite shore of the river saw naked men forced around the burning stake with spears, and heard their heart-rending shrieks and dying groans."

I pass over the troubles and sacrifices which befel the women and helpless children in their flight from the valley. Their husbands and fathers and brothers were nearly all slain. Of the army which went out in the morning, fifty did not return alive. Of the fifteen officers, eleven were slain. Every captain

12

of the six companies, including Ransom and Durkee, were found dead at the front of the line, with the exception of Bidlack, whose charred body was found among the burned débris of Wintermoot fort.

The women and children of Plymouth started on the night of the battle for Fort Augusta, at Sunbury. The roads in every direction leading from the valley were thronged with fugitive women and children—and as they ascended the high hills skirting the valley, they looked back upon their burning homes and inhaled the tainted breeze from the battle-field of their slaughtered husbands, brothers and fathers.

On the preceding day, July fourth, the British Butler marched to Forty Fort, where he found Colonel Denison with a small remnant of the men who had escaped the horrors of the day before. Captain Franklin, with his thirty-five men, had reached there on the evening of the battle. These soldiers and the women and children composed the garrison. Articles of capitulation were drawn up and signed. But except as to the commission of any other deeds of murder, the conditions were almost totally disregarded. The Indians were still Indians, and the British commander pretended he could not control them. They robbed the women of their clothing and the children of their bread. What they could not carry away they burnt and destroyed. After the signing of the treaty, bands of Indians and Tories traversed the valley and destroyed by fire nearly all the buildings.

To show the brutal character of the British commander, we will give an incident. In entering the gateway of Forty Fort, he recognized Sergeant Boyd, a deserter. "Boyd," said he, with the sternness of savage ferocity, "go to that tree."—"I hope," said Boyd, imploringly, "your honor will consider me a prisoner of war."—"Go to that tree, sir." And then summoning an Indian squad he ordered them to fire upon him. The poor sergeant fell dead.

In this we read the temper and disposition of the man. He had it in his power to have checked the slaughter of his prisoners; he had it in his power to have saved the people of the valley from plunder, and their homes from the brand. He was under Tory influence and acted from savage impulses.

And after all these examples of monstrosity, he sought the honorable distinction of knighthood. It was too much for even George III. to grant!

Brandt was not in the battle. It is somewhat remarkable that almost every survivor of the massacre was under the impression that the Mohawk chief was at the head of the Indians on the third of July. Chapman took up the same idea from revelations undoubtedly made to him by the survivors, and such was and is the tradition of this matter. I have been told, time and again by them, that they saw him and they would describe his dress and person. Miner followed Chapman, but doubtingly, and in a note he submits the question to the judgment of his readers. Pearce says that he was not in the battle, and Dr. Peck is of the same opinion.

In order to satisfy my own mind, some years since I wrote a letter to Mr. Bancroft, the historian, on this subject. He had come down in the chain of his history to the eve of the Wyoming battle. I wrote stating to him that there was a difference of opinion on the question whether Brandt was in the battle of Wyoming.

I give the copy of his reply to my letter on the subject:

"NEW YORK, April 15, 1867.

"*My Dear Mr. Wright :* I had already written the account of the Wyoming massacre, and having had before me very full contemporary materials, I had avoided the error against which you so kindly caution me.

"Brandt was not in the valley ; your party was of the Seneca tribe, and led by a great Seneca chief. Brandt led an expedition in New York, as the enclosed papers will show.

"Very truly yours,   GEO. BANCROFT."

The enclosed paper which is here referred to, is a copy of a report, of the massacre, made by Colonel Guy Johnson to Lord George Germain, at the time Secretary of War under George III., dated at New York, on the twentieth of September, 1778, two months after the battle. The following is the report :

"Your Lordship will have heard before this can reach you of the successful incursions of the Indians and Loyalists from the Northward. In conformity to the Instructions I conveyed to my officers, they assembled their force early in May, and one division under one of my Deputies, Mr. Butler, proceeded with great success down the Susquehanna, destroying the Posts and Settlements at Wyoming; augmenting their number with many Loyalists, and alarming all the country; whilst another Division under Mr. Brandt, the Indian Chief, cut off two hundred and ninety-four men near Schoharie, and destroyed the adjacent settlements, with several Magazines, from whence the rebels had derived great resources, thereby affording great encouragement and opportunity to many friends of the Government to join them."

This document would seem to settle the question that Brandt was not in the battle of Wyoming. He took his two hundred and ninety-four scalps at Schoharie, "and destroyed the settlements" in that country at the same time that "Mr. Butler" took nearly or quite the same number of scalps at Wyoming, "and destroyed the settlements" on the Susquehanna, as well as "alarming all the country."

How idle was it, therefore, for "Mr. Butler" to allege to Colonel Denison that he could not control the Indians in their destruction of property in the valley. His master, Mr. Guy Johnson, says that such were the orders he gave. Butler, therefore, when his Indians and "Loyalists" (Tories) were destroying the entire settlement of Wyoming with the brand and the sword, was but carrying out the orders of the agents of a Christian King.

It is well that this part of the history of Wyoming, as to the presence of Brandt, is fully settled and understood, though at a very modern date.

I have in this statement of the battle of Wyoming not gone into it as fully as I should have done, because it did not have a material bearing on the subject I have in hand. The local history of Plymouth, however, became so much connected with it, that I was compelled to give it a short examination.

I have already stated the number of our people slain in the massacre, and the circumstances under which they were marshalled into the ranks, and that they did not flinch from the duties which events imposed upon them. The Williams family alone contributed four of their number to the slaughter.

Our people should know the spot where their ancestors fell in the battle. When any of them hereafter shall, through curiosity or motives of regard, visit the field, they will find the particular locality about a mile above the Lackawanna and Bloomsburg depot, at Wyoming station, and very nearly on the bed of the track of that road. There our townsmen, Captain Samuel Ransom, Captain Asaph Whittlesey, and some twenty-five of our people were outflanked and slain by Indians and Tories on that ever-memorable day.

The following statement of Daniel Washburn, a Plymouth man, was kindly furnished me by Steuben Jenkins, Esq., as written down by him in 1846, from the mouth of the old man. I give his precise language. It is an interesting statement of the thrilling events of the times, from one of our own people :

"I lived in Shawnee. The Nanticoke company came up to Shawnee and I joined in with them under Captain Whittlesey. We all marched up to Forty Fort that night. The next morning we saw the flag of the enemy coming with two men; one carried the flag and the other played upon the fife. They had a letter for our Colonel, from what I could learn, telling us to give up the fort. The Colonel told them he would not give up the fort, and they left. After they had left, orders were given by our Colonel, Butler, that we must go and meet the enemy." (Here follows an account of the massacre.) * * * "We then started, and steered a straight course for the Shawnee fort (Garrison Hill), through fields and woods, till we came to Ross Hill, where we came in the main road, and went to the fort. We came to the fort about midnight, and to our great surprise .it was occupied by no one except my father, Jesse Washburn, and my brother Caleb, my step-mother with two small children, and Mrs. Woodring, the wife of William A. Woodring, who was killed in the battle. Mrs. Woodring had five children, four sons and one daughter. We all remained till daybreak, when we could see no one else around. The fort was full of provisions and store-goods, bedding and house furniture. In the morning we three, father, Caleb and myself carried

rails and made a raft.   At nine o'clock we had our
raft finished.   About this time we heard the report of
the enemy shooting at the Wilkes-Barré fort (*and
we knew it to be the enemy*).   We then got aboard of
our rail raft; my father and mother, Caleb and the
two children, and Mrs. Woodring and her five children, taking with us provisions to last us across the
Blue Mountains.   We then set sail with our rail raft
and went on very well till we got to Nanticoke Falls,
when we saw two boats fast on a rock.   They called to
us to help them loose.   There were in these boats
men, women and children.   We then landed our raft
on the Shawnee side and went and helped them loose,
and helped them below the riff safe, for which they
paid us.   When we were getting the boats loose we
saw a man come out of the woods.   He was naked
and had not a stitch of clothes about him.   He said he
swam the river about Forty Fort, and had come down
through the woods.   He spoke to us from the other
side and told us of his happy escape, and then went
on again.   When we had them all loose—it was
about twelve o'clock in the day—then we pushed off
our rail raft again and sailed on very well till night,
when we landed at, or a little above, the mouth of
Little Wapwallopen, and put up for the night in a
small cabin that stood where Jacob and Joseph Hess
now live (1846).   A man by the name of Dewey had
moved out about two days before.   Here we stayed
over night.   In the morning we again pursued our

journey along the old Indian path. This day we travelled beyond the Buck Mountain and put up for the night in the woods, Mrs. Woodring and her five children being still with us. The next morning we again renewed our journey, and on the third day we landed at a place called Greaden Head (*Gnadden-Hutten*), in Northampton county. I was about fifteen years old at the Wyoming battle, and went for my father. I am now nearly eighty-three. When we got to Wapwallopen we met a man with a horse and some cows which he wished us to assist him in driving to Northampton. The women and children rode alternately upon the horse. We had much trouble in driving the cattle."

There seems to be no definite account preserved of the number killed of the enemy in the battle. They removed their dead and wounded. It is probable that fifty would include the enemy's loss—possibly a less number. We are left to conjecture as to the fact.

CHAPTER VIII.

A LESS number of our townspeople were murdered or carried into captivity by the Indians than in other parts of the valley, compared with our population. The records we have, though probably incomplete, show but two murdered and fourteen carried away as prisoners. Some of those taken prisoners were not afterwards heard from, and were probably murdered.

This number does not embrace those slain in the Wyoming battle.

Mr. Miner's list of the murdered within the town of Westmoreland contains the names of sixty-one, and his prisoners' list sixty, making a total of one hundred and twenty-one; and while this catalogue was made with great caution and with much research and labor, we do not find upon it the names of Louis Harvey and Lucy Bullford, of Plymouth, who were captured at the time Colonel Ransom and the two Harveys were. He, however, admits that the num-

(200)

ber, including those killed and captured, was larger
than the list he furnishes.   There can be but little
doubt of this, as sixty years had passed by from the
time of these slaughters and imprisonments to the
period in which he wrote.   The one hundred and
twenty-one would probably bear an addition of fifty,
and come nearer to the true state of the facts.   Our
people of Plymouth, therefore, were remarkably fortunate considering the terrible sacrifices that their surrounding neighbors were subjected to, for the three
years succeeding the Wyoming battle.   Before the
occurrence of this event, there was not an instance
of murder or capture in the town.   It was after the
battle that the Indian character took on those terrible
and remorseless features of cruelty, the exhibitions of
which, in some cases, are too shocking to relate.

To the natural feeling of revenge and the thirst
for blood, the policy of the British king had imbued
the Indian heart with the new elements of avarice and
cupidity.   These were before unknown to the red
man.   He was proud and haughty in his manners, indifferent to any luxuries, content with the bare necessaries to sustain life, and in the language of Camp-
bell,

"A Stoic of the woods ; a man without a tear."

In his intercourse with the white man he had acquired a new appetite.   He tasted of the cup which
intoxicates, and he became unscrupulous as to the
manner of gratifying it.   The scalp of an American,

whether of man, woman or child, had a market value
under British law.   The Indian dealt in the commodity; he could make more money in the traffic of the
white man's scalp than he could in the peltry of the
chase.   He could sell them on presentation; the
market was never dull; there was no credit; the gold
was paid over the counter on delivery of the merchandise.   This would buy rum, and rum made the red
man happy.   The new appetite supplanted all the
others, and his natural savage ferocity became increased tenfold.   Before this it was prescribed by
limits.   True, the boundary was frail, but still the
line was discernible; the scalp bounty removed all restraint.   The king gloried in the accumulation of his
new article of traffic; and the Indian, made more
savage in his cups, sharpened the already keen edge
of his knife with the exultant feelings of a monster.
The minds of purchaser and seller were in accord, and
so the trade went on for the mutual profits of each.

The voices of such men as Chatham, Wilkes and
Barré, in the English Parliament, were impotent.
There was no mercy to be shown to rebels; they were
outside of the pale of humanity—their crime did not
entitle them to " the benefit of clergy."

It is therefore not a matter of surprise that the
savage, nerved up to acts of cruelty by the example of
a nation professing to be governed by rules of Christianity, and basking in the sunshine of a high civilization, would stop to scrutinize the mode or manner of

executing his new calling. His well strung girdle of reeking scalps was not ornamental merely to the savage warrior, but it possessed a specific value in pounds, shillings and pence—which the British treasury paid on the production of the article.

The dull and obtuse faculties of the Indian mind could not be made to comprehend that there was any immorality in the mere act of murdering the victim for the value of the scalp upon his head, when the transaction received the endorsement of so renowned a dignitary as George III.

The conduct, therefore, of this inhuman prince gave license to the commission of the most terrible and revolting brutalities. He gathered his harvest of three hundred scalps at the massacre of Wyoming— and while this scene was being transacted upon the Susquehanna, his friend BRANDT strung upon his belt two hundred and ninety-four, taken from the heads of the defenseless people of Schoharie, upon the Mohawk.

In the two expeditions under the orders of his Majesty, one intrusted to "Mr. Butler," on the Susquehanna, and the other intrusted to "Mr. Brandt," on the Mohawk, his royal tannery was replenished with about six hundred fresh scalps; some of them, it is true, from the heads of women and children, but all in a good state of preservation—all marketable!

Now when we consider that this course of conduct was in the eighteenth century, and in not merely a civilized but an enlightened age, we are confounded and amazed. There is one redeeming feature in it, however, and which will ever redound to the honor of English statesmen, that the high-toned men of the Lords and Commons denounced the act of their Sovereign in the most bitter and scathing invective.

The untutored wild man of the woods, without the pale of civilization as to the knowledge even of an accountability to a supreme ruler in the world to come, or being clothed with the mantle of Christianity, may plead these things in palliation of his beastly murders; but with the memory of George III. rest the curses and anathemas of the enlightened world.

Immediately succeeding the Indian battle where the great harvest of scalps had been reaped by Butler and his allies, bands of straggling, marauding Indians and Tories commenced their incursions upon the now desolate people of the desolate valley of Wyoming.

Colonel Zebulon Butler was in command of the fortifications, but his force was inadequate to suppress the raids which were frequently made by the enemy; and instances of murder and capture were often occurring within sight of the people in these fortifications.

The following letter from Washington, in reply to one from Colonel Zebulon Butler asking for aid, I found many years since among some old papers of Colonel Butler. It has never before been published. The original is still in my library, and is in a perfect state of preservation.

"HEADQUARTERS,
"MORRISTOWN, April 7, 1780. }

"SIR: I received yesterday your letter of the 2d instant, and am extremely sorry to find that parties of the enemy have appeared and committed hostilities in the neighborhood of Wyoming. It is not in my power to afford any troops from the army, and I should hope those already there, and the inhabitants, will be able to repel at least incursions by light parties.

"It was my intention, as I informed you, that you should join your regiment immediately after your return: however, I am inclined from the face of things to let you continue where you are for the present, and you will remain till further orders. Should further depredations and mischief be committed by the enemy, you will take occasion to inform me of them.

"I am, sir,
"Your most obedient servant,
"G. WASHINGTON."

"To Colonel Zebulon Butler."

This letter fully shows that the people of the valley could not depend upon Washington for any assistance. The defense of the valley was left with Colonel Butler, his command consisting of Captain Spalding's company, composed of the remnant of the two independent companies of Durkee and Ransom, with a few stragglers which Sullivan had left the year previous. Death and slaughter had intimidated the living, and the people were a helpless prey to the predatory bands of Tories and Indians who were continually prowling about the valley. And it now became the lot of our townspeople to submit to their share of the pains and penalties in reserve for them.

John Perkins, a Plymouth man, was murdered by the Indians on the seventeenth of November, 1778, in the lower end of the township, shortly after the battle.

In March following, a band of twenty Indians appeared on the Kingston side of the river, in sight of the Wilkes-Barré fort, in broad daylight, and murdered three valuable citizens: Mr. Elihu Williams, Lieutenant Buck and Mr. Stephen Pettibone. Frederick Follet, who was with them, fell pierced by seven wounds from a spear, and with the others was scalped and left for dead. Instantly a detachment of men was sent over: the Indians had fled. Follet, sweltering in blood, gave signs of life and was taken to the fort. Dr. William Hooker Smith, on examining his wounds, said that while everything should be done that kindness and skill could suggest, he regarded his recovery as hopeless. Yet he did recover. One spear thrust had penetrated the stomach, so that its contents came out at his side. Mr. Follet lived for many years, and removed to Ohio, where he left a large family.—*Miner's History,* p. 263.

It would afford me much pleasure to speak of Dr. William Hooker Smith at length. He was the pioneer physician of the valley; a man of good qualifications as a physician and surgeon, and possessed of a knowledge of the prospective value of anthracite coal far beyond his contemporaries. The numerous deeds made to him in early days of coal privileges and mineral rights, prove him to have been a man of great forecast and sound judgment. His history, however, does not properly come within our limits.

Elihu Williams was a Plymouth man. His son had fallen in the massacre the year previous. The residence of the Williams family, and where the Rev. Darius Williams, a descendant, lived for many years, was on the south side of the Plymouth road leading from Wilkes-Barré to Ross Hill, and immediately below the machine shops of the Lackawanna and Bloomsburg Railroad Company.

Darius Williams was for many years a local Methodist Episcopal preacher, and a man of strong mind and peculiar powers of pulpit eloquence. The writer has often heard him preach. He had great earnestness of manner, and his language was strong and well chosen. He earned, and very justly too, the reputation of not only being a good and exemplary man, but also of possessing a high order of talents. He died at the old homestead, probably about thirty years ago.

Captain James Bidlack, a Plymouth man, father of the Captain James Bidlack who fell in the Wyoming battle, at the head of his company, was taken prisoner on the second of March, 1779, in the upper end of the township. He made his escape, or was released about a year afterwards.

Captain Bidlack had another son, the Rev. Benjamin Bidlack, who served the whole period of the Revolutionary war, and was discharged at Yorktown

13

upon the surrender of Cornwallis. The Rev. Benjamin Bidlack resided many years in a small log house on the north side of the main road, immediately below the Joseph Wright homestead. My mother, now living at an advanced age, informs me that Mr. Bidlack occupied this house when she first went to Plymouth to live, about the year 1795 ; that Mr. Bidlack was then a Methodist preacher, and travelled the circuit. I shall have occasion to speak of him hereafter.

Our local historians agree mainly as to the circumstances attending the capture of Rogers, Van Campen and Pike, but they are wide apart as to the incidents attending their release and escape. My own memory is somewhat imperfect as to the account I have heard of the circumstances, though I have probably listened to Mr. Rogers' statement of them more than a score of times. But this is long ago, fifty years at least. I shall, however, rely more upon my own memory—as I have learned the story from the actors of the drama —than the written accounts of it by others.

A band of ten Indians, on the twenty-seventh of March, 1780, made their appearance in Hanover. This was ten days preceding the date of the letter I have introduced from General Washington to Colonel Zebulon Butler; and their acts, together with another band of six, who made their appearance on the same day in Kingston, carrying off three prisoners, probably gave rise to the correspondence. The ten who visited Hanover shot and killed Asa Upson about two miles below Wilkes-Barré, on the main road. On the day following, two men were engaged in making sugar near Nanticoke : one of them was killed on the spot, the other taken prisoner. This was the work of the same party, undoubtedly; the man taken prisoner was never heard of again. On the twenty-ninth they passed over the river, near Fish Island, and found Jonah Rogers, a boy then fourteen years of age, who had been sent by his parents on an errand to the lower end of the valley. They took Rogers and went down the river to Fishing Creek, in the vicinity of Bloomsburg, and on the following day they surprised the family of the Van Campens. Moses Van Campen, a young, athletic man, they took prisoner, having murdered and scalped his father, his brother, and his uncle. On the same day they captured a boy by the name of Pence, whom Rogers says was older than he—probably eighteen years of age. From Fishing Creek they passed northerly through Huntington. Here they were opposed by a scout of four men under the direction of John Franklin. A skirmish ensued; two of Franklin's men were wounded. The Indian party being too numerous for Franklin to contend with, they continued on to what is known as "Pike's Swamp," in the southern part of what is now Lehman township. Here they found Abraham Pike, a Plymouth man—and known for the rest of his life as "*The Indian Killer*"—and his wife, making sugar. Mrs. Pike had an infant some four months old.

Here they staid over night. In the morning they took Pike and his wife prisoners; binding the child up in a blanket, they threw it on the roof of the sugar cabin and hastened on with their prisoners. The lamentations of Mrs. Pike for her poor child, thus left to exposure and certain death, seemed to excite the feelings of the savages. After travelling a few miles they halted, and upon consultation, they painted Mrs. Pike, saying, "joggo squaw"—go home, woman. She returned to her cabin, got her child, and fled to the settlement and gave the alarm; but the Indians were out of reach.

It is an interesting fact that the bottom logs of this old cabin are still visible; and a gentleman informs me, who visited the spot within the last year, that in the centre of it stands a beech tree some two feet in diameter. Ninety-one years is a long time for the foundation logs of Pike's cabin to resist the encroachment of the seasons. I remember seeing it a great many years since : it was then three or four courses of logs high.

About the third of April, they encamped for the night upon the Susquehanna, some fifteen or twenty miles below Tioga Point. The Indians feeling that they were now safe from pursuit, and upon the borders of their own possessions, made arrangements for a night of quiet repose. Not so with Abraham Pike; he was a British deserter. He had fought under that flag at Bunker Hill, and received a wound there. An

Irishman by birth, and full of the idea of liberty, he made his escape and volunteered for a term of two years in the American army, at the end of which time he came to the Susquehanna. He had also been in the battle of Wyoming, thus not only deserting the British ranks, but having openly fought against the British flag.

His Indian captors knew these things. He was now on the way to the British lines, and he would soon be handed over to the men whose cause he had abandoned. He knew his fate; his position was one of desperation. We may, therefore, readily understand who was the originator of the bold scheme which took place on the night of that encampment. There was no one of the party who had the same issue at stake that he had, and we must rely upon the statement of Rogers and Pike, in opposition to that of Van Campen. The two former died before the latter, and he strangely asserted the claim of the whole credit of the escape, and there was no one to contradict.

As I have had the story from Mr. Rogers, he says : "That in the afternoon of the day before we reached the place of encampment, we came to a stream; I was tired and fatigued with the journey; my feet were sore, and I was just able to proceed; Pike told the chief of the gang that he ' would carry me over on his shoulders.' The old chief in a gruff voice, said ' well.' Pike whispered in my ear as we were crossing the stream : *'Jonah, don't close your eyes to-night;*

*when they sleep take the knife from the chief's belt
and cut the cords with which I am bound.'* I was
the only one of the prisoners who was not bound, and
every night the old chief took me under his blanket. The nights were cold and raw, and though protected in this way, I thought that I should perish."

This much of the project was communicated to the
other prisoners by Pike. Towards nightfall, they
halted on the banks of the river, kindled the camp
fire, partook of their meal, and were soon extended
upon the ground, five Indians upon each side and the
four prisoners in the middle.

Mr. Rogers says : "In a few moments the old
chief was asleep, and in the course of half an hour, the
savages were all snoring, but he knew his friends
were awake, from their occasional half-suppressed
cough. Pike was the nearest to me, and not over two
feet in distance. It was a terrific effort for me to
make up my mind to perform my part of the business,
for I knew that instant death would be the penalty in
a failure. But as the time passed on, and the snoring of the savages grew louder, my courage seemed to
gather new strength. I had noticed that when the old
chief laid down, that the knife in his belt was on his
side next to me. I peered out from under the blanket and I saw the embers of the fire still aglow, and a
partial light of the moon. I also saw the hands of
Pike elevated. I thought the time had come, and
these two hours of suspense I had passed were more

terrible than all the rest of my life put together. I cautiously drew the knife from the scabbard in the old chief's belt, and creeping noiselessly out from under the blanket, I passed over to Pike, and severed the cords from his hands.

"All was the silence of death, save the gurgling noise of the savages in their sleep. Pike cut the cords that bound the other prisoners. We were now all upon our feet. The first thing was to remove the guns of the Indians ; the work for us to do was to be done with tomahawks and knives. The guns were carefully removed out of sight, and each of us had a tomahawk. Van Campen placed himself near the old chief and Pike over another. I was too young for the encounter, and stood aloof. I saw the tomahawks of Pike and Van Campen flash in the dim light of the half-smouldering flames ; the next moment the crash of two terrible blows ; these were followed in quick succession, when seven of the ten arose in a state of momentary stupefaction and bewilderment, and then came the hand-to-hand conflict in the contest for life. But our enemy was without arms, still they were not disposed to yield. Pence, however, seizing one of the guns, fired and brought down his man, making four killed, and two of them were very dangerously wounded; they fled with a terrific yell on the report of the gun. As they were retreating, Van Campen hurled his tomahawk, which buried itself in the shoulders of one of the retreating foe. And this Indian, with the terrible scar in his shoulder-blade, I saw years afterwards, and who acknowledged that he got the wound upon this occasion."

This is the story, as near as my memory retains it, and which I have so often heard from the lips of my old school-master, Jonah Rogers. It would appear from this that four were killed, six escaped, three of whom were wounded, two probably fatally.

Van Campen represents that the whole number were killed, and chiefly by his own hands. This is wholly improbable, and it is a matter of much doubt if any one of the prisoners knew precisely the condition of the battle-field after the conflict. It was night; it was of course the most exciting state of affairs in which men could possibly be placed.

The prisoners, now free, collected together immediately the arms of their savage captors, their blankets, the scalps of their friends, and the provisions at hand, and left the camp. In the morning they found a canoe. Getting into this they plied the paddles with celerity, and, in two days after, were at the fort at Wilkes-Barré.

It is unfortunate that there should have been any spirit of rivalry on the part of Van Campen, inducing him either to confuse the state of facts connected with this gallant exploit, or by misrepresentation, to have diminished its thrilling character. There was glory enough for them all.

I knew Abraham Pike well, and towards the close

of his life, I made several attempts to get his version of this startling adventure; but he became extremely intemperate in his old age, and his mind was impaired and his eye wandered in vacancy, and he failed to give a satisfactory statement. But his account of the affair, as I have heard it from others, agrees substantially with that given by Rogers.

I am inclined to make him the hero of the transaction, and I think the facts fully sustain the conclusion.

Colonel Jenkins—and who by the way may be regarded as a safe authority, a man of much intelligence, and one of the leading men in those days in the valley—says in a memorandum made by him at the time: "Pike, and two men from Fishing Creek, and two boys that were taken by the Indians, made their escape by rising on the ground, killed three, and the rest took to the woods and left the prisoners with twelve guns," etc.

This statement very nearly agrees with the account of Mr. Rogers which I have given, with the exception of making one prisoner more and one Indian killed, less.

Van Campen, as late as 1837, in his petition to Congress for a pension,—in which he gives a narrative of the transaction,—represents himself as the principal man, giving Pence some credit, but stating that the others were terrified and inactive. At this time he was the only survivor, and the mouths of his fellow-prisoners were sealed. We can afford to allow an old man—and at the time in poverty—considerable of a margin, but we can hardly justify him in so gross a misrepresentation of the case. Mr. Miner thinks " there was honor enough for all, and that there could be no motive but excessive self-glorification for representing Pike and Rogers as cowards."

Rogers does not pretend that he took an active part in the melée, but the share assigned to him—considering that he was but a lad of fourteen years—was performed with great adroitness and uncommon courage.

The statements of Pike and Rogers connected with the journal of Colonel Jenkins, agreeing with them in the main features, must establish the true history of the matter.

Reviewing the whole subject from this standpoint, it presents a case of the exhibition of wonderful courage based upon a cool, deliberate, and daring resolution. This fearless and courageous act, accompanied at about the same time by a corresponding one by Bennett and the prisoners arrested with him in Kingston, and attended with nearly the same results, served as a salutary check to Indian incursions. While prisoners were taken afterwards, there were no such acts of brutality attending them as were practised by the band who arrested Pike and his companions.

Poor old Abraham Pike, who had been a sergeant in the British army—a soldier of the Revolution—fought bravely in the Wyoming battle ; a scout for Sullivan's army in its expedition into the Indian country, became in the latter years of his life a wandering mendicant, going from door to door for charity, and finally died a pauper, by the roadside, November eleventh, 1834, with no kindly hand even to close his eyes after his spirit had departed. His habits of extreme intemperance in his old age had blasted and destroyed a mind quick, discriminating, and very sensitive to honor ; and utterly prostrated a stout and well-knit frame, which in its hour of development had undergone great hardships and endured the most oppressive fatigues.

It is probable that there is no one left in the valley who can point out the spot where repose the bones of the old " Indian killer."

Jonah Rogers remained in Plymouth till within a few years before his death, when he removed to the Township of Huntington. He was a man highly respected, as also a man of comfortable means. His death occurred about the year 1825, though as to this, I speak only from vague memory. His residence was upon the back road, about midway between those of the late Calvin Wadhams and Captain James Nesbitt. But I suppose this designation will hardly be intelligible to the majority of the people of Plymouth of this day.

Pike may be said to have had no residence during

the last years of his life. He was a wanderer, and while his citizenship was in our town, the blue vault of heaven was the roof, and the solid earth the floor, of his cabin.

There is one circumstance which is related both by Pike and Rogers, which does not reflect much credit upon Van Campen, and weakens materially his credibility in the narrative which he furnishes us.

On the night of their escape from the Indian camp, Rogers became so disabled that he could not walk. Van Campen proposed to leave the boy in the wilderness, and the rest of them make their journey without him. To this proposition Pike solemnly protested, and said "that he would carry the boy back to his parents or he would die with him." And he accordingly took him upon his shoulders, and thus saved him from desertion, and very likely, from death.

Probably this circumstance should not now be noted, as all the parties are dead; and my only excuse is that Van Campen, in his published statement, deliberately branded Pike and Rogers with cowardice.

The capture and arrest of the two Messrs. Harvey, Colonel Ransom and the two young women, Louis Harvey and Lucy Bullford, are not involved in any questions of doubt or perplexity.

Benjamin Harvey was an aged man at the battle of Nanticoke, December twenty-fifth, 1775. He had three sons, Benjamin, of Captain Ransom's Independent Company, Revolutionary service, who died at

Valley Forge from the severity of the winter; Silas, who fell in Captain Whittlesey's company at the battle of Wyoming; and Elisha, father of the gentleman of that name, and till very recently a resident of Plymouth.

Old Benjamin Harvey resided in 1780 in a log house standing on a little elevated spot on the north side of the main road, opposite the old Indian burial-ground, and between the Christian Church edifice and the small stream I have heretofore noticed.

On a cool evening on the sixth of December, 1780, the elder Mr. Harvey, his son Elisha, Miss Lucy Bullford and his daughter Louis, and George Palmer Ransom, were seated around a bright wood fire in the house I have named. Colonel Ransom was then a young man of some twenty years, of pleasant personal address, had been with his father in the Revolutionary war acting in the capacity of orderly-sergeant, and gained some credit for his valor at Millstone, Boundbrook, Germantown and Brandywine. On this evening he put on his best regimentals and went up to Mr. Harvey's, as he has frequently told the writer, "*a sparking.*" Now this word, which in old times meant the civil attentions of a young gentleman to a young lady with a view of marriage, if all things went on mutually agreeable, is not probably quite so euphonious as our word courting, yet still its significance is entitled to the same consideration.

Our young soldier, dressed in his blue coat, with

buff lappels and gilt buttons, had just made his best bow and laid aside his cocked hat, when there was a gentle knock at the door; but while the knock was just audible, the party inside knew that it did not proceed from the knuckles of a closed hand. There was a shriller tone to the sound, very much as though it were made with the head of a tomahawk. The practised ear becomes very sensitive in discriminating sounds.

The party about the fire looked at each other, and read in each others looks "the cause of that alarm." Old Mr. Harvey broke the silence by saying, "they had better invite them in, as resistance might make the matter worse;" and as the gentle knock was again repeated, he bade them enter.

A band of six Indians came in, and immediately bound the whole party and set out towards Canada. This was the route the Indian always travelled with his bale of scalps, or with his prisoners of war. There his *friends* resided, and there his human peltry brought a better price than in any other market of the world, barbarous or enlightened.

Arriving on the top of the Shawnee mountain— and out of danger of immediate pursuit—the party made a halt for consultation. Of the Indians, one of them was past middle age, two others were some years younger, and the remaining three were mere youths, this probably being one of their first expeditions.

To the credit of humanity, this consultation re-

sulted in the release of the two young women. The
old chief taking them aside from the rest of the party,
painted their faces in true Indian style, and discharged them in the dark and gloomy wilderness, with
directions to go to Colonel Butler, and tell him that
"*I put on this paint.*" To this they did not, of
course, take exceptions; so parting with their friends,
whom they never again expected to see, they commenced their descent down the mountain, arriving at
the fort at Wilkes-Barré on the following morning.
The cannon was fired as the signal of alarm, but the
captors and the captured were by this time far on their
journey, and out of the sound even of the signal which
fell upon the ears of the people of the valley as a no-
tification, that somebody had been murdered or carried into captivity; a sound that not unfrequently informed them of terrible deeds as well as reminded
them of human suffering and woe during the three
years immediately succeeding that fearful massacre
upon the Wyoming battle-field. The report of the
cannon meant torture, death or bondage.

The Indians and their prisoners moved on their
trail after the girls had been released. The inclemency of the weather, or the snows and the wilderness
were obstacles not to be considered. They travelled
on that night, and the close of the day which followed brought the party to the head waters of the
Mehoopany Creek, which empties into the Susquehanna, some fifteen miles above Tunkhannock.

Benjamin Harvey was an old, feeble man, and not able to meet the exposures he had already incurred. He was nearly seventy years of age. It was evident that he could not endure the march on the following morning.

After spending the cold and chilly night of December as they best could, in the morning the Indians held a council of war as to what was to be done with old Mr. Harvey. The value of his scalp in the British market preponderated the scale against his life. The savages bound him to a tree with thongs, and fastened his head in a position that he could neither move to the right nor to the left. The old chief then measured off the ground some three rods, called the three young braves, and placing a tomahawk in the hand of each and stepping aside, pointed his finger to the head of the old man. All this was done in silence and without the least emotion depicted upon their stoic countenances.

The first one hurled his tomahawk—after giving two or three flourishes in the air—with a piercing whoop. It fastened itself in the tree, five or six inches above the old man's head. The second and third made the same effort, but with like effect ! The whole Indian party now became furious; the young warriors, for their want of skill in this, probably their first effort, and the older ones from some other impulse. An angry scene ensued, and they came nearly to blows. The old chief approached the victim, unloosened his bands, and pointing to the trail they had passed over, told him to "go." The rest of the party moved sullenly on their way, and old Mr. Harvey took his.

The old gentleman in giving an account of this said, "that as each tomahawk came whizzing through the air, it seemed as though it could not but split his head in two. That so far as he could understand from the Indian dispute—having some knowledge of their language, though imperfect—the old chief took the ground that "the Great Spirit had interfered and prevented his death," while the others imputed it wholly to the unpractised hands of the young braves, and that "the Great Spirit had no hand in the matter." The stubborn will of the old sachem, however, prevailed, and though in the minority, his counsel in the affair decided the issue.

Mr. Harvey, through fatigue and weariness, and the effect of the terrible shock to his nerves, became bewildered, and after travelling the whole day found himself at night at the point from which he had set out on that fearful morning. Overcome with exhaustion, he rekindled the fire at the encampment of the night before, and on the following morning started with a better prospect, as he thought, of finding his way out of the woods.

He wandered the most of that day without any better prospect, and by this time hunger began to make loud demands upon his already exhausted
14

frame. Towards evening a small dog came to him. This was a subject of alarm as well as comfort. He did not know who might be the owner of the poor creature. The dog stuck to his new friend, as he supposed, *i. e.*, if instinct can form conclusions— a matter somewhat doubted now, but may not always be.

On the third morning, still travelling without any idea of his whereabouts, following the example of Byron's shipwrecked crew who dined upon poor "Pedrillo," he made a meal of his new friend, saving the remainder of the carcass for future necessities. On the fourth day, however, he came to the river, and getting upon a float, arrived safely at the fort at Wilkes-Barré, where he met his daughter and Miss Bullford, with whom he had parted on the Shawnee mountain.

Our Indians travelled on with Ransom and Elisha Harvey towards their point of destination. The only incidents I shall notice were, that the old chief would make Ransom, who was a good marksman, shoot a horse or two on their long journey for their commissariat, and require him to make the fires and prepare the banquet, giving him secretly now and then, as a mark of especial favor, a pinch of salt with which to flavor his diet of horse meat! The regimentals made an easy disposition of Ransom; when they reached the British lines he was handed over to the servants of King George, and sent to a prison at Montreal. For the present we leave him and follow Harvey to the far distant waters of Green Bay.

Harvey had not yet reached his majority; he was about seventeen years of age. Young, sprightly and active, he won upon the good opinion of his master, who proved to be a sachem of the Seneca tribe, and had been with his people two years before at the Wyoming battle. The three young Indians were novitiates, whom this brave had taken out on their first expedition. It was well for old Mr. Harvey that they had not yet become proficient in hurling the tomahawk.

During the remainder of the winter our prisoner remained with the Seneca chief, and in the spring following, a large Indian party set out for Green Bay to spend the summer and following autumn in hunting game.

The expedition turned out very favorably, and in the beginning of winter the party returned to Montreal. Here the Indians disposed of their furs, but in the course of a month they had used up the proceeds in riot and dissipation. Our Seneca brave began casting about for a market for his prisoner, which he found became necessary, as he had not the means of subsistence for himself, much less for poor Harvey.

He finally stumbled on a Scotchman, who was a small dealer in Indian commodities, and after a half day's bantering and talk, in which the good qualities of Harvey were highly extolled by the old chief, they at last settled upon the price to be paid for Elisha, which was a half-barrel of rum !

He now went behind the counter of his new master, and was duly installed in the mysteries and secrets of an Indian trader. Among the first lessons he learned the important fact that the hand weighed two pounds and the foot four ! Under this system of avoirdupois there never occurred any fractions. The weight always came out in even pounds ! Human peltry went by the piece; the peltry of beasts by the pound. Our Scotch merchant did not deal in the former; the depot for it was over the way, and a gentleman with a red coat and lace collar stood at the counter, in that establishment, to wait on his customers.

Our prisoner became a great favorite with his new master, who was a bachelor, and promised to make him the heir of his estate if he would assume his name and become his child by adoption. Elisha *openly* favored the idea, but his *secret* thoughts were centred on old Shawnee. He managed to communicate with his family; and his father, in 1782, procured his exchange for a British prisoner held at the Wilkes-Barré fort by Colonel Butler.

The authority upon which this exchange was made is still in existence—a venerable looking paper, now in the custody of Jameson Harvey, the son of our prisoner, and which he has permitted me to copy.

" These certify that Adam Bowman, now a prisoner of war to the United States of America, was taken by the Inhabitants of Westmoreland and brought to this Garrison some time in 1780, when I commanded this post; and upon application made to me by Mr. Benjamin Harvey, for the prisoner, to send him to Montreal in exchange for his son there, and yet in captivity. Which request I granted, and Mr. Harvey, at his own expense, did take the prisoner from this place to Saratoga for the above purpose. I have been informed that he has for some reason been sent from there down to West Point, or its vicinity, and I should yet request that Mr. Harvey may be indulged with the prisoner for the purpose of redeeming his son.

"ZEB'N BUTLER, *4th Connecticut Regiment.*
"*July* 29*th*, 1782.
" To the officers in whose custody the prisoner may be "

From the date of Colonel Butler's order, it will be seen that Elisha Harvey had been a prisoner for nearly two years. In the first effort of conducting Bowman from Wilkes-Barré to Canada, it appears that under some question of the legality of his papers, the prisoner had been taken from him on his arrival at Saratoga and sent to West Point. Upon the return of Mr. Harvey, and procuring the letter already recorded, he went back to West Point, and taking Bowman with him to Montreal, procured the release and exchange of his son.

Notwithstanding the many hair-breadth escapes of Elisha Harvey, it was his destiny to die a natural death in Plymouth, at his long-occupied and peaceful home, in the lower end of the town, in March, 1800. I am not able to say whether the old stone tenement still stands; probably not, as progress has big eyes glaring in every direction where a dollar can be made, without regard to the memory of the living or the dead; and it would be exceedingly strange if what was once the rather aristocratical stone mansion, in early days, of Elisha Harvey, had not disappeared. I do not like to make the inquiry whether the old house still stands. I am afraid that along with the old threshing-floor and the stone barricade, between the two chestnuts, this too had disappeared under the itching palms of modern levelling hands.

And now let us visit Montreal and find what has become of our prisoner in the Continental uniform— the boy who went "a sparking" at a terrible *discount*, as the sequel too plainly showed.

Ransom and the other American prisoners at Montreal were removed in February, 1781, to Prisoner's Island, situate some fifty miles above Montreal; and as an account of this imprisonment was given at length by Colonel Ransom to Mr. Miner, which was reduced to 'writing at the time, and published under the head of "The Hazleton Travellers," I shall give his text up to that time, in the narrative, when he swam the St. Lawrence; from that up to his restoration to his friends, and as to subsequent events, I shall rely on my own memory, as I have frequently heard them from his own lips, being his next door neighbor for a period of twenty years, and intimately acquainted with him for more than thirty years.

He says:—"In February, 1781, I was in Canada, forty-five miles up the St. Lawrence river from Montreal, on an island with about one hundred and sixty-six American prisoners. We were guarded by the refugees, or what was called Tories, who belonged to Sir John Johnson's Second Regiment. The commanding officer of the guard on the island was a young Scotch officer by the name of MacAlpin, about eighteen years of age. The winter was very severe, and a great snow-storm drifted before the door of the guard, who sent for some of the American prisoners to shovel it away. They refused, saying that they were prisoners of war, and he had no right to set them to work for his pleasure. Enraged at this, the officer ordered them into irons, and directed others to get shovels and go to work; these also refused, and were put in irons.

"So he went on commanding and meeting with resolute disobedience to what they considered a tyrannical order. They had taken up arms and perilled their lives to resist British tyranny, and would not now, though prisoners, submit to it. Some were ironed together; thus he kept putting into irons as long as he had handcuffs left. Among the last who refused were myself and one William Palmeters. We

were then put into an open house, without door, floor
or windows, and directions given that we should have
neither victuals, brandy nor tobacco; but our faithful
friends contrived to evade the guard, and we were
furnished with all. There we remained all night, suffering extremely from the cold.

"The next morning MacAlpin came, thinking our
spirits were broken, and demanded if we would not
shovel snow? One word all answered: 'Not by order
of a d—d Tory!' He then took us out of that place
and put us in a hut just finished, with a good floor,
and we sent for a black man, a good fiddler, for we
had two on the island. We then opened our ball,
dancing, to keep ourselves warm, jigs, hornpipes, four
and six-handed reels. Where four were ironed to one
bar, they could dance the cross-handed, or what we
called the York reel.

"We continued in this merry mood till our Scotch
gentleman found the place was too good for us. He
then took us out and put us into the loft of one of the
huts, which stood so low that a man could stand up
only under the centre of the ridge. Here we were kept
in extreme suffering two days and two nights. In the
mean time MacAlpin sent for Charles Grandison, our
fiddler, and ordered him to play for his pleasure. The
black went, but firmly declared that he would not play
while his fellow-prisoners were in irons. The officer
then ordered a kind of court-martial, composed of
Tories, who of course brought in the poor negro guilty.

The sentence of the court was that he should be stripped, tied up, and receive ten lashes on his naked back, which was done. Smarting with the lash, the officer then demanded if he would fiddle as he was ordered? 'No, not while my fellow-prisoners are in irons!' Again he was tied up and ten lashes laid on, but his firmness was not to be shaken, and the officer sent him to his hut.

"MacAlpin then sent a party of soldiers to bring up some of the prisoners, several of whom were flogged severely; and one, against whom the Tories had a particular spite, was tied neck and heels, and a rope put around his neck, and he was thus drawn up to the chamber floor and so kept till he was almost dead— let down and then drawn up again.

"One John Albright, a Continental soldier, was flogged almost to death for being a kind-hearted man and speaking his mind freely. But no American was found to shovel snow.

"We remained here till the ninth of June, when myself and two others, James Butterfield and John Brown, made our escape from the island and laid our course for Lake Champlain. On the eleventh, at noon, we came to the lake, and three days after we got to Hubbardstown, Vermont; the next day to Castleton, to a fort; from that to Pultney, where I had an uncle living. My companions went to Albany and I to Connecticut."

This statement of facts, in a plain way, gives the reader an idea of the gross and barbarous character of the times as well as the severe trials to which the people of the last century were exposed—and especially that part of them who fell under the denomination of rebels. The gracious influences which were produced by the elevation of the masses, in after times, had not then become visible. The freedom of man was the severe taunt and ridicule of tyrants. And if the man of the lower orders asserted a single privilege with which nature endowed him, he became the especial object of persecution. We have abundant occasion to thank the All Wise ruler of the universe that in his Providence the result of the American Rebellion placed man upon a solid, and, it is to be hoped, a perpetual foundation of equality.

And as we, the descendants of the bold and fearless men who had the courage to proclaim the principles of freedom in the face and teeth of tyranny, are now the recipients of the vast and indefinable blessings which flow from the effort, should we not only cherish but revere the memory of the men who were the direct cause of it all?

Colonel Ransom's statement, so far given, has but little reference to himself. The trials he passed through in his escape from the island during the three days and three nights in the wilderness, before reaching Lake Champlain, are not given.

He passed from the island with Butterfield and Brown upon a rude raft which they had been for several days collecting the materials of, and concealing by day in the sand upon the beach from the observation of the sentinel! When they reached the American shore they were in a state of great exhaustion.. They had been able to procure but little food, and were chilled through by the exposure upon the water, their little raft with its human freight being a foot or more submerged. When they landed, a vast wilderness lay before them, and they were to make their experimental journey without chart or compass. It was a wilderness that had not yet been penetrated but by wild beasts and savage men. They had made the desperate effort to regain their freedom, and great obstacles lay in their path; but they were young and had the power of endurance, and so they left the river and entered the forest before them. The thick underbrush and swamps which they encountered made it almost impossible at times to proceed. The first day exhausted their slender stock of provisions, with their keen appetite but half appeased. They travelled with forked sticks, and with these they captured snakes and frogs, upon which they sustained life. From fatigue and hunger one of the party gave out, and declared that he could go no further. They halted at a spring, and providing their sinking companion with some vermin, they built a brush covering to protect him at night, and shook hands with tears

in their eyes, and without speaking a word they separated.

"The heart feels most when the lips move not."

Towards the close of their last day in the wilderness, as they approached a trail or obscure path, they
saw two poor and half-starved horses browsing upon
the sparse herbage. Daylight had partially dawned.
Here was food. The first thought was to kill one of
them and satiate their ravenous cravings of appetite.
The second thought was to mount the horses, and by
giving them their own road, they might conduct them
to some habitation. This they adopted. The horses
brought them to a log hut not far distant, the only
occupant present being an old woman. Upon the
representation of their condition, she gave them each
a half pint of milk, mixed with an equal quantity of
water, and a mouthful of bread only.

They laid themselves upon the floor, but they
were awakened in the night by the most voracious
cravings of appetite. They aroused the old woman.
The small quantity of food she had given them only
enkindled the raging fire in their stomachs, and had
not in the least degree assuaged it. They told her that
she must give them some more milk, that they could
not live, and their words of entreaty assumed the
language of threats. "Well," said she, with much
composure, seated by the rude hearth, with the dim
light flickering up now and then, where she had

posted herself as a kind and protecting guardian, "you may have what I've got to eat, and you may dispose of it at once, but mind you, I wash my hands of the murder which will be the result." This made us ashamed of our conduct, and "we apologized to the good old soul."

They finally compromised with the old lady "for three swallows of milk each, unmixed with water, and a piece of bread for each the size of one's hand."

"But," as I have time and time again heard it from the old gentleman's lips, "such swallows have never been repeated since that day when the whale engulfed poor Jonah! I would not have exchanged my chances at that bowl for one of the same size filled with diamonds."

By degrees the woman of the log hut restored them to their usual condition. Her husband had gone to the settlement, some twenty miles away, for food for their household. The John Franklin of the wilderness, or more properly, the Daniel Boone of the frontier.

But while they were here the companion whom they had left behind them, recovering from the stupor in which they had left him, and reinvigorated by his refreshing diet of vermin, took up their trail and joined them again—an event as unexpected when they separated as though the dead were to come to life.

In this connection I must name one incident fresh

in my mind: "One day," said the old gentleman, "faint and famished by hunger, sitting upon a decayed fallen tree, I saw a small striped snake make its appearance from under it. I fastened my eyes upon the reptile and made a pass to catch it, but getting hold near the tail in the struggle, with the tight grip I gave, it separated, leaving me with six or eight inches of its little end in my hand; the rest of the body disappeared under the tree. At this misfortune I cried like a great booby."

In a couple of days or so of kind attention by this good Samaritan woman, they were all fully restored, and being now out of the wilderness, they begged their way to their different destinations. Butterfield and Brown went to Albany, and Ransom to Litchfield, Connecticut.

Soon after this, Colonel Ransom returned to the valley, joined his company—Captain Spalding's—went from here to West Point, where he remained to the end of the Revolutionary struggle, and was honorably discharged. He was not in the battle of Wyoming. He was with Spalding's company on Pocono the day of the battle, and thus escaped that carnage. He was here afterwards and helped to collect the mutilated bodies upon the battle-field. He said "there were but few of them that we could recognize; the stench was very offensive; we put them on sledges with pitchforks and shovels, and hauled them to one common grave and put them into it." The body of his father they found near Fort Wintermoot, with a musket shot in the thigh and his head severed from his shoulders, and his whole body scarred with gashes. He says, "I counted twenty-seven mutilated bodies around Queen Esther's Rock—old men and lads of fifteen." Scattered over the field they lay in a state of far-advanced decomposition. In all cases the scalp was removed.

The winter after the battle he obtained a furlough. He stayed with his mother and family at the old Plymouth homestead, the chief subsistence of them all being the milk of one cow. The loss of the entire crop of that season, with the effects of the Indian and Tory devastations, completely deprived the people of food and nearly of raiment.

Colonel Ransom was born in Canaan, Litchfield county, Connecticut, in 1761. This was the same town in which Franklin was born, and there was ever a strong intimacy between the two families. His father was chosen a "Selectman" for Plymouth, at a town meeting for Westmoreland, on the second of March, 1774. He probably came here in 1771 or 1772.

The following anecdote, which I have often heard repeated, I will give in the language of Dr. Peck, as it is very cleverly related by that gentleman :

"While in one of the old taverns in Wilkes-Barré" (Arndt's he might have added), "when quite advanced in years, he heard a windy young man speak very disrespectfully of General Washington. The General, he said, was not a great man nor a great soldier, but had taken advantage of fortunate circumstances to palm himself off upon the world as such. This was more than the old soldier could bear, and he lifted his cane and felled the impudent young sprig to the floor. The whipped puppy prosecuted the Colonel for assault and battery.

"When the cause came on, Colonel Ransom appeared in court without advocate, and simply pleaded guilty, and flung himself on the mercy of the Court. Hon. David Scott was Presiding Judge, his associates were the venerable Matthias Hollenback and Jesse Fell. Judge Scott remarked: 'This is a case which I choose to leave to my associates, as they are old soldiers, and can fully appreciate the circumstances of the case,' and then left his seat. Judge Hollenback asked Colonel Ransom 'where he was at such a date?' The answer was, 'in my father's company in Washington's army.' 'And where on the third of July, 1778?' Answer. 'With Captain Spalding, on my way to Wyoming.' 'And where the following summer?' Answer. 'With General Sullivan in the Lake country flogging the Indians.' 'And where the next fall and winter?' Answer. 'A prisoner on the St. Lawrence!' 'Ah!' said the Judge, 'all that is true enough, Colonel Ransom. And did you knock the fellow down, Colonel?' 'I did so, and would do it again under like provocation,' was the answer. 'What was the provocation?' asked the Judge. 'The rascal abused the name of General Washington,' was the answer. The Judge coolly said, 'Colonel Ransom, the judgment of the Court is that you pay a fine of one cent, and that the prosecutor pay the costs!' This sentence was followed by a roar of applause."

My earliest recollection of Colonel Ransom brings back to my mind a stout built, square-shouldered man about five feet eight inches high, light complexion and blue eyes. I remember when he was the colonel of a militia regiment, and have been present at his annual regimental parades. He was then in the prime of life, probably not over fifty years of age. He had a pleasant and agreeable manner, very communicative, and was a most obliging neighbor. He was a man who liked mirth, and nobody enjoyed a joke better than he. He was quiet and peaceable; a man of thoroughly domestic habits. He raised a large family of children and brought them up respectably, giving them all a good common school education.

I never knew him, during my long acquaintance, to have been more than twice in the court; one occasion I have already noticed, the other was in a civil suit.

In the last ten years of his life he became feeble, and would hobble about his premises with a cane in each hand. His house was always open to hospitality, and no man more thoroughly and keenly relished a convivial assemblage than he. He possessed the

15

highest sense of honor.   His long training in the revolutionary service made him very punctilious in his
intercourse.   His word was his bond.

He lived to a very advanced age; he died in 1850,
in the full enjoyment of his mental faculties.   He was
therefore in his eighty-ninth year.   I attended his
funeral.   We buried him with military honors at the
cemetery near Ross Hill.   And when the smoke of
the musketry over his last resting-place cleared away,
and we moved off in silence from his grave, the reflection came home to the heart of one at least I know,
that we had consigned to earth a man of many virtues,
and whose strong arm and resolute will had made
their impression in the frame work and superstructure
of Free and Republican America.

Daniel McDowal, one of our townspeople, was
carried away by the Indians to Niagara some time in
1872; but I am unable to ascertain where his residence was located.   A daughter of his married General Samuel McKean, of Bradford county, and at one
time a Senator from this State in Congress.   I cannot
say either how long he was held in captivity.

Mr. Miner mentions the capture at the same time
of the arrest of the two Harveys, Ransom, and the
two girls, Louis Harvey and Lucy Bullford, of Nathan Bullock, Jonathan Frisby, James Frisby, Man-
asah Cady, and George Palmer.   I am inclined to
think there is an error in this statement.   The name
of Bullock has been confounded with Bullford, and

that of George Palmer, with George Palmer Ransom. This, however, would not explain the matter as to the two Frisbys and Cady. But as he fixes the same date, December sixth, 1780, of the capture of Ransom and his party, he is most certainly incorrect.

It is not surprising by any means that this confusion may have occurred in the multiplicity of facts that Mr. Miner grouped together for the material of his history.

The only remaining instance of Indian atrocity committed on our people of which we have knowledge, was that upon Samuel Ransom, brother of George P. Ransom. The house of his deceased father was attacked on the tenth of March, 1781, in the night, the following spring after his brother had been carried into captivity.

Being aware that the house was surrounded by Indians, he took his gun and walked out; the moon shining brightly, the Indians discovered him and fired upon him, breaking one of his arms. He coolly and deliberately rested his gun against the house, and with his remaining arm fired and brought down his man. This success, accompanied by the discharge of a gun, at random, within the house, by Jonah Rogers, at the same time, induced the marauding party to fly, leaving their dead comrade upon the field.

CHAPTER IX.

THE WAR OF 1812.

SOON after the commencement of the war of 1812, between the United States and Great Britain, a volunteer company, principally composed of Kingston men, with a few from Plymouth, under the command of Captain Samuel Thomas, offered their services to the United States government and were accepted.

This company, on the thirteenth of April, 1813, embarked on board of a boat at Shupp's Eddy, in the upper part of Plymouth, on their way to join General Harrison's army on the western frontier. They numbered thirty-one men. They proceeded to Danville in their boat, and thence they went overland to Lake Erie. In passing through Bedford county, Captain Thomas procured the addition of thirty-seven recruits, and in Fayette twenty-seven more, thus making his full complement of ninety-four men.

On their arrival at Erie, the company (artillery) of Captain Thomas was attached to a Pennsylvania regiment under Colonel Reese Hill.

Of this company the following were Plymouth men: Abraham Roberts, John Blane, Festus Freeman, James Devans and William Pace.

The company had not been long at the point of

their destination before they had occasion to test their courage.

The harbor of Presque Isle—now Erie—contained a part of Perry's squadron upon the lake, which had been built there, but which could not join the rest of the fleet. A bar extended across the mouth of the harbor, and the British fleet under Barclay had no trouble in a contest for the supremacy of the lake, while the fleet of Perry was thus divided. Perry made a desperate effort to reach the harbor in order to form a union of his fleet. He accomplished it; but in this he was materially aided by the cannonade from the shore of Captain Thomas' battery; and as these shots were answered from the British squadron, a lively cannonade was kept up for some time, and for the coolness and courage of Captain Thomas' men, they received especial commendation.

In consequence of the bar, however, Perry could not get his heavy ships out, and dared not meet the enemy without them. To his great relief, however, Barclay moved to the Canada shore, not supposing that his adversary was ready to go to sea.

Perry immediately taking advantage of the absence, passed his flag-ship, the Lawrence, and the Niagara, his largest vessels, over the bar with lighters, the schooners following; and within twenty-four hours after the departure of Barclay, he had his ships ready for action. He lacked, however, his complement of men.

And here comes in the Plymouth feature of the great battle of the Lakes, small, comparatively, it is true, but nevertheless so important as to be stamped upon medals of silver to be held in perpetual memory.

The tenth of September was approaching, when the gallant young officer of but twenty-seven years was to measure swords with the mistress of the seas. The crews of his new ships were to be replenished. Time was short, and the slow progress of enlistment in the ordinary way would not meet the emergency. He sent an invitation ashore for volunteers to fully man his quarter-decks. The proportion which fell to Captain Thomas' company was four. He ordered out his company, read the request, and desired four men to volunteer by stepping four paces to the front.

William Pace, Benjamin Hall, Godfrey Bowman, and James Bird advanced to the line of honor. They were immediately placed on board the Niagara. A thousand cheers for old Shawnee and Kingston. Revolutionary sprouts ; they bore high aloft the fame of their ancestors. The blood of the Ransoms, the Harveys, the Gaylords, or the Bidlacks had not soddened the Wyoming battle-field in vain. The shore of Lake Erie was about to chronicle new feats of valor of men of the same soil, after the lapse of a third of a century.

On the morning of the tenth of September, the British fleet of sixty-three guns weighed anchor in the port of Malden. Perry, with his fleet of fifty-four guns, was waiting to meet it. He hoisted the flag upon his own vessel, on which were inscribed the last words of Commodore Lawrence: "DON'T GIVE UP THE SHIP." This was the signal for action, and cheer upon cheer rolled down the line.

When within a mile and a half of the enemy's line, the blast of a bugle came ringing over the water, the signal of battle. This was followed by a single gun, whose shot went bounding by the Lawrence, and then followed the discharge of the long guns of the whole British squadron. Perry was unable to use his carronades, and was thus exposed for a half hour before he could bring his guns within range.

"Steering straight for the Detroit, a vessel a fourth larger than his own, he gave orders for the schooners that lagged behind to close up within half cables' length. Those orders, the last he gave during the battle, were passed by trumpet from vessel to vessel; the light wind having nearly died away, the Lawrence suffered severely before she could get near enough to open with her carronades, and she had scarcely taken her position before the fire of three vessels were directed upon her. Enveloped in flames and smoke, Perry strove desperately to maintain his ground till the rest of the fleet could close, and for two hours sustained, without flinching, this unequal contest. The balls crashed incessantly through the sides of the ship, dismounting the guns and strewing the deck

with the dead, until at length, with every trace and
bowline shot away, she lay an unmanageable wreck on
the waters.   But still through the smoke, as it went
before the heavy broadsides, her colors were seen flying, and still gleamed forth in the sunlight that glorious motto : 'Don't give up the Ship !'   Calm and
unmoved at the slaughter around and his own desperate situation, Perry gave his orders tranquilly as
though executing a manœuvre."—(*Headley.*)

After every gun had been dismounted, and out of
the one hundred men who entered the action with him
but eighteen stood before him unwounded, when peering through the smoke, he saw the Niagara, apparently uncrippled, drifting out of the battle. Leaping
into a boat, he exclaimed: "If a victory is to be gained,
I will gain it!" and amidst a perfect storm of shot and
shell he boarded the Niagara, faced her about, and
flung out his signal for close action.   He immediately
bore down upon the enemy's centre, reserving his fire
till in the midst of the enemy's fleet; with the Detroit
and Lady Provost within pistol shot on the right and
left, he opened his broadside. Headley says, that "the
shrieks that wrung out from the Detroit were heard
even above the cannonade; while the crew of the Lady
Provost, unable to stand the fire, ran below, leaving
their wounded, stunned and bewildered commander
alone on deck, leaning his face on his hand, and gazing
vacantly on the passing ship."

An action conducted in this manner could not last

long, and within fifteen minutes after the desperate charge, the British flag struck—the proud and haughty "Mistress of the Seas" had met more than her equal; and so Perry notched it down upon the tablets of history, before the smoke had cleared away, or the last echo of his guns rebounded from the shore : "WE HAVE MET THE ENEMY, AND THEY ARE OURS."

One of the most brilliant naval engagements of the world, and the victory at the time was almost decisive of the war. Three hundred men were killed and wounded upon both sides.

Our townsman, William Pace, has very frequently given me an account of the engagement, and as he would dilate upon the conduct of Perry and the terrible charge of the Niagara upon the two vessels, the little man's frame would shake with emotion. He assisted to raise Perry from his boat to the deck of the Niagara. He was also upon the Lawrence immediately after the action, and saw the fifty men, whose bodies were mangled, still lying there, the blood and gore covering the entire surface of the deck.

The Legislature granted those who volunteered for the naval action and citizens of this State, silver medals. He brought me his in 1847, with the view of obtaining for him a pension. It is a circular plate, probably four inches in diameter, and the eighth of an inch in thickness. On one side is the raised profile likeness of the American commander, with the inscription: "Presented by the Government of Penn-

sylvania. Oliver Hazard Perry; *Pro patria vicit.*"
Upon the other side : " To William Pace, in testimony of his patriotism and bravery, in the Naval engagement on Lake Erie, September Tenth, 1813."

He was a short, thick-set little man, probably five
feet four inches in height, with a pleasant smile generally on his face. He remarked, "that so long as he
had been able to support himself he would not accept
a pension from his State; but now, as he was getting
old, he thought the State ought to assist him." And
so I thought, and I sent the medal to General Ross,
who was then our representative in the Senate of
Pennsylvania, who procured the passage of a law on
the fifteenth of March, 1847, granting him a pension.

Pace lived in the back part of Plymouth, known
as Blindtown, at the time of his enlistment, and died
but a few years since an humble and unpretending
man; upright in his conduct, and held in the esteem
and good opinion of all his neighbors.

Our company was in several engagements before
they were discharged. At the battle of the Thames
the company behaved well under the command of
Lieutenant Ziba Hoyt, who by the way was a most
excellent and worthy citizen. Captain Thomas, being
detained at Detroit with a part of the company and
the field-guns, for its defense, the rest of the company,
under Lieutenant Hoyt, followed the fleeing enemy to
the Thames.

They were honorably discharged after the expiration of the term for which they enlisted.

During the time I was engaged in preparing these sketches for publication, I received the following very interesting letter from Captain Thomas, now a resident of Wyoming, State of Illinois, and in good health at the age of eighty-five years. I insert the letter, as it will be not only a reminder of an old and valued acquaintance to the citizens of this county who knew him, and where he spent the greater part of his life, but also testimony of some of the facts about which I write.

"WYOMING, ILLINOIS, Nov. 23, 1871.

" *Colonel H. B. Wright:*

" DEAR SIR.—Mr. Charles Myers (formerly from Wilkes-Barré) brought to my notice a statement under your name, in the Luzerne *Union* of the first of this month, giving a short sketch of the company that marched under my command to Lake Erie in the year 1813.

" In reading your remarks it brought vividly to my mind all the circumstances of the part I had in that campaign, although fifty-eight years have passed. and the years of my age will be eighty-five on the second of February next. While you have given a more favorable as well as accurate account of the behavior of the company while in the service of our country than has been written or published, yet I see that you are in fault in some particulars.

" One instance I mention : you state ' that the company marched with the army to the river Thames under the command of Lieutenant Hoyt.' This requires explanation. The fact is, that when we crossed the Lake and marched up opposite to the city of Detroit, the hostile Indians appeared in strong force on the bank of the river in a warlike and threatening attitude. I was ordered to cross the river with my company and drive the Indians from the

city, and to remain there and guard the place while the main army
followed in the pursuit of the retreating enemy.   This service was
faithfully performed, although the Indians tried to prevent our
landing, firing at us with their rifles ; but when we opened upon
them with our field-guns, they scattered like a flock of sheep.
While we were guarding the city we had several alarms, but the
Indians finding us always in readiness to meet them, never ven-
tured to come within reach of our guns.

" I would like to relate many incidents that I recollect connected with this service, but I have been wholly out of the practice of writing many years ; still, I must mention one circumstance.
We went down the Susquehanna on a board raft that Elihu Parrish was taking to market.   We ran into Shupp's Eddy, and landed,
for the purpose of taking in some men in that vicinity who were
members of my company.   Among them was a man by the name
of Moyer.   All of them had got aboard of the raft but him, and we
were impatient to get off.   He did not come, and I went to his
home near by to hurry him on.   I opened the door and entered,
when a scene presented itself that requires one of better descrip-
tive powers than I have to describe.   Moyer stood there in his uniform, and apparently ready to march.   His wife and a number of
children surrounding him, crying bitterly, and as though their
hearts would break at the parting—they literally held him so fast
that he could not move.

"James Bird, whose sad fate has been commemorated in song,
was standing by, and seeing the family in such distress, it touched
his generous sympathies, said to Moyer, 'GIVE ME YOUR UNI-
FORM COAT AND I WILL GO IN YOUR PLACE.'   Moyer was so overpowered by the generous and noble act that he could not say a
word, but silently took off his coat and gave it to Bird ; when we
immediately went upon the raft and proceeded at once on our
journey to Lake Erie.   Very respectfully yours,

"SAMUEL THOMAS."

The correction of General Thomas is not very material.   The point of discrepancy is, whether the

whole of his company passed over the river to Detroit, or a part of it only. The tradition of the affair is that Lieutenant Hoyt, with a part of the company, left Captain Thomas at this place and proceeded on with the army to the Thames, and participated in the battle there.

The noble conduct of poor Bird, in taking the military coat of Moyer and joining the company as a substitute, cost him his life, and that too under a state of facts that shocks the mind. It is true he was convicted of desertion, but it was not desertion through cowardice or a desire to shun the service of his country. It is, indeed, passing strange, how the man should have been convicted, or what the officer meant, in command, who could affirm such a finding.

Bird was a patriot and a man of unquestioned courage. He had voluntarily left the ranks of his company and went on board the Niagara at the moment, when every one knew that a desperate action was about to be fought.

And when severely wounded, was ordered to "leave the deck" by Perry—

> "No," cried Bird, "I will not go,
> Here on deck I took my station :
> Ne'er will Bird his colors fly;
> I'll stand by you, gallant Captain,
> Till we conquer or we die!"

This was the language of a man who a few days afterwards was condemned for desertion by a "drumhead " court-martial and shot down like a dog ! And what was the charge ? Certainly not an offense that corresponded with the awful character of the penalty inflicted. Was it cowardice ? No. Was it a desire to flee the service ? No. It was charged upon him that he had deserted the ranks, but it was after the battle was fought and the victory won—a victory too that was sealed by his blood.

I well remember, though then but a lad of six years of age, that the report of the execution of this man sent a thrill through this valley. Grief pervaded the entire population. He was a great favorite with the people, and the sensation produced by his death was as sincere as it was intense. The people of the valley could not believe the rumor; and when the facts of the case became known, it only added fuel to the burning fire of excitement.

He was promoted on the Niagara for deeds of courage. Shortly after the naval engagement on the lake, and in which he had exhibited so much courage, he learned of the intended attack by the British on New Orleans; that the South were arming for resistance, and he made up his mind to be with them. In company with some of his men, he left without orders; he was overtaken at Pittsburg, where he had made arrangements with a few bold and congenial spirits to join him, and enter Jackson's army.

Tried by a court-martial, he was condemned for desertion, and shot to death, kneeling upon his coffin !

The poor fellow's prayer to be allowed time to lay his case before Perry was denied him, and his execution immediately followed the unrighteous sentence.

It makes one's heart sick at such savage and inexcusable conduct. Such a penalty for such an offense! It might have suited an age of barbarism, but is not to be tolerated in this.

It was the untimely death, and the inexcusable circumstances which surrounded it, that inspired the muse of Hon. Charles Miner, from whom we have already quoted, in the production of that commemorative, and, at the time, most popular ballad, commencing :

"Sons of Freedom, listen to me."

Deeds are sometimes done under the sanction of law that shock our senses, and make us feel the utter imbecility and total want of qualifications in human jurisprudence. A more glaring case in proof of this cannot be cited than in the conviction and execution of James Bird!

More than fifty years have passed by since the tragedy; but these same fifty years have not erased from my memory the deep and lasting impression the sad event indelibly stamped upon my mind. I am but one of the multitude that shared this feeling at the time, yet all of those who are now gone, as well as those who survive, never changed their opinion of the cruelty of this judicial murder.

Upon the attack upon Baltimore by the British, in

1814, a requisition was made upon our northern counties for a draft. Five companies were raised in pursuance of this order. The Plymouth men were in Captain Peter Halleck's company. Those who were
drafted from Plymouth were: Adjutant of the regiment, Noah Wadhams; Second Lieutenant, Jeremiah
Fuller; Third Sergeant, Joseph Wright; First Corporal, Ezra Ide; Privates, George D. Nash, Thomas
Lynn, John Hunter, Anson Car Skadden, Aaron Van
Loon, Wm. Blane, Philip Group, Luke Blane, Samuel
Harvey and Aaron Closson.

The company of Captain Halleck marched to
Danville, and was there attached to a regiment under
the command of Colonel James Montgomery. But
before full arrangements were made at Danville, the
northern rendezvous, in making the necessary organi-
zation for a march, news came of the gallant defense
of Fort McHenry and the expulsion of the British
from the Chesapeake; and the regiment was discharged, the men of the northern companies returning
to their homes.

Among the papers of my father, I find one of
which the following is a copy. It seems that he was
not only a member of Captain Halleck's company,
but also an *officer*. I give the paper as a relic of the
past.

"*Joseph Wright, Third Sergeant:*
  " Take notice, that you are hereby required personally or by sufficient substitute to appear at the house of Jonathan Hancock, in

the Borough of Wilkes-Barré, properly armed and equipped for service at the hour of ten o'clock A. M. on the ninth day of November next, to march when required. Appeals to be heard at the house of Jonathan Hancock, on the ninth day of November next.

"Given under my hand, the twenty-eighth day of October, A. D. 1814.

"STEPHEN VAN LOON, Captain."

It appears, as I find by a memorandum in a small diary of his made on the fourteenth, that "on this day I eat my first rations of bread and beef furnished by the United States."

In years after I procured his land warrant, as also for most of the others, who were at, as they termed it, "the Siege of Danville!"

As to the part our people took in the war with Mexico and the late rebellion, I leave it to be recorded by some other pen.

CHAPTER X.

TOWN MEETINGS.—EARLY SYSTEM OF LAWS.—FIRST TOWN OFFICERS.

THE "town-meeting" of our ancestors was an important affair, and so it was within my own recollection in Plymouth.

In the early days of the valley, the town meeting of Westmoreland assembled the "Freemen" of all that territory between the Delaware river east and the

16

present Sullivan county line west, and from the Lehigh south to Tioga point north, embracing more than seventy miles square.

Within this town of Westmoreland, Plymouth had been early designated and named one of the first five, as already stated, and set off by the Susquehanna company in 1768. Other townships from time to time were set off and designated as districts. Plymouth was known outside of the public records as Shawnee—Shawanee or Shawney—Franklin's journal spells it Shawney; the Indian name being provincialized from *chuanois,* which is a very pretty appellation.

The town of Westmoreland was governed by a digest of laws, or more properly called rules and regulations. These were prepared by the Susquehanna company, at Hartford, Connecticut, on the second of June, 1773, with the acquiescence of the settlers.

The principal authority under these rules, as to the township or district municipal government, was vested in a board of directory, " to be composed of three able and judicious men among such settlers." These were to be elected annually on the first Monday in December; and their duties were, " to take upon them the direction of the settlement of each town, under the company, and the well-ordering and the governing the same; to suppress vice of every kind; preserve the peace of God and the King therein; to whom each inhabitant shall pay such, and the same, submission, as is paid to the civil authority in the several towns of this colony." The rules provided for the election of a constable, "to be vested with the same power and authority as a constable by laws of this colony is, for preserving the peace and apprehending offenders of a criminal or civil nature."

These directors of each town were required to meet "on the first Monday of each month, and oftener if need be, with their peace officers, as well to consult for the good regulation thereof, as to hear and decide any differences that may arise, and inflict proper fine or other punishment on offenders, according to the general laws and rules of this colony, so far as the peculiar situation and circumstances of such town and plantation will admit of ; and as the reformation of offenders is the principal object in view, always preferring serious admonition and advice to them, and their making public satisfaction by public acknowledgment of their fault, and doing such public service to the plantation as the directors shall judge meet; to fines in money or corporal punishment, which however, in extreme cases, such directors shall inflict as said laws direct."

The directors of all the towns were required to meet quarterly "to confer with each other on the state of each particular town, and to come into such resolutions concerning them as they shall find for their best good; as also to hear the complaints of any that shall judge themselves aggrieved by the decisions of their directors in their several towns, who shall have the right to appeal to such quarterly meeting."

The rules further provide, "that no one convicted of sudden and violent breach of the peace, of swearing, drunkenness, stealing, fraud, idleness and the like, shall have the liberty of appeal without first procuring good security for his orderly and sober behavior," etc., and in civil proceedings an appeal was confined to matters in controversy exceeding twenty shillings.

In this way petty matters were to be disposed of; but when it came "to the high-handed crimes of adultery, burglary and the like, the convict shall be sentenced to banishment from the settlement and a confiscation of all their personal effects therein to the use of the town where such offense is committed; and should there still be the more heinous crime of murder committed, which God forbid, the offender shall be instantly arrested and delivered into the hands of the nearest civil authority in Connecticut," etc., etc.

No appeal lay " from the doings of such quarterly meeting, or their decrees to the Susquehanna company, save in disputes as to land."

And thus we find the character of the tribunal and the mode of administering justice in Plymouth ninety-eight years ago.

As the frame of law was adopted and promulgated by the Susquehanna company in June, 1773, and the time named for the election of directors in December in each year, a general town meeting is warned, *i. e.*, of the whole territory of Westmoreland, which on assembling appointed three directors to act till the following December, in the towns of Wilkes-Barré, Plymouth, Providence, Kingston, Pittston and Hanover.

The appointments for Plymouth were Phineas Nash, Captain David Marvin and J. Gaylord. These gentlemen, therefore, we may consider as the first judicial officers who ever sat in judgment upon the Plymouth bench. But only reflect, if these three civil magistrates were alive to-day, and in commission, what labor would devolve upon them in disposing of all the cases of "breaches of the peace, swearing, drunkenness, gaming and *idleness.*" Would they have many spare hours out of the twenty-four, that is, if they faithfully discharged their duties?

And this is a question we have no right to ask, as all officers in those days discharged their official duties personally. Those were days when there was no pay and competent men held office, and their character was at stake to do the duty faithfully. Is such the case now? This is a question we have a right to ask.

But as I am writing history, I must confine myself to the past, and let some one who shall follow me comment upon the present! Each district was thus empowered on the December following the general town meeting, to elect its three directors, composing a municipal court, and its constable; the appointing power for all other officers was vested in the general town meeting, and so remained up to the time when Westmoreland was set off into a county.

At a town meeting held on the first of March, 1774, the districts were established and all the officers appointed. I copy from the journal the following :

"MARCH yᵉ 2d, 1774.

" *Voted*, That yᵉ town of Westmoreland be divided in the following manner into districts, that is to say, that yᵉ town of Wilkes-Barré ' be one entire district, and known by the name of Wilkes-Barré district;' and that Plymouth, with all yᵉ land west of Susquehanna river, south and west to the town line, be one district, by the name of Plymouth district." And at the same time defining the limits of Kingston, Pittston, Hanover, Exeter, Providence; also making Lackaway, Blooming Grove, Shehola and Coshutunk districts on the Delaware.

After defining the boundaries of each, the meeting proceeds to appointing officers. I shall only name those appointed for Plymouth. Seven selectmen were chosen, one of them was Samuel Ransom ; seven collectors of rates, one of them, Asaph Whittlesey; twenty-two surveyors of highways, three of them, Elisha Swift, Samuel Ransom and Benjamin Harvey; fourteen fence viewers, two of them, John Baker and Charles Gaylord; fifteen listers, *i. e.*, persons to make enrolments, two of them, Elisha Swift and Gideon ·

Baldwin; twelve grand jurors, two of them, Phineas Nash and Thomas Heath; seven tything men, one of them, Timothy Hopkins; eight key keepers, one of them, Thomas Heath.

And so the civil list was filled up. The representatives to the Connecticut Assembly were chosen semi-annually—they had probably been chosen at a former meeting. Two hundred and six persons took the freemen's oath at this meeting, which shows that there were not a dozen absentees of the whole male voting population of the town of Westmoreland at the time this meeting assembled.

It was "voted at this meeting that for ye present, ye tree that now stands northerly from Captain Butler's house, shall be ye Town Sign-Post."

The year following, a strife grew up between the people on the two sides of the river, the Plymouth and Kingston people demanding that the Sign Post should be on the west side of the river, and accordingly they met to take a vote. The west side carried it by a small majority, and designated a certain tree in Kingston, "ten rods north of the house of Mr. Ross, the Public Sign-Post." The proceedings of the few succeeding meetings, and important ones too, for there were chosen at them representatives to the General Assembly of Connecticut, do not state at which Public Sign-Post they were held. Bad blood grew out of this strife. A compromise was finally made, and at a general town meeting it was

" *Voted*, That for the future the annual town
meetings and Freemen's meetings shall be held half
the time on the east side of the river, and the other
half on the west side of the river, for one year."

In this vote they had a precedent, for the home
government of Connecticut had settled a like difficulty between New Haven and Hartford, in designat-
ing each of these towns as the alternate places of the
meeting of the Legislature.

The Public Sign-Post in these days meant something; it was the public hall for conducting the public business and holding elections; the place for post-
ing notices, for newspapers had not yet made their
appearance there; the public whipping-post for punishment of petty offenses, and it may be well doubted whether our reform in this particular has bene-
fited the public morals; it was the central place
of business transactions, the exchange, the auction
mart, the forum, the hustings, the recruiting depot,
and the general centre of all public affairs.

It don't precisely conform to our modern ideas of
things, but nevertheless did very well ninety-eight
years ago.   There is one thing about which there
cannot be much question, and that is, that at these
Public Sign-Posts they elected better men to office
than now; and that if some of the men who now hold
places, had lived in the days of Sign-Post elections,
and used the effrontery and despicable practices they
now do to procure them, they would have been tied

up to these same Sign-Posts and enlightened with the cat-o'nine-tails.

Those were the blessed days when the office sought the man, and it was sustained in its dignity by his acceptance; not as is the case now, frequently, when the office gives the incumbent the only claim he has to notice.

These annual town meetings furnished the occasion for not only a general assemblage of the voting population, but of the young men also. It was a day of jubilee and amusement. The young men would engage in feats of physical strength — wrestling, throwing the bar, playing ball, foot races, and like amusements.

In later years I can well remember myself, that the annual town meeting day in Plymouth was a day of amusement as well as of business. This was held, if I remember, on the third Friday in March, at which time the township officers were elected. All turned out, old and young, and made it a general jubilee. The practice, I suppose, came down from the precedents of the town meetings of old Westmoreland.

But there was one thing always done at these annual meetings which did not very much redound to the credit or humanity of our early settlers ; that was the selling of the town poor to the lowest bidder, to be boarded for the year. Along from 1812 to 1820, Jerre Allen, a deranged man, would be brought to the place of holding the town meeting, in chains, and thus put up for sale. Speedy Nash, a poor, simple, foolish creature, also. The bidding on the paupers, for the year's keep, would generally begin at a hundred dollars and go down to fifty or forty-five, and would be generally struck off to some mountaineer, living in a log hut, and the town contribution would sustain pauper and purchaser. The practice was not local; it reached throughout the State. Finally, however, Judge Burnside caused the overseers of the poor of some district to be indicted in his court, and the penalty he imposed on this offense of inhumanity, put a final stop to the selling of the township poor annually, at auction, to the lowest bidder.

The town meeting, however, is one of the institutions of the past. The last twenty-five or thirty years have changed its features to such an extent, that one of our old settlers, were he to return, would not recognize it any better than he could divine the meaning of a telegraph wire or a locomotive!

In a careful review of the system of laws applicable to Plymouth a hundred years ago, we can hardly say that there has been much improvement for the better. That they were better administered I think there cannot be a doubt. If drunkenness, and gaming and idleness were upon our calendar of this day, and made the subjects of punishment, there cannot be a question but the moral tone of the community would occupy a higher standard.

We cannot therefore say that we are ahead of our plain and unpretending ancestors in this particular. Idleness, perhaps, should not be classed as a crime, and yet the example it furnishes to those who cannot afford to be idle, is of the most pernicious character.

I have not been able to ascertain, after diligent inquiry, where our first Triumvirate held their court. Phineas Nash, Captain David Marvin, and J. Gaylord, clothed as they were with the municipal power of Plymouth, must have had a court, and undoubtedly a whipping-post and stocks; but the locality o, these things deemed necessary in a past age, has become somewhat obscure. These men and their successors were to Plymouth what the three triumvirs were to Rome after the fall of Cæsar, or the three Consu's to France who preceded the first Empire. Holding therefore the commissions of the peace, and the balances of justice for old Plymouth, it is to be regretted that not only the records of their court but the place of administration are gone.

Nor can we find any record of the acts of their successors, or even the names of them. The floods and the ravages of the common enemy have left but little to enlighten us.

A friend has furnished me with a very venerable looking paper, but well written, and in a hand too which I recognize as that of my old schoolmaster, of which the following is a copy:

" At a meeting of the proprietors of the commonfield in Shawney, legally warned, and held on the twenty-fourth of March, 1786,

"*Voted*, That John Franklin, Esq., be moderator for said meeting.

"*Voted*, That all such houses as are within the limits of this commonfield, and occupied with families, be removed out of said field by the tenth of April next; the committy to give speedy warning to any such residents and see it is put in execution. The house now occupied by the widow Heath excepted, provided the said widow Heath shall run a fence so as to leave her house without said field.

"[A true copy].

"Attest: JONAH ROGERS, Clark."

It is probable that this commonfield, as it is called, may have had something to do with the place of the administration of justice. One or two of the oldest people, now resident in Plymouth, have a perfect recollection that the general parade-ground was on the brow of Ant Hill. The fences in those days had not so far encroached upon the common. This was the commonfield referred to in the memorandum of the meeting, for Mrs. Heath's house, afterwards Mrs. Morse, still stands near the elm tree; and here was a common place of assembling within my own recollection; and it is more than probable that the elm tree still standing there was the Public Sign-Post of the town. My own recollections do not go further back than fifty-five years; and while I remem-

THE OLD ELM, OR WHIPPING POST.

ber well the tree standing there fifty years since, of large size then, I do not remember the tradition of its being the Public Sign-Post of the town. The sign post, commonfield, and house of justice, were probably all on this parade-ground.

In those days there was a public school-house on the opposite side of the road, a few rods below the locality of the elm. Here I first went to school, to John Bennet, Esq., late of Kingston. The benches and desks were removed from that to the academy, and the old house was torn down about 1815.

I have but little doubt, therefore, but the old school-house upon Ant Hill was in early days the forum of justice, and the old elm, the Public Sign and whipping-post of Plymouth, ninety-eight years ago.

Will you spare it? It stands there now, erect, green and vigorous; a glorious old landmark of the early days of Plymouth, and it is to be hoped that it may be permitted to remain. The eyes of our ancestors rested upon it in days agone. To me it is a pleasant reminder of the plain and primitive days of the town.

CHAPTER XI.

OCCUPATIONS AND HABITS OF THE PEOPLE IN EARLY
DAYS. — INDUSTRY. — ECONOMY. — CHURCH. —
SCHOOL-TEACHERS. —ROGERS, PATTERSON, CUR-
TIS, SWEET AND OTHERS.

I COME now to that time in our history when I
write chiefly from my own knowledge and personal observation. I have reached the point where it
was my original design to have begun.

Starting out in company with our people, in 1768,
from Litchfield, Connecticut, we found a tribe of red
men in the possession of old Shawnee. This led to
the inquiry who they were, where they came from,
and what finally became of them. Disposing of this,
it was very natural to ascertain if there had been any
white people there ahead of us. Before I had fairly
got through the mazes in which these inquiries involved the thread of my story, I found myself in the
midst of the Pennamite and Yankee war, and then
in the Revolutionary struggle. And while pursuing
the red line of battle, I at last found myself on board
the Niagara, alongside of our gallant and brave old
friend, "Billy Pace," charging under the command
of young Perry, the British fleet on Lake Erie.

And into all these different positions I found myself compelled to go because the people were there of whom I was writing.

And this must be my apology, if an apology is necessary. My readers may well conclude that I have given them a long introductory chapter. But those of them who are the descendants of Plymouth men must blame their ancestors and not me. So long as they were fighting men, if we speak of them at all, we must speak of them in the battle as well as on the farm, or in other occupations.

We have seen how they behaved themselves throughout the most trying and disheartening difficulties that it was ever the destiny of men to encounter. War at their own thresholds; war throughout the land; murder, captivity and torture: these made up the yearly calendar.

Their valor and courage at Millstone elicited the especial notice and public commendation of Washington. Butler put Whittlesey and his Plymouth men at the post of honor, as well as danger, at the battle of Wyoming. The officers of this company fell in the front ranks; the rank and file were literally overpowered and cut to pieces by a vastly superior force. At Lake Erie, the conduct of a private in the ranks is singled out as the object of especial notice by the Government, and the deeds of his bravery recorded upon a plate of silver.

Wherever the exigency of the exciting times called them, there they were, and they maintained their

honor.   It is a pleasant thing indeed to be able in after years to record such facts.   They showed themselves men of high tone and remarkable valor; great
self-reliance, and unflinching patriotism.   These traits
of character were alike exhibited upon the field of
battle, as well as in Indian captivity.

We are, therefore, by no means afraid to lift up
the veil and disclose them to the world in their private employments and domestic relations.

The war of the revolution had taught the lesson
of personal as well as national independence; captivity
the lesson of submission, as well as the important feature of self-reliance; and the final result of the long
and bitter conflict as to the question of the title to
their lands, that a just cause should never be abandoned.

When universal peace therefore dawned, and domestic strifes were healed at their own homes and
firesides, those of them who had survived the crash
of war, and could breathe in repose, free from the re-
straints of fear, were in a condition, if any people ever
were, to enjoy the luxuries of a plain, simple and un-
obtrusive life.   The sons of those who had fallen in
the public service, or in defense of their own private
rights, knew well the cost of the soil they inherited
and therefore how to appreciate it.

When, therefore, peace reigned and titles were con-
firmed, they immediately set themselves down with
no other view than to live by their labor.   This they

were not only willing to do, but it was to them a source of perfect happiness. The musket and the sickle did not now require partnership. The field could be planted with the expectation of gathering the crop it produced.

The occupation of the people of the town fifty years since was agriculture. A retail store, a couple of blacksmith shops, a wheelright shop, and a carpenter's shop, were about the only exceptions. The coal business was then in its swathing bands. It may have been used in a dozen houses, partially, but upon the big kitchen hearth blazed the wood fire.

The people had but little to do with the store. They lived upon what they produced by their own labor from the earth. The food they eat and the clothing they wore, they produced with their own hands—a little tea, some spices, salt and molasses were the chief articles of their purchases. The best of them drank rye coffee, unless upon some holiday or other extraordinary occasion. They dressed in homespun. I do not think that I wore an article of clothing till I was sixteen years old, that did not come out of my mother's loom; and I suppose that my father's means were as ample as a majority of the people. A shirt made of homespun linen was a little scratchy at first, but after being washed a few times it sat very easy. In its new state it kept the pores open, and that was beneficial to health.

In these times there was not much inducement for
17

merchandising. Even the article of tobacco was a home product. I presume that the Plymouth merchant of those days considered that he had done a good business for the year, if his sales reached two thousand dollars.

Most of the early settlers owned a lot on the flats. Here was the broad field of their labor; and daily labor in those primitive days began at sunrise and ended with the approaching stars. One common highway led to the flats. Upon this road could be seen almost the entire male population of the town wending their daily way, at early dawn, during the season of planting and harvest, to the productive fields of the broad plain. Old and young made up this line. The summer school was for small children not yet of sufficient age for the requirements of the field. There was a common equality between master and man. They were clad alike; they ate the frugal but substantial meal from the same board. To save time, they carried with them their noon meal, so that on leaving home in the morning they made provision for the whole day, and did not return till evening.

And so along the main thoroughfare and through "the old swing gate," passed and repassed for the six days of the week of the summer, a long line of industrious and contented people. All labored. There were no drones in the busy hive. No man was above work. Labor was respectable; labor was inviting; and more than all that, labor was the true and genuine test of social position in those good old primitive days in Plymouth—God bless them. A hard hand was the index of manhood; and if the countenance did happen to be a little burned in the rays of the sun, it detracted nothing from the social status of the person. The homespun garment did not derogate from the character of the man who wore it.

In harvest time the minister, the schoolmaster, the blacksmith, the wheelwright and the carpenter lent a hand, and all went "merry as a marriage bell."

No one in these days, in our town, lived upon the perquisites or *the spoils of office.* The seeds of corruption had not been sown even, and there was of course no crop. One idea of obtaining a livelihood only prevailed. The door opened to this the path of honest and simple toil, and this was the one they all pursued. The primitive door of the Plymouth homestead a half century ago needed no locks, no bolts. These are the precautions of a higher state of civilization! The days of simplicity and integrity and honesty required no defensive walls for the protection of the humble castle. A lock upon the door! It would have implied that thieves and robbers were about; that some one of the community was under the ban of suspicion.

All being occupied, there was little time either to think of, much less to commit crime. Noah Wadhams, for a great number of years the sole justice of the peace of the town, held his court on Saturday afternoons to hear any cases that were to be tried; but a half day's work had to be done in the field before the parties litigant could be heard. And at these trials there were no persons present save the parties and their witnesses. There were no idle loungers thronging the tribunal to gratify their curiosity or waiting their chances, if need be, on either side for witnesses. This is a commodity more in demand, I am told, in modern days; and the article is cheap.

The dwellings were very generally on the main road; a few of which are still standing; the barns were on the opposite side. The bountiful harvest was stowed away in these, and when the winter set in, the sound of the flail resounded from the one end of the long road to the other. Modern invention has almost totally supplanted this implement. But I like the music of the flail, and with the accompaniment of the keen whirr of the spinning-wheel, and the measured beats of the old square loom, which was in motion in almost every house, it was infinitely ahead of the tones of the piano. This may be in bad taste upon my part, but I am now too old to be taught otherwise ; nor do I desire to be.

The principal crop in those days was wheat. Upon the sale of this, the farmer relied for all the money he received. The remaining products of the farm were used in barter and exchange. There was very little money: what there was came from Easton, on the Delaware, the market for the wheat of the whole valley. There were no banks. Easton bank bills made up the entire currency.

When the winter set in, the first matter was the thrashing of the wheat. It was put away in bins, awaiting the fall of the first snow for transportation. When this occurred, all was commotion. The moment the snow fell in sufficient quantity to warrant the journey, the teams were started. The distance by the Easton and Wilkes-Barré Turnpike, and then the only avenue of travel out of the valley toward the east, was sixty miles. The round trip could be made in three days. The load was usually about thirty bushels.

It was an exciting and pleasant excursion in early days, this Easton journey. I have hauled many a load, and I have counted on Pecono a hundred sleds in line. The jingling of bells, the mirth and laughter, and sometimes the sound of music, gave it a charm that made it very agreeable. Besides this, every tavern upon the roadside had its fiddler, and we generally had a dance for half the night, and then off in the morning, our horses steaming in the snow flakes, and the merry songs and shouts made the summits of Pocono and the Blue Mountain ring with their echoes!

Ah! if we could only always be *young!*

I noticed, however, in these " trips to Easton," as they were called, that the "old settlers" enjoyed them quite as much as the boys. The first segar I ever smoked was while walking behind my sled up the Blue

Mountain. I remember it well, for the effects were not so agreeable. I was then a boy of some eighteen years; I am told that young gentlemen commence smoking now at eight and ten years of age. So much for progress.

But I am wandering.

Every farmer in the days I am writing about, raised his own flax. From it the linen of the household was manufactured; he grew his own wool; he, in fact, produced from his land almost everything consumed in the family. Luxuries were few, the necessaries of life were abundant. I have no reason to question, but that under this mode and manner of life the masses enjoyed themselves and were quite as happy as they are now. Nay, more so; for no debts were incurred then as now, in apeing the follies and the vices of those who assume a higher social position on account of their money.

Fifty years ago equality was the rule; caste in society had not reared its head; there was no necessity of striving for the highest round in the ladder because all were perched upon it. Every man was as good as his neighbor, that is if he behaved himself well. He was not set back for the reason that his hands were soiled with labor, or that he wore a homespun coat.

Little was known in the primitive days of our town about distinction in the social relations of life. There was a common scale of friendly and personal intercourse which was very generally acknowledged and observed. The exception to the rule was immoral and vicious conduct. The man who conformed to the proprieties of a well-ordered social system, and was industrious in his habits, ranked with the best, without regard to his calling or occupation, or the amount of property he possessed. The tradesman, the merchant, the mechanic, and the farmer, as to social caste, all stood upon the same platform. Grade was unknown, except measured by industry and moral excellence. The same board was spread for the whole household. The homespun cloth furnished the material for the whole family wardrobe; the hired man, the hired girl, and the apprentice came in for a share upon the equality principle with the employer and master.

Industry was the common theme, and hence very few holidays were observed. New Year's day, Christmas, and the Fourth of July embraced them all, and pressing engagements on hand would often overrule the observance of those festive periods. Industry the year round was the universal creed, and to it all yielded implicit obedience. Idleness was disreputable. And for the reason that crime was extremely rare, it was therefore regarded with more abhorrence. It is familiarity with this, and when of frequent occurrence, that relieves it of half of its repulsive character.

This general social intercourse brought the people closer together, and gave them a deeper feeling of interest in each other's affairs. It was not an unusual thing for the whole farming community to turn out and gather the crop, which would otherwise have gone to waste, of some unfortunate neighbor who was prostrated upon a sick bed. This I have very frequently witnessed, and scarcely a year passed that an instance did not take place.

Bees were very common with the men, chopping new ground, raising buildings, corn husking, and a variety of other branches of manual labor; with the women, quilting, spinning, sewing, etc.

These frequent assemblages of the people were a means of uniting industry with pleasure. They would generally conclude with a supper, succeeded by games and other amusements; sometimes by a dance This, however, was of rare occurrence, as the Puritan mind had not yet come down to the belief, that dancing was altogether a harmless recreation !

The settlers were very generally New England people, and the social customs of their ancestors were pretty generally adhered to. Dancing, therefore, was an innovation, and its progress was slow. But in the end it was regarded with more favor, and very properly too, so that at this day, in our town, there are few probably of the "straightest" religious sect who would condemn the amusement.

Buildings for the purpose of religious worship and for education were erected by common contribution. All gave their mite in these enterprises, and those

THE OLD ACADEMY.

... coming ... ... part ... ... the ... ...
of ... ... have ... ... that new and expec-
... ... rather ... the
... ...
... ...
... the ... ...
... ... and they ...
... the ... ... of ... ...
... ... were not ... in ... the ... ... by
this ... ... It may be said, however,
that this ... ... of ... ...
... ... to a people ... ...
civilization. It is particularly ... ...

... ... that ... and summer
... ...
... ...
... ... two ...
... ...

... ...
... ...
... ...

who had not money gave their labor, so that there
was no tax imposed, and consequently no sinecure for
the indolent, in its collection.   No one grew suddenly
rich because he was fortunate enough to hold the tax
duplicates.   There was but one road open to compe-
tence and respectability, and that was honest, diligent
and persevering labor.

All denominations of religion worshipped in the
second story of the old Academy for a great number
of years.   The fact that a particular sect had occupied the common benches on one Sabbath day, did
not require their purification before another sect could
use them on the next.   Presbyterian, Methodist, Baptist, Episcopal, Christian, Catholic and Congregational
in turn, all knelt at one common altar, and they were
none the worse for it.   The public morals and private
virtues were not dimmed in the least particular by
this familiar intercourse.   It may be said, however,
that this state of things was better suited to a primitive, simple people than to a people more advanced in
civilization.   It is possible, barely possible.

The schools were kept open winter and summer;
in summer, however, they were taught by female instructors; in winter, by male.   It was small children
only who attended the summer school; the larger ones
were at labor.

The school-master "boarded around."   And as
most of my readers may not know what this means, I
will explain it.   He would go from house to house

for board and lodging, among the patrons of the
school, and remain according to a schedule of time,
which he based upon the number of his pupils, and in
the proportion which each patron sent to him.   It was
frequently said, however, but I do not pretend to assert upon what ground of authority, that the master
did not always adhere to his schedule time with all.
He would ever incline to exceed his limit where he
fared best, and shorten it where he fared worse.   And
it was not unfrequently the case that the master in entering into his contract, which was a monthly allowance, "board and lodging in," provided to be relieved
from sojourning with certain families; though this was
a kind of confidential arrangement, and charity would
ascribe it to distance, a large family, or sickness.
And this .was the way in which the kind-hearted,
burly old settlers would dispose of a knotty question;
and their memory is to be held in generous remembrance for it.

Among those who may be classed as the early permanent instructors, were Jonah Rogers (of whom notice has already been made), Thomas Patterson and
Charles C. Curtis.   Dr. Thomas Sweet, an eminent
physician afterwards, and now a resident of Scranton,
taught occasionally; and, by the way, the doctor
presented me with a thin, flat ruler, a few years since,
which he said he broke over the shoulders of the writer
for misconduct, and had retained it some fifty years as
a *souvenir* of early days.   The circumstance had passed

my memory, as flagellations in the remote days of which we are writing were of too frequent occurrence to be held in memory. The old idea, and one by no means to be scouted, pretty generally prevailed, "that if you spared the rod you spoiled the child."

Jonah Rogers never called up a poor urchin for punishment that this quotation was not a matter precedent; and the consequence was that he came very nearly making his whole school unbelievers in the divine doctrines of the revelation! But I must say that while the good old man made a great deal of fuss and talked very loud, and looked uncommonly ferocious, his blows were exceedingly light. He taught in the public school of Plymouth probably fifteen years, commencing, I am informed, not far from 1800.

Thomas Patterson succeeded him, and he continued as the principal instructor for probably ten years. He spent his summers upon his farm, and his winters in Plymouth in the capacity of teacher. He possessed a very good education; in all the English branches he was very proficient, and he had some knowledge, though limited, of the classics. He had much energy of character, and was a man of strict integrity and honor. He was an Irishman. Having taken part in the Rebellion of 1798, he fled in disguise from his native country and made this one his home. He would often tell his scholars of the marked and bloody events of the noble effort of the Irish people to rid themselves of their English oppressors; and in speaking of the execution of Robert Emmet—with whom he was acquainted—upon his conviction of high treason, the old man would shed tears.

His reverence and love for the free institutions and government of the United States were unbounded. He would say, "that the only hope for the amelioration of the condition of man was centred in the American Republic; that when this system failed, debasement and slavery would follow in its train."

I attended his school when he commenced teaching in Plymouth. This was not far from 1817. He was then a man of near fifty, stout, broad-shouldered, and nearly six feet in height. He had a well-developed head, prominent features, a keen blue eye, heavy bushy eyebrows, and when his countenance was lighted up, he exhibited evidence of great intellectual power. The old gentleman always had lying upon his desk, before him, a bound volume containing the speeches of Curran and Grattan, with the speech of Emmet delivered before his judges, when the question was propounded as "to what he had to say why the sentence of death should not be pronounced against him." A boy of sixteen, I committed this speech to memory, and would declaim it occasionally in school exercises, which was very agreeable to his feelings; and I have no doubt but that this fact led to the liberal education which I afterwards received, as the old gentleman never ceased his importunity with my father to give his son a collegiate course. And his arguments prevailed. It is due, therefore, that I, at least, should honor the old patriot's memory, and I do.

He came to the valley soon after the conclusion of the Irish Rebellion, selected this spot as his home, married a daughter of the late Colonel Nathan Denison, of Kingston, and settled in Huntington, where he ended his days. He died some twenty years since. On a visit to Huntington some years ago, I went some distance out of my course to visit the old man's grave. He left a comfortable estate to his family. Three of his sons held prominent positions of trust in the Lehigh Coal and Navigation Company, in the days of Josiah White and Erskine Hazard. One of them, Ezekiel, is a prominent man in New Brunswick, New Jersey.

Charles C. Curtis was the successor of Thomas Patterson. He continued several years in the public school as instructor. He was a kind and affable man in his deportment, and very highly respected for his probity of character. He married a daughter of Colonel George P. Ransom, who still survives her husband. Mr. Curtis, after the close of his occupation as school-teacher, settled down with his family upon a farm in Jackson township, inherited by his wife from her father, where he died about the year 1850.

And thus much for the early instructors of the youth of Plymouth. There were others, but they were of more recent date, and I cannot therefore speak of them from my own knowledge.

The languages were taught in the old Academy as early as 1829. Mr. Nyce and Mr. Patterson, graduates of Dickinson College, were engaged three or four years in the capacity of teachers—they were succeeded by Mr. Seiwers.

I am not aware that the dead languages have been a part of the system of education in Plymouth since Mr. Seiwers left.

As it is not my purpose to bring the Historical Sketches of Plymouth down to a later period than 1850, it will be no part of my labor to speak of the later progress of the school system, and which has been attended with very cheering and hopeful prospects, not only as regards our town but the country at large.

CHAPTER XII.

OLD LANDMARKS. — POUND, SWING-GATE, COMMON-FIELD, SIGN-POST, MILLS, ETC.

IN early days, the "Shawnee Flats" were all within one common enclosure. The several lots composing the great field were divided by surveys, with stone monuments at the corners, but there were no fences dividing as well as protecting the respective ownerships. The annual floods, caused by the rise of the Susquehanna, were deemed too formidable to permit the idea of erecting fences. Since the great ice flood of 1784, which removed all the buildings from Garrison Hill, no owner has presumed to put up buildings for any purpose upon the lower plain.

About the year 1820, my father made the first experiment of inclosing his land by fencing. The other proprietors, waiting a year or two, and seeing that the fences remained, followed his example, and in a short time each owner had at least the exterior lines of his lots protected by inclosures. These, from that time down, have been pretty generally maintained.

Before this, the river was the only barrier on one side, and the fence, which skirted the main road, on the other. The two ends of the plain coming to an acute angle, the highway and river were very close together at each.

After the crops were gathered in the fall, the whole field was thrown open to the public. This was bad farming, as the winter crops were very much injured by being eaten off and trampled upon by the herds of cattle grazing over them. This led to the necessity of enclosures, and a good farmer would be well satisfied if he did not have to replace his enclosures oftener than every seventh year—about half the ordinary time they would have lasted without the accident by floods.

But while the plain was thus in common, and which continued from 1784 to 1820—nearly forty years—some extraordinary means had to be adopted to prevent the trespasses of cattle running at large.

To obviate this, the proprietors of the flats—and this embraced very nearly two-thirds of the taxable inhabitants—erected a public Pound. This structure was built of hewn logs. It was of an octagon shape, covering an area of probably a thousand square feet, and some ten feet in height. It stood on the lower side of the flat road, and at the junction of it with the main thoroughfare, upon land of the late Colonel Ransom, and a few rods east of the old red mansion house, in which he resided many years, and in which he died.

In this stronghold were impounded all the cattle which were found running at large upon the Flats, before the season of their being thrown open to the public. The owners could only procure their release on the payment of a fine. This averaged probably about twenty-five cents a head, which was paid to the " Key Keeper." This officer, at the first date of my own recollection—over a half century ago—was Hezekiah Roberts. He occupied a house upon the little rise of ground on the opposite side of the way from the pound—now the estate of Oliver Davenport, Esq.

Hezekiah was an active, dapper little man, and supposed that the running gear and the machinery of the whole universe, and the United States in particular, depended very much on the faithful discharge of his duties as keeper of the municipal keys.

You might see him every morning during the summer, at the dawn of day, mounted on his gray horse, making a reconnoissance of the big field, and if he made a large haul, it was a pretty profitable day's work. He did not become, in this tour of a Sunday morning, liable to a fine for pursuing worldly employment on the Lord's day. It was a work of necessity. For while the forefathers were very exemplary, and extremely exacting in the observance of the Sabbath, they still had an eye to the security of their crops. All very proper, undoubtedly. This office of "Key-Keeper," at the first settlement of Plymouth, was considered a matter of especial trust, and was a mark of distinction that no one of them would refuse. I have already mentioned the fact that at a town meeting of the people of Westmoreland, held on " March ye second, 1774," Thomas Heath, one of the prominent men of the town, was chosen for this office. Next to the selectman and the board of directors, came this functionary. His duties were to hold the keys of the garrison, the church, the school-house, the pound, and the swing-gate. And it was a mark of the public confidence for which any man of reasonable ambition might very properly feel elated. He may have been said to have carried the state and the church in his breeches pocket; at all events, the key which opened the door to each. And I can well re-

member the impression the display of these bright
shining evidences of power, as well as personal dignity, made upon my mind. No less, probably, than
that produced by the distinguished personage entrusted with the keys of Dover or Calais, upon the humble people of the wayside.

As these were the days of summary justice, the
public sign-post in its double capacity of gazette and
whipping-post, supplied the place of criminal records
and prison, and there was no occasion for a jail key on
the official ring. Whipping and banishment were the
two penalties for crime. Our early pioneers went
upon the principle that it was not worth their while
to be bothered with lock-ups, and taken from their
useful occupation to lounge about courts, waiting days
and weeks for a trial, in the case of some miserable
fellow who was of no account to the community, in
prison or out of prison. So for a small offense they
tried the culprit, and if found guilty, tied him up to
the whipping-post and gave him ten or twenty lashes;
and thus fifteen minutes ended the whole matter, and
the court, the constable, the complainant, witnesses,
and the criminal could all go to work, and probably
in the same field. A pretty efficacious, if not sensible, way of doing things. The fellow who committed
felonies they sent off to Connecticut to be dealt with
according to his deserts, and for the intermediate
grade of crime they banished. So that dispatch was
the order of the day, and moderate taxation.

My own memory does not reach back to the time when the whipping or sign post, or the town fortifications were in use. So that when I first became acquainted with the town key-keeper, in the person of Mr. Hezekiah Roberts, he only had on his ring the key of the pound, the school-house and the swing-gate. Troublesome men had crept into the church; it now had two doors to it, so that the old office—which in the days of Thomas Heath was of great honor and importance—I am sorry to say, in the days of Hezekiah Roberts, had become very much curtailed, though still respectable; and people who did not have "just at that moment" the ready money to pay over for the redemption of their impounded cattle, were very obsequious to Mr. Roberts.

The old pound was one of the institutions of its day, and its locality and purposes were well understood by every man, woman and child over six years of age, fifty years ago in Plymouth.

Some thirty years since it disappeared; the inclosures on the flats, and the people beginning to learn that it was not lawful to permit their cattle to run at large, seemed to have diminished the necessities for its continuance. It was a landmark, and I could not well pass by it in silence.

Famous as is the memory of the *Pound*, the "old swing-gate" is quite as much so. That and its children have survived a hundred years. It opened to the flat road, and through it passed and repassed

daily during the summer season, going to and returning
from their labor; the substantial representative men
of the township; men who were an honor to their race
because they lived by the sweat of their brow, and
whose word did not require to be written down or at-
tested by a witness.   And through it rolled too, upon
creaking wagons, the annual produce of a thousand
acres of as fertile land as the sun ever shone upon.

Why this should have been particularly called the
swing-gate, I do not understand, as I am pretty sure
that there was not in the township any other gate,
public or private, that did not swing upon hinges.
This too will probably disappear in time.

" The commonfield," so called because it was the
parade-ground, the place where the common sign-post
was located, and the spot of general rendezvous, was
upon Ant Hill.   The ground was originally eight
rods wide, and extended from the brow of the hill
above the house of J. W. Eno, Esq.   The fences
upon the west side have gradually encroached upon
the " commonfield," and it is now by no means what
it was fifty years since.   We find so long ago as the
twenty-fourth of March, 1786, at the meeting at
which John Franklin was chairman and Jonah Rogers clerk, that the people owning land on the borders
of the commonfield were encroaching upon it, and
that they warned them off, with the exception of the
Widow Heath.   Her house was made a special case,
probably because her husband had been entrusted at

one time with the responsible office of holding the public keys. This commonfield has long since ceased to be occupied for public purposes.

I can remember when it was used for military parades, but for no other purpose.

But on this field stood a hundred years ago, and stands to-day, the lofty old elm which was the public sign-post of our ancestors. There is no reason but wantonness why this old landmark should be removed. Like the Charter Oak of revolutionary memory, now standing upon the Boston "commonfield," it should be nursed and preserved with the same care that it is. It should have a strong barricade put about it, that its life may be prolonged to the latest possible day.

If the old elm had a tongue and could speak, strange stories to our ears, at least, would it relate. It could inform us that on such and such days, such and such offenders, who stood charged and convicted of sundry and divers crimes of "swearing, drunkenness, frauds, gaming, and idleness," were lashed to its rough bark, and soundly whipped, as they deserved to be, for these and all like crimes and offences!

Wise men were the good, solid men of Plymouth. Labor was honorable, and idleness a punishable crime. They knew how to keep down taxes; and honor to their memory, for their independence of character in adopting and enforcing, too, the means to prevent idleness and dissipation. But I fear that the wisdom and courage of these old patriarchs, were they back to-day, would not be equal to the task of reformation.

Mr. Pearce informs us, in his "Annals of Luzerne," that "Robert Faulkner erected a log grist-mill in 1780, on Shupp's creek, below the site of the old Shupp mill; and the same year, Benjamin Harvey erected a log grist-mill and residence on Harvey's creek, which was occupied by his son-in-law, Abraham Tillbury; and that about the same time, Hezekiah Roberts erected a saw-mill on Ransom's creek; and in 1795 Samuel Marvin built a saw-mill on Whittlesey's creek, on the Calvin Wadhams farm." The foundations of these old mills have passed away. I remember the old log grist-mill of Mr. Tillbury, and the saw-mill on Whittlesey creek: the others had disappeared before my day.

The Shupp mill must have been erected as early as 1800. That, when I was a boy, was the principal flouring mill of the town, and many a time have I carried my grist on horseback to it. One horse wagons were unknown till after the close of the war of 1812. Mr. Philip Shupp, the grandfather of the present gentleman of that name, now a resident of Plymouth, then owned the mill and mill farm. A short, stout-built old German, from Northampton county, and a man of the strictest integrity. I have known three generations at that mill. It has also disappeared.

Having spoken of the stone threshing-floor, the barricades, and the old Academy, with a notice of the other old landmarks of Plymouth, I conclude the subject, in the earnest hope and prayer that the old Academy and the big elm sign-post may be permitted to remain as venerable indexes, pointing back to the good old days of our ancestors. They are not here to speak for them, and in humble supplication I do, in their name, and on their behalf.

CHAPTER XIII.

SHAD FISHERIES.—GAME.

WHEN the State of Pennsylvania commenced the building of her public canals, it put an end to the shad fisheries. It became necessary to use the large rivers for the purposes of feeders; and the erection of dams to accomplish this, created a barrier which totally interrupted the annual ascent of this delicious fish up the Susquehanna. Before that, this stream had become famous for its shad fisheries, and, in fact, this product was one of the chief staples of food in the early settlement of the country. The system of internal navigation commenced in 1825; since then the fisheries have been abandoned. It was in one sense a public calamity, for the people along the shores of the Susquehanna looked forward with as

much interest to the fishing season as to the time of
their harvest. The crop, indeed, was quite as important to them. Many poor families the fisheries
supplied with the chief article of their food, for at
least a third of the year. By a reference to Franklin's
diary, it will be seen that one of the causes of the
wrongs inflicted upon the Plymouth settlers by
Wilkes-Barré magistrates, as far back as 1784, and
of which he complains, was the destruction of their
fishing-nets and seines.

From that time down to 1825, a period of thirty-
nine years, the shad crop was relied upon by the
people as one of the utmost importance. Large numbers of the people of Plymouth were shareholders in
the shad fisheries. Those who were not, were supplied at a mere nominal price. Previous to 1800,
the price probably did not average more than two
cents a piece, and from that period up to 1825, when
the dams were put in the river, the highest price did
not exceed eight or ten cents apiece. Thus a laboring
man, who had no interest in the fisheries, could lay
in his year's supply for the receipts of a week's wages.

And while the whole population along the Susquehanna were exceedingly anxious to have the canal,
they indulged in feelings of deep regret at the idea
that it would result in the total destruction of their
fisheries. The great advantages they contemplated
from the inland navigation, overbalanced the conse-
quent loss of the fisheries. They submitted, but a

great many of the old settlers could hardly reconcile their minds to the exchange. They did, however, but with extreme reluctance.

The day of railroads had no existence forty years ago. "De Witt Clinton and the grand canal," were the watchwords of progress. New York led off, and the other states followed in her wake. The motto was interwoven upon handkerchiefs and vest patterns. I well remember of wearing a vest with these words interwoven all over it. And so with the ordinary water pitchers; they would be decorated with the profile likenesses of Washington, Lafayette, Decatur, Lawrence, Perry, or Scott, so that every time the old pioneer brought the cider mug to his mouth, he had looking him in the face some one of the land or marine heroes of the country. A good reminder! It may be said these were days of primeval simplicity. I would they could return to us again. Particularly if they would bring along with them those habits of honest rusticity, when jails were tenantless, and the scaffold a thing of the imagination only.

But our subject is not to theorize, but to jot down facts and things connected with the past, and blended with the lives and transactions of our ancestors.

Plymouth was noted for its good shad fisheries. There were three of them. "The Mud Fishery," nearly opposite the old Steele ferry. The point of "hauling out" was on the west bank of the river, and probably a half mile below "Garrison Hill," called also a "night fishery." They never drew the seine in the daytime. I have taken part in the work here a great many nights, in years gone by, and have shared as many as a hundred shad for the labor of a night.

Another fishery was located at "Fish Island," sometimes called "Park's Island." Its last name came from the residence of an old rheumatic man who hobbled on two crutches, one under each arm-pit, with a bag slung over his shoulders, in which he carried herbs. He was an herb doctor, and was known far and wide as Dr. Parks. Some time about the year 1835, he made a voyage to Washington, D. C., in his canoe. He went for a pension, and he got it. He came back with his canoe by the way of the Chesapeake and Delaware canal; thence up the Delaware to Easton, and then up the Lehigh navigation to White Haven, within twenty miles of his home. Canoes in past days were an important river craft. I have already stated that this was the vessel Colonel Franklin navigated when he went on his mission from the valley to Annapolis, to present the settlers' petition to Congress. He informs us that he left his canoe at Conawago Falls, near Harrisburg, and proceeded the rest of his journey on foot, by land.

Dr. Parks being unable to walk, or with very great difficulty, passed through the falls and landed at the wharves on the Potomac at Washington. The doctor gave a circumstantial and interesting account of his voyage on his return, and exhibited his pension certificate; as to the propriety of granting it, the people of the valley generally entertained very grave doubts. And I believe it never has yet been ascertained, and probably never will be, for what particular military service this bounty was granted. He said "it took him just two months to make the voyage; and the rheumatics enemost killed him, too; the tide water seemed to baffle the vartu of all his yarbs, and at one time he nearly give in."

Dr. Parks had a slab hut some ten feet square, and six feet high, on Fish Island. This was his domicile and home, except during high floods, and when these occurred, the doctor, along with the exodus of his friends and neighbors, the muskrats, would seek refuge on the main land. His cabin was fastened by a cable to a huge sycamore hard by.

The old name of Fish Island became partially obscured; the long residence of the root doctor attaching to it his own patronymic. Before the erection of the dam immediately below, this island was much larger than it is now, the back flow of the water has submerged probably two-thirds of the original surface.

This was a day fishery, and in early times there were some most extraordinary "hauls" made. One of them, somewhere between 1790 and 1800, tradition informs us, yielded "nine thousand nine hundred and ninety-nine shad." I have been informed by persons who were present, that this haul was made on a Sunday morning; that in bringing the seine to, on the point of the island, it soon became apparent that the twines of the meshes would not withstand the pressure of the load, and that two other nets were put around it, and in this way only a part of the immense catch was secured. That the number of fish taken at this haul was nearly or quite ten thousand, there is no question. I have heard the relation of the story from the mouths of credible persons who were present at the time.

The third was known as the "Dutch Fishery," located at the lower end of the narrows below Nanticoke; the upper end of the Croup farm was the point of "hauling out." The fishing was done most generally here during the night, though occasionally they dragged their nets in the daytime. My father said that his share at one night's catch, at this fishery, was nineteen hundred. He was the owner, however, of the seine, and drew a fifth of the product.

I think that it may be fair to estimate that these three fisheries, in an ordinary season, would yield not less than two hundred thousand shad. The state, therefore, in closing up the natural channels of the Susquehanna, did an immense injury to the people along its shores. The policy, however, which caused it may have made a full equivalent for the damage in other ways. The generation, however, who immediately preceded us, could not forget the annual luxury which the shad fisheries of the Susquehanna had afforded them. With them it was ever a subject of regret, that they had exchanged their fisheries for the canal.

An attempt has been made within the few past years to so arrange the schutes of the Susquehanna dams that the shad may pass up them; but the result thus far has been an almost total failure. The people of this valley will probably never have the satisfaction of seeing the river stocked with this most delicious fish, so long as the waters are made contributory for feeders of the canal. The shad fisheries, therefore are among the things of the past.

The Susquehanna, but for its shad, was not remarkably celebrated for its fish. Eels were pretty abundant in the fall of the year, but the season for taking them was very short; and its waters contained but few other specimens, and those comparatively insignificant in number. "The Oswego bass," however, were common in its waters, and sometimes obtained a large size. I have seen them of fourteen pounds weight.

Within my own recollection the Plymouth mountains, and the broad stretch of forest between them and the Blue Ridge, contained a great abundance of game, Deer were remarkably plenty ; and wild turkeys might be seen in large flocks. Pigeons, particularly in the spring of the year, would alight upon the Shawnee flats in countless numbers. Peter Gould, who resided in a log house a few rods above the Academy, was celebrated for his skill and success in taking these birds. · He sold them at a shilling a dozen, with a dull demand at that price. I have occasionally heard the wolves howl by night on the Plymouth mountain.

The clearing up, however, of the forest land, and its occupation by the husbandman, drove off the remnant of these denizens of the wood; the deer and the wild turkeys, with the red man, have disappeared.

Our town does not chronicle the names of any very celebrated hunters. Those people lived a step further towards the " green woods." Joseph Worthington, of Lake memory, was a renowned hunter, as was James Wandel of Union township. The exploits of these two men would fill a small volume. They would make contracts with the early retail dealers of merchandise to furnish them game by the wagon load, which was sent to New York and Philadelphia in exchange for goods. The price of venison in those days was four and five cents a pound, for the saddle.

These two men, when the game disappeared, wended their way west. They had been so long accustomed to a life on the border, that they felt the encroachment of the pioneer's axe. Worthington went first to Illinois, then to Kansas, and the last heard of him was in California, still in pursuit of his old and darling occupation. Though now if living—

and he was a year since—waning towards eighty, still upon the track of the quarry! A Daniel Boone of the wild woods. Wandel also went·west under the same impulses which moved Worthington, and was also living at a very recent date.

It is a marvel to what an extreme old age these hunters will attain. We would suppose their occupation would be very prejudicial to health. George Sax, the great panther hunter of "the shades," is living at over eighty. I think that John McHenry, of Fishing creek, is still living. Mr. Pearce, in his Annals, informs us that the old hunter told him in 1840, that his registry then numbered nineteen hundred deer and sixty-five bears, besides immense quantities of other game.

The forests of the Susquehanna and its tributaries were alive with game. When we reflect that the streams also were well stocked with fish, and that the natural prairies bordering the river were free from trees and incumbrances, so that the Indian could easily till his cornfields, we may well conclude that he left his wigwam with as keen an anguish as the most intellectual and enlightened white man would his houses, his fields and his herds. Human natures are alike in their attachments. The Indian was happy in the occupation of his wild domain. He roved over it with all the conscious pride of a conqueror. He acknowledged no allegiance but to Manitou. The Great Spirit was, in his judgment, his only superior.

To him alone he acknowledged submission. To the white man he was too proud to pay tribute.

When the German missionary, prompted by the most elevated piety, and ready to meet almost any sacrifice, approached the wigwam of the Shawnees, the keen and penetrating glance of these children of nature saw, that in the professions for the good of their spiritual wants, they were coming in contact with a people who, though they might tender kind offices, still might inflict great harm; they brandished their scalping-knives and exhibited every demonstration of dissatisfaction. They were probably in the right. Events which followed show but too plainly that the advance of the white man was to them, the signal of extermination and death.

But civilization came, and the Indian and the forests and the wild game vanished before it. And in all this change it is probably for the best. The territory of old Plymouth to-day furnishes employment, and its industrial pursuits feed some ten thousand intelligent people. Churches and seminaries of learning, and manufactories and machinery, all tell the story of the advance of knowledge and the useful arts. The exchange of these for the occupations of the trapper and hunter, bespeak a better state of things. It is the enlargement of the area for the more useful employments of free and enlightened men. Though this may have been a sacrifice to a few, the general good which the multitude has reaped is a consummation which is to be approved. Broad and diffusive as the rays of the sun, the blessings of high civilization reach and permeate the great masses; thousands are made happy and independent, instead of the comparatively small number of the past. We will conclude the chapter with the remark of Othello to *honest* Iago, that "it is better as it is."

CHAPTER XIV.

EARLY MERCHANTS.

BENJAMIN HARVEY, Jr., of Captain Ransom's Independent Company revolutionary service, and who died from exposure at Valley Forge, seems to have been the first merchant of Plymouth. In 1774 he started a small retail store in the log house of his father, which has been already mentioned, and located very near the site of the Christian Church building. Here, for a couple of years, he dealt in a small way in articles of absolute necessity—salt, leather, iron, a few groceries, etc. At that time, and for many subsequent years, all articles of merchandise were transported upon the river in " Durham boats." These boats were some forty feet in length, with a beam of some ten feet, and would carry from fifteen to twenty tons burden. They were propelled with long "setting-poles," with iron sockets at the ends, three men

19

on each side, with a steersman at the stern.   Ten or twelve miles up the stream was considered a fair day's work.

These boats were the only means of transportation of merchandise until the making of the Easton and Wilkes-Barré turnpike.   This thoroughfare was completed about the year 1807.   Thence down to the time of the canal navigation in 1830, the merchants of the entire valley received all their goods, either by " Durham boats " on the river, or by wagons on the turnpike.   The turnpike company was chartered in 1802, and the road was constructed at a cost of $75,000.   This road was regarded as a very important matter by the early settlers of the valley; and indeed such was the fact, as it gave a much shorter outlet to the seaboard.   The corporation was a joint-stock company, and it required the contribution of nearly every landholder in the valley to accomplish the construction of this important link of intercommunication.   Seventy-five thousand dollars in 1802 was a large sum of money to be raised, and it required a united effort of all the people to accomplish it.

The old "Conestoga wagon," drawn by four horses, was the vehicle of transportation on the turnpike.   It has disappeared; but it was a goodly sight to see one of those huge wagons drawn along by four strong, sleek, and well-fed horses, with bearskin housings and "winkers tipped with red."   It was very common to have a fifth horse on the lead.   I have seen trains of these wagons, miles in length, on the great road leading to Pittsburg, as late as 1830. It was the only way of transportation over the Allegheny chain westward. A wagon would carry three, four, and sometimes five tons. The bodies were long, projecting over front and rear, ribbed with oak, covered with canvas, and generally painted blue. There were several persons, residents of the valley, who made it their only occupation to carry goods for the early merchants here. Joshua Pettebone, one of this number, is still living in Kingston at an advanced age.

But in the days of the first merchant of Plymouth, the "Conestoga wagon" was not known. His transport was the "Durham boat." It will be remembered that Benjamin Harvey, Jr., that same first merchant, was at Fort Augusta, near Sunbury, with his boat, in December, 1775, when Colonel Plunkett impressed him and his vessel into the Proprietary service, immediately preceding the battle of Nanticoke. He was then on his way down the Susquehanna for a supply of goods for his log store.

After the enlistment of Mr. Harvey in the United States army, his father took charge of his small stock of goods and sold them out, but the store was never replenished.

From this time down to the year 1808, there seems to have been no store kept in Plymouth. In February of that year, my father, the late Joseph Wright, opened a small retail establishment in the

east room of his residence, in the lower end of the
village; the same building is now standing there,
in a good state of preservation.   By a reference to his
ledger, which is in my possession, I find the first entry bears date the twenty-sixth February, 1808.

"ABRAHAM TILLBURY, DR.

" To one qt. of rum, at 7-6 per gallon, £0. 1s.
10 1-2d."

It is well for our young people, therefore, to
know, that even as late as 1808, accounts were kept
in Plymouth in pounds, shillings, and pence.

Mr. Jameson Harvey informs me, and to whose
kindness I am indebted for many interesting facts
concerning the early settlement of our town, that he
made the first purchase at the new store.   He bought
"a Jew's Harp, and paid sixpence for it in *cash*."
He being at that time a minor, it is probable
he did not deem it prudent to ask for credit.   Mr.
Tillbury therefore, must be placed as second upon
the list.

These old books, which tell in plain and simple
language the plain and simple habits of a race of
people gone, I cannot lay aside without permitting
them to speak out.   In the first place, the handwriting is dear to me; for it brings before me the benev-
olent and honest countenance of the man who noted
down the memoranda upon these venerable pages,
nearly seventy years ago.   And in the next place,
are the names of all the hardy old settlers of the

THE WRIGHT HOUSE, AND BIRTH PLACE OF AUTHOR.

town, with the faces of nearly every one of whom I was familiar. And their economy, and that all important question of living within one's means, are spread out on every page of the ancient ledger. It is true that the accounts against Abraham Pike, William Hodge, Thomas Car Skadden, Benjamin Rumsey, Adolph Heath, John L. Shaw and some others, have rather too much of a sprinkling of rum about them ; but then we must remember that it was wise lips which uttered the sentence—" Let him that is without sin, cast the first stone."

The logic of the old ledger shows us that people can live comfortably and happy without money. Barter and exchange seem to have been the rule in the primitive days of the town. The old ledger shows the payment of a small, very small sum of money, occasionally. Abijah Smith was one of the principal customers of the store. He was then making a small beginning of the trade, and engaged in the development of an article which later years has increased to a wonderful magnitude. He paid money, while nearly all the other customers of the store paid in the product of the farm. The accounts exhibit the fact that of an annual sale of probably two thousand dollars, there was not paid in cash, exclusive of the money of Abijah Smith, ten pounds. The credits are for wheat, rye, corn, oats and flax. The last article particularly is a large item. And this is by no means singular, as tow and linen cloth were staples of old Plymouth in those remote days. Credit also for bear and deer skins, venison and wild turkeys, appear here and there, but cash rarely. The goods bartered in exchange were mostly the absolute and necessary wants of life; iron, leather, salt, molasses (generally sold by the pint and quart), sugar, tea, coffee (in small quantities, a quarter and half pound at a time), cutlery, spices; no cloths of any account, thread, needles, pins, calico, muslin and cambric (in small quantities), to the most opulent; and these made the bulk of the necessaries. The luxuries may be summed up in rum, whisky, tobacco and snuff.

The old settlers of that day generally smoked their tobacco in pipes. The charges of pipes, at three-pence a piece, are numerous. The only entry I find of cigars are several charges to John Turner, at the very moderate price of three-pence a dozen.

The accounts embrace the names of the people generally of the town—Calvin and Noah Wadhams, Benjamin Reynolds, Abraham and James Nesbitt, Samuel and James Pringle, Thomas Davenport, William Currie, George P. Ransom, Mrs. Rosannah Harvey, Abraham, Nicholas and Stephen Vanloon, Hezekiah Roberts, Joshua Pugh, Jonah and Joel Rogers, Charles Barney, John and Daniel Turner, Jesse Coleman, Moses Atherton, Jacob and Peter Gould and Philip Andrus. These, with names already given, and a few others, were the principal customers at Joseph Wright's store in 1808.

JOHN L. SMITH'S OPERA HOUSE.

There is not one of them except Abijah Smith whose annual account amounts to a hundred dollars. We do not find in this fact a want of ability to pay, but it exhibits a frugality and a disposition of the men of that day to contract no debt that they could not pay. And to show how little our ancestors knew about paper money, every note paid in is registered in the back of the ledger, giving the name of the bank issuing the note, from whom received, and its date and number.

In 1812, Joseph Wright sold out his stock of goods to the Reverend George Lane, who continued the best part of the year at the old stand, then taking Benjamin Harvey, a son of Elisha, and whom we must designate as the third of that name, into partnership with him, they commenced business in a small frame building, lately removed by Mr. John B. Smith, and on the site of the new Music Hall. They continued on at this stand until 1816, when Mr. Lane removed to Wilkes-Barré, put up a dwelling and store at the north-west corner of the public square and Market street (Osterhout property now), where he carried on the business of a merchant for several years. Mr. Harvey the same year removed to Huntington, where he still resides.

The next mercantile adventure in the township was a firm composed of Joseph Wright, Benjamin Reynolds, and Joel Rogers. This firm opened a store in a small frame building on the east side of the road, opposite the present residence of Mr. Henderson Gaylord. This was in the year 1812. They employed Mr. Gaylord, then a young man and resident of Huntington, as the clerk and salesman. And this young gentleman here commenced the pursuit of an occupation, which he carefully and industriously followed up in after years, with a very prosperous result.

This firm was dissolved in October, 1814, and the business continued by Mr. Rogers and Mr. Gaylord, under the firm of Joel Rogers & Co., up to 1816.

In this year a new firm of Reynolds, Gaylord & Co. was formed, consisting of Benjamin Reynolds, Henderson Gaylord and Abraham Fuller, which continued to December, 1818, when Abraham Fuller died. From this period down to the fall of 1824, Mr. Gaylord continued the business, and then entered into a partnership with the late William C. Reynolds. This partnership lasted for a period of ten years, under the firm name of Gaylord & Reynolds. During this time they had established a branch at Kingston.

Shortly after the dissolution of the firm of Gaylord & Reynolds, in 1836, Mr. Gaylord and Draper Smith formed a partnership, which continued down to 1839, when it was dissolved.

In 1816, the business stand was removed to the premises now occupied as a hotel by John Deen, and continued there to the year 1827. In that year Mr. Gaylord erected a store-house on the opposite side of

HENDERSON GAYLORD.

the street, in which he and Mr. Smith carried on the business till they dissolved, and Mr. Gaylord alone from that time up to 1856, when he retired.

About the year 1828, John Turner opened a store where Turner Brothers now are. Soon after that he sold his stock to Gaylord & Reynolds. Asa Cook, now a resident of Ross township, commenced business in the Turner store, and was soon followed by John Turner, in the same building, and the establishment has been continued down to the present time either in his name or the name of his sons.

Samuel Davenport and Elijah W. Reynolds opened a store where A. S. Davenport, son of Samuel, now keeps, in the year 1834. This firm was dissolved in 1835, and the business continued by Samuel Davenport to the year 1840, when he formed a partnership with John B. Smith; this firm lasted till the death of Mr. Davenport, which was in the year 1850, and for several years succeeding the store was continued by Mr. Smith.

Ira Davenport opened the establishment he now occupies in the year 1845. Chauncey A. Reynolds also opened a store in 1850, which was continued by him some four or five years.

And this completes the history in a few paragraphs of the early merchants of the town. It is an agreeable reflection that none of them failed or became bankrupt. All of them were successful, and the most of them, though beginning with small means, became men of wealth.   I am not aware that any of them were addicted to habits of intemperance, and being acquainted with them all, with the exception of Benjamin Harvey, the pioneer, if such had been the case, it would not have escaped my knowledge.   They were, too, men of correct business habits, and enjoyed the confidence and respect of the people of the town.

It is certainly worthy of record, that among so considerable a number of men engaged for so long a period of time, that there should have been no failures, and that sobriety and temperance should have been a characteristic of every one of them, and each successful.   It may be a very difficult task to find a parallel.

The business character, enterprise and upright conduct, therefore, of the merchants of Plymouth of earlier days, furnish a good model for the imitation of their successors; and if he who writes the history of the merchants of Plymouth at the end of the next fifty years, will be able to truthfully state what is here recorded of the fifty and more years past, it will not merely be to him an agreeable duty, but will illustrate the fact that moral precept and good examples have had their influence.

CHAPTER XV.

IN the fall of the year of 1807, Abijah Smith purchased an ark of John P. Arndt, a merchant of Wilkes-Barré, which had been used for the transportation of plaster, for the price of $24.00. This ark he floated to Plymouth, and loaded with some fifty tons of anthracite coal, and late in the same season he landed it safely at Columbia, Lancaster county, Pa.

This was probably the first cargo of anthracite coal that was ever offered for sale in this or any other country. The trade of 1807 was fifty tons; that of 1870, in round numbers, sixteen millions! It may be fairly estimated that the sale of 1880 will reach twenty-five millions.

Abijah Smith therefore, of Plymouth, was the pioneer in the coal business. Anthracite coal had been used before 1807, in this valley and elsewhere, in small quantities in furnaces, with an air blast; but the traffic in coal as an article of general use, was commenced by Abijah Smith, of Plymouth. The important discovery of burning coal without an air blast, was made by Hon. Jesse Fell, of Wilkes-Barré, one of the Judges of the Luzerne county courts, on the eleventh day of February, 1808, and less than six months after the departure of the first cargo from

the Plymouth mines.   This important discovery,
which led to the use of coal for culinary and other
domestic purposes, enabled Mr. Smith, in the year
succeeding his first shipment, to introduce it into the
market.   But even then, as is the case in most new
discoveries, the public were slow in coming to the
conclusion that it would answer the purposes of fuel.
Time, however, has fully demonstrated its usefulness;
and the rapid increase of its consumption, from fifty
tons annually, to sixteen millions, in a period of a little more than fifty years, is one of the wonders of the
nineteenth century.

The statistical tables of the trade, which yearly
appear in the public press, date the commencment
in 1820.   It is put down in that year at three hundred and sixty-five tons, as the shipment from the
Lehigh region to market.

In this there is error, for thirteen years previous
to that time, as we have already stated, Mr. Smith
had shipped coal from his Plymouth mine.   But in
fact the article had been put in the market long previous to 1820, by other persons than the Messrs.
Smith.

Charles Miner, Jacob Cist, John W. Robinson
and Stephen Tuttle, all of Wilkes-Barré, had leased
the old Mauch Chunk mines, and in August, 1814,
had sent an ark load of it down the Lehigh.   Mr.
George M. Hollenback sent two ark loads down the
Susquehanna, taken from his Mill creek mines, in

1813. The same year, Joseph Wright, of Plymouth, mined two ark loads of coal from the mines of his brother, the late Samuel G. Wright, of New Jersey, near Port Griffith, in Pittston. This was an old opening, and coal had been mined there for the smith's forge as far back as 1775. The late Lord Butler, of Wilkes-Barré, had also shipped coal from his mines, more generally known of late years as the "Baltimore mines," as early as 1814, and so had Crandal Wilcox, of Plaines township.

My object in making these references is to show that the coal-trade actually began in 1807, and not in 1820, as is now generally believed.

But while the persons I have named did not follow up the business, Abijah and John Smith, his brother, continued the business down to the period of their respective deaths; and their children continued on the trade long afterwards.

Abijah Smith came to the valley in 1806, and in that or the following year he purchased some seventy-five acres of coal-land on the east side of Ransom's creek, for about five hundred dollars. In 1807 he commenced mining; and coal has been taken almost yearly from the opening he made down to the present period.

In the year 1808, his brother John came to the valley. He bought the coal designated in the deed, from Wm. Curry, Jr., as "Potts of Coal," on the adjoining tract of one hundred and twenty acres, for the consideration of six hundred dollars. This mine was soon after opened, and workings have been uninterruptedly continued ever since. Abijah and John were partners in the coal business for many years. They were natives of Derby, in the state of Connecticut. From the time they commenced coal operations, they continued on in trade, as a means of living, for the remainder of their lives. It was their sole occupation. They prosecuted their employment with great energy and perseverance, and amid a great many difficulties and disappointments; and although neither of them lived to see their anticipations realized, their descendants—who are still the owners of the estates they purchased more than a half century ago—are enjoying the advantages and comforts which resulted from their ancestor's foresight and judgment.

Abijah died in 1826, at his residence, the site of which is now occupied by the new brick Music Hall, recently put up by his son, John B. Smith, of Plymouth. His brother John died in 1852.

I knew them both intimately for a great number of years. They were industrious, upright and worthy men. They started the coal trade, and their names will ever be blended with it.

It is proper that we should examine into the details of the mode and manner of mining and transportation, as pursued by these early pioneers in the business. There are but few now engaged in the great

GOLDSMITH.

trade who are aware of the troubles and sacrifices which attended it in its infancy. We will look at the child when in its swathing bands; it is now a giant, but fifty years ago it was in its infancy. The experiment which was perseveringly followed up, and beset on all sides by difficulties and hazards, resulted in a grand success.

The annual trade, which at the commencement was limited to hundreds of tons, has now become tens of millions of tons. The price of coal land of five dollars an acre, in the days of the Smith purchase, is now a thousand per acre. What the future demand for the article may be—or the annual production—the future alone can determine, human foresight cannot; nor can it be said that the field is inexhaustible. There is a limit to it; and those who will occupy our places five hundred years hence, will say that our prophecy is not entirely fiction.

In the early process of mining, there was no powder used: this, under the present system, is the chief agency. It was all done with the pick and wedge. The miner did his labor by the day, and received from fifty to seventy-five cents. The product of his day's labor was about a ton and a half; his time was from sunrise to sunset. The coal was transported from the mine to the place of shipment, in carts and wagons, and deposited upon the banks of the river, to be put in arks, in the time of the annual spring freshets of the Susquehanna.

The process of mining with the pick and wedge was too slow and too expensive. Mr. Abijah Smith came to the conclusion that the ordinary powder blast might be made available in mining. He must have some one, however, who was accustomed to the quarries. There was no one here who understood the business.

In the year 1818 he found that he could get a man for the work. This man was John Flanigan, of Milford, Connecticut. His occupation was quarrying stone with the powder blast. He wrote to Mr. Flanigan to come and make the experiment,—we say experiment, because it was contended that coal had not enough of strength and consistency to be properly mined with a blast. That the explosion would not reach far enough, and loosen and detach a sufficient quantity to make the blast economical in mining.

In March of that year, Mr. Flanigan came on. The result of the experiment was a success. We may therefore chronicle the name of John Flanigan as the first man who ever bored a hole and applied the powder blast in the anthracite coal of Pennsylvania. An important era in the commencement of a trade that has become so immense in later years.

In August of the same year he returned to Milford in company with Samuel French, a step-son of John Smith, for the purpose of removing his family to Plymouth.

I am obliged to Mrs. Flanigan, who is still living

with one of her sons in Kingston, at a very advanced age, for an account of their journey from Milford to Plymouth.

She says, "that on the sixth of September, 1818, my husband, myself, and five children, in company with Samuel French and Henry Gabriel, set out for the Susquehanna. Our conveyance was a two-horse covered lumber wagon, in which myself and children and a few traps were deposited; the men walking. At the end of eleven of the longest days of my life, we landed at Abijah Smith's, in Plymouth. I bore up under the dreary journey, and preserved my courage pretty well, till we struck the log way, on the Easton and Wilkes-Barré turnpike, when I was forced to give vent to my feelings, and wept like a child. Had I but foreseen, before starting, the trials and misery of the long journey ahead, I should never have consented to have left my old home and friends."

Of this party, Henry Gabriel was one. He was a blacksmith, and made Plymouth his home and residence. He married respectably, and spent a long, laborious and useful life there. He was a man of integrity, and a most excellent and exemplary citizen. He accumulated some property, and died but a few years since, beloved and regretted by the whole of the community, in which he spent the greater part of his life.

Samuel French afterwards became one of the principal coal operators of Plymouth. He was engaged in the trade for several years, and at a time when the

20

profits arising from it, conducted in the most skilful and economical manner, would afford a living only. Mr. French, through much prudence and great industry, accumulated some property in coal lands, which have recently been sold by his family at a thousand dollars an acre.

He died some ten years since. He was a man very highly esteemed, and his conduct and manner of life most richly warranted it. Two of his sons are now business men of prominence in Plymouth. A daughter of his is the wife of Elijah C. Wadhams, Esq.

The annual average of the business of the Messrs. Smith, from 1808 down to 1820, was from six to eight ark loads, or about four to five hundred tons.

The old Susquehanna coal ark, like the mastodon, is a thing of the past. The present men of the business should understand the character of the simple vessel used by the pioneers of the trade. Its size and dimensions, cost and capacity, must be chronicled. And the difference between it and the present mode of transportation is as wide as the rough old grate of Jesse Fell—still to be seen—compared with the costly heating fixtures of the modern palace, of the modern coal prince.

The length of the craft was ninety feet, its width sixteen feet, its depth four feet, and its capacity sixty tons. Each end terminated in an acute angle, with a stem-post surmounted by a huge oar, some thirty feet in length, and which required the strength of two stout men to ply it in the water. It required, in its construction, three thousand eight hundred feet of two inch-plank for the bottom, ends and sides; or seven thousand six hundred feet, board measure. The bottom timbers would contain about two thousand feet, board measure, and the ribs or studs, sustaining the side planks, four hundred feet; making a total of some ten thousand feet.

The cost at that time for lumber was
$4.00 per M. $40.00
Construction, mechanical work. . . . 24.00
Running plank, oars, caulking material,
hawser (made of wood fibres), bailing
scoops, etc. 6.00
_____
Total cost. $70.00

The ark was navigated by four men, and the ordinary time to reach tide water was seven days. The cost attending the trip was about $50.00. Two out of three arks would probably reach the port of their destination; one-third was generally left upon the rocks in the rapids of the river or went to the bottom. The following estimate, therefore, of sixty tons of coal, laid down in market, is not far from the facts:

Cost of mining 60 tons. $45.00
Hauling to the river. 16.00
Cost of ark. 70.00
Expenses of navigation. 50.00
_____
Total. $181.00

or equal to $3.00 a ton. To this must be added one-third for the perils of navigation, which will make the actual cost of the ton at tide water, $4.00. Commissions on sales, transhipment from the ark to coasting vessels and other incidents, would probably make the whole outlay upon a ton, about five dollars.

The average price of sales at this time was probably $10.00, leaving a profit of $5.00 on the ton. If, therefore, three hundred and fifty tons of the five hundred annually transported by the Messrs. Smith reached the market, it left them a profit of seventeen hundred dollars, not taking into the account their personal services. ·

Eight hundred and fifty dollars each. A modern family would consider themselves in very straitened circumstances, if limited to this sum for their yearly support. Times have materially changed, it is true; but foolish and unnecessary wants have multiplied beyond all rules of propriety or necessity. These men lived comfortably and respectably upon the product of the business they were engaged in; and this did not sum up a thousand dollars annually to each. If the primitive days of our fathers did not spread their tables with unnecessary luxuries, or their wardrobe with tinselled tawdry decorations, they slept as soundly, enjoyed themselves as well, and were quite as happy as the most favored and wealthy of the present time; nay, a thousand times more so ; for their wants were few, and their ambition did not require curbs and fetters to prevent its "overleaping itself."

In this small way the coal trade continued on from 1807 to 1820, when it assumed more importance in the public estimation. The years preceding that of 1820, were the years of its trials, and the men during that period who were engaged in the business, were merely able to sustain themselves with the closest economy and the most persevering and unremitting labor. Some of the Plymouth men who embarked in the business, made total failures; and others encumbered their estates with debts which required subsequent years of labor to wipe out. It was the work of forty years to convince the people that "black stones" could be made available for fuel. The problem at this day is fully solved.

The following account current, rendered by Price & Waterbury, of New York, to Abijah Smith & Co., composed of Abijah and John Smith, in 1813, and furnished me by Mr. John B. Smith, is a remarkably interesting relic of the coal business in its infancy. It very clearly exhibits two facts: one, the demand, price and consumption of coal, in the great city of New York, at that period; and the other, the wonderful zeal manifested in the pioneer dealers to introduce the article into the market.

The coal was sent to Havre de Grace, Maryland, and thence by coasting vessels to New York.

"NEW YORK, February, 1813.
"Messrs. ABIJAH SMITH & Co.—Gentlemen: Having lately taken a view of the business we have been conducting for you this

sometime past, we have thought it would be gratifying to have the account forwarded, and therefore present you with a summary of it up to the eighteenth of January, 1813, containing, first, the quantity of coal sold and to whom; second, the amount of cash paid by us from time to time; third, the amount of interest, cash on the various sums advanced, the credit of interest on sums received, and lastly, the quantity of coal remaining on hand unsold. Should you, on the receipt of this, find any of the items incorrect, we need hardly observe that the knowledge of such an error will be corrected with the greatest pleasure. As it respects our future plan of procedure, we shall expect to see one of your concern in the city sometime in the spring, when a new arrangement may be fixed upon. Our endeavors to establish the character of the coal shall not at any time be wanting, and we calculate shortly to dispose of the remaining parcels of coal unsold.

1812.

June 8.—By cash of Doty & Willets for 5 chaldrons coal $100.00

By cash of John Withington for 5 chaldrons coal 100.00

By cash of Coulthaid & Son for 10 chaldrons coal.... .... 200.00

By John Benham's note (60 days) for 10 chaldrons coal.... ....; 200.00

By cash of G. P. Lorrillard for 1 chaldron coal   20.00

By cash of J. J. Wilson for 4 chaldrons coal....   80.00

June 13.—By cash of Doty & Willets for 5 chaldrons coal.. 100.00

By cash of G. P. Lorrillard for 11½ chaldrons coal.... .... 230.00

By A. Frazyer's note (90 days) for 25 chaldrons coal 475.00

By cash received of T. Coulthaid for 5 chaldrons coal 100.00

By M. Womas's note (90 days) for 20 chaldrons coal.... .... 380.00

By half measurement, received for 9 bushels....   6.33

June 13.—By B. Ward and T. Blagge for 1¼ chaldrons
at $20 .... 25.00
   By Wittingham for 1½ chaldrons coal 10.00
June 25.—By Pirpont for ½ chaldron coal 11.00
   By Mr. Lands for ½ chaldron coal 12.00
July 16.—By Robert Barney for 17½ chaldrons at $22
per chaldron 385.00
Sept. 15.—By cash for 1 chaldron coal 12.50
Oct. 9. —By William Colman for ½ chaldron coal 12.50
   By Sexton & Williamson for 1½ chaldrons coal 37.50
Oct. 24.—By cash for 1 chaldron coal 25.00
Oct. 29.—By cash for ½ chaldron coal 12.50
Nov. 7. —By cash for ½ chaldron coal 12.50
Nov. 12.—By cash for 1 chaldron coal 25.00
Nov. 16.—By Mr. A. Le Briton for 12 chaldrons at $25 per
chaldron 288.50
Dec. 5. —By cash for ½ chaldron coal 12.50
Dec. 11.—By cash of A. Daily for ½ chaldron coal 12.00
Dec. 14.—By cash for ½ chaldron coal 12.50
 1813.
Jan. 4. —By cash for 1 chaldron coal 25.00
Jan. 18.—By J. Curtiz for 9 bushels coal 6.27
   By amount of balance this day 763.12

     Total $3,691.20
Errors excepted.   PRICE & WATERBURY."

It will be seen by this account current that coal
was sold by the chaldron: thirty-six bushels, or
nearly a ton and a third, to the chaldron. The sales,
therefore, for the New York supply in 1812, were inside
of two hundred tons. Though the price was liberal,
about $15.00 a ton, most of the early coal operators
of Plymouth were unsuccessful. The risk attending

the navigation, and the system of barter and exchange of those days, instead of cash, were serious obstacles in the coal trade. And even at a later period, when the canal opened a new thoroughfare of transportation, the trade was not remunerative. The demand for the article was limited, and it required years of struggle to establish the cash in the place of the credit system.

Mr. Daniel Davenport embarked in the trade about the year 1826. He pursued the business for several years, but the result was the final loss of the greater part of his estate. Ziba Davenport also made the attempt, but with no better result. And to the unsuccessful catalogue of coal men may be added the names of Thomas Borbidge, Francis J. Smith, John Ingham, John Flanigan, and Martin Brenan.

At a later period, some of the merchants connecting the coal trade with their business, turned it to some account; but still down to 1840 the coal business in Plymouth could by no means be regarded a success. And with the exception of the Messrs. Smith, nearly all of the men engaged in the trade at its commencement, or immediately after, met with disasters.

The Smiths pursued the business steadily, with great economy and energy of purpose. These qualities, combined with the knowledge which they had gleaned from long experience, enabled them to live merely, but not to accumulate money. They held on to their

mines, which in subsequent years became very valua-able. The Messrs. Smith worked what is known as the great red ash seam, and which is thicker and the coal of a much better quality than the same seam on the east side of the river. On the east side of the river this seam crops out near the summit of the Wilkes-Barré mountain, and is not exceeding eight feet in thickness, while at the Smith mines, Avondale and Grand Tunnel, it averages twenty-six feet of pure coal. During the entire period that the Messrs. Smith worked this vein, some twenty years, and their successors a quarter of a century after them, the whole space cleared out has not reached ten acres.

Modern mining and modern facilities of transportation to market, and the demand are, of course, making deep inroads upon the red ash vein, and it is difficult to anticipate what the next quarter of a century will have produced in the extent of mining in this very valuable coal seam.

It is the underlying seam of the coal measures of the valley, and on the west side of the river by far the most valuable, because the largest. The John Smith part of the old mine is now owned by Mrs. William C. Reynolds, his daughter, and the Abijah Smith part, by his sons and the writer of this notice, and both under lease to Messrs. Broderick, Conygham and Walter.

Among the later coal men, I must not omit the name of Freeman Thomas. He came to Plymouth, from Northampton county, about the year 1811. He purchased the Avondale property. He gave it that name fifty years since. But when the old farmer conferred upon it this poetical cognomen, he was not aware of the vast mineral treasure which its surface concealed.

Mr. Thomas was in advance of most of his neighbors in his knowledge of coal measures. At an early day he commenced driving the " Grand Tunnel " into the mountain side, with the purpose of striking the coal. This was probably as early as 1828. This was the first experiment of tunneling in the Wyoming valley through rock. He labored on very assiduously for several years before the object was accomplished. His neighbors regarded the enterprise as utopian, but amidst all obstacles, and against the counsel and advice of his friends to abandon the tunnel, he moved steadily and persistently on; and after three or four years of persevering labor, and with his credit almost sunk, he struck the big red ash vein.

This experiment established a new theory, new at least in this valley. And the " Grand Tunnel," as its constructor named it, will long be remembered as one of the most expensive efforts of the early days of the coal pioneers, as also a monument to commemorate the name of the man whose sagacity and foresight were far in advance of his contemporaries. In the toiling years which he devoted to the excavation of the tunnel, he constantly encountered the opposition of his friends; and many of them failing in argument to convince him of what they called his error, would laugh at and deride him, as the last means of driving him from his fixed and determined purpose. But to all this he meekly submitted, still holding on to his own convictions, and finally proved to them all that the error was with them and not with himself.

Freeman Thomas lived to a good old age. He died in 1847, at his home in Northumberland county, in his eighty-eighth year. He left the valley for his new residence some ten years since. His children are still the owners of the "Grand Tunnel" property, and they also own an undivided interest in Avondale.

Not long after the construction of the "Grand Tunnel," Jameson Harvey discovered coal upon his premises near by. And these two coal properties being most eligible to the canal, were more extensively worked than any other mines in the township. William L. Lance became the lessee of the "Grand Tunnel" property in the year 1851. He carried on the business of mining and transporting coal from this mine for several years, and became otherwise very largely engaged in the trade.

But although I did not commence my sketches of Plymouth with a view of speaking of its present prosperity, and the vast business that is now done in coal operations, I must mention the fact that probably six thousand tons are now daily mined, prepared and shipped to market.

There is not in the whole coal field of the valley as much merchantable coal embraced in the same area as there is within the region of "Old Shawnee." It is a favored spot in the great basin; and the fact that every acre within the measures will readily find sale at a thousand dollars, is conclusive proof of the allegation.

When we compare the present trade (October, 1871), with the business in 1812, it strikes us with surprise. There are now in Plymouth fifteen breakers in active operation, yielding an aggregate of six thousand tons a day, and producing annually a million and a half of tons. The probability is, from present prospects, that this will be increased to two millions in the course of a couple of years, and the increase of production has not exceeded the increase of values. Coal lands upon the mountain side fifty years since were considered of no. account. While it was manifest that coal was present in large quantities, the fact of there being but a small demand, and no facilities of transportation, made the article a drug; and any one would have been deemed the fit subject for a mad-house and a straight-jacket who would have predicted the coal trade of Plymouth in 1871, at a million and a half of tons annually. The results have exceeded the anticipations of the most sanguine; and were Freeman Thomas alive at this day, he would find his air-built castles of forty years since more than reality. Men would laugh at his predictions, "that the man with a beard on his face," when he made them, "would live to see fifty thousand tons of coal shipped yearly from the Plymouth basin !" If the old gentleman had said fifty thousand weekly, he would have approached more nearly the result. But his estimate of "fifty thousand tons yearly," lost him the confidence of his neighbors, and they concluded, and so whispered among themselves, that "the man's mind was waning, and that it was a pity it was so."

The men who condemned the sagacity and foresight of Freeman Thomas, lived, many of them, to see the most extravagant of his speculations far exceeded by the results. He was a man of much reflection, and he made the coal measures his study; and while by his expenditures he encumbered his estate, he lived to realize the fact that all his theories had become fixed realities, and he could well afford, therefore, in the day of his prosperity, to retort upon those who had suggested that his mind was "waning" and his judgment was at fault.

Mr. Thomas was a man of placid and even temper, kind, hospitable, and generous to a fault. The likeness we present of him was taken at seventy-one, and while not so perfect as it should be, still shows the resemblance and features of the man.

I made every effort to procure a likeness of Abijah Smith, but he died before photographing became a science, and there is no painting representing him to be had.   It would have been exceedingly gratifying, if the face of this man, who was pre-eminently, the pioneer in the coal trade, could have been preserved to us.

That a member of his family should be placed in my gallery, I thought proper: and therefore I procured the consent of his son, John B. Smith, and who very much resembles his father, to consent that I might introduce his photographic likeness.

CHAPTER XVI.

EARLY PHYSICIANS—MORSE, MORELAND, CHAMBERLIN, GAYLORD.

THE first settlers of the town did not require the attendance of the doctor as frequently as their descendants.   They were but little accustomed to that luxurious course of life which is pretty sure to be followed by severe pains and penalties.   They lived upon plain fare, and their hours of labor and rest were regular:—they therefore did not have much occasion for medicine.   Every garret was an herbarium in itself, and carefully supplied with medicinal plants and roots—catnip, balsam, elderberries, pennyroyal, hemlock; and the whole family of roots and herbs were methodically arranged, tied up in bunches, and suspended from the rafters, and the matron of

the establishment pretty well understood how to prepare, apply, and administer them. It was a part of her education, and she took pride in this branch of knowledge. Apothecary shops did not, in those days, occupy the corner of every cross-road. The consequence was, that under this system, health was the general rule, and disease the incident. Modern custom and habit have reversed it.

Dr. William Hooker Smith, though not a resident of the town, was the earliest practitioner of medicine in it. He was the only physician of note of the whole valley, in the first settlement of Westmoreland; and the limits of his circuit extended throughout its broad territory. He has left behind him the fame and renown of a most skilful surgeon and able physician. The old settlers of the valley were all accustomed to speak of this man with great respect. He was, undoubtedly, a man of learning in his profession, and entertained the public confidence to a wonderful degree. With such a man within a reasonable distance, there was but little occasion for local doctors.

I do not learn that until in the beginning of the century, that Plymouth had an established resident physician. My own memory and observation go back nearly sixty years: at that time the physician was Dr. Anna Morse, a stout, waddling old lady of two hundred pounds avoirdupois, with a green medicine bag pendant from her girdle, on one side, and the keys of

the tap-room on the other. This was the same lady
known as Mrs. Heath, of early times, and who was
permitted to leave her house stand within the boundaries of "the commonfield," provided that she put
a fence about it. The house is still standing in jux-
taposition with the old rough barked elm, upon Ant
Hill, a sketch of which appears in the back-ground
of the elm-tree photograph, and a modern coal-breaker
on the right of the picture. It may possibly have
been enlarged since the time of holding "ye meeting
on ye twenty-fourth March, 1786," at which Colonel
John Franklin appeared as moderator, and Jonah
Rogers, "clark." But the old two-story double
frame house, was an old house when I first knew it,
and Mrs. Doctor Morse was then the tenant and owner.
Her first husband was Thomas Heath, the "town
key-keeper," and grand juror, elected at the town
meeting of Westmoreland, held "ye second March,
1774," and but five years after the first settlement of
the town.

At the time I speak of, Anna Morse, as an M. D.,
she had survived her second husband, and the old
double-framed house was a licensed tavern. Before
it creaked, on rusty hinges, a capacious sign-board, on
which were painted in bold characters:—"Entertain-
ment for Man and Horse!" The north-east room, on
the first floor, contained the chest of drawers wherein
were deposited the mysterious cures for all diseases.

I have an occasion to remember the treatment of

Dr. Morse; for when a child I was a patient of hers, and I distinctly remember listening to the conversation upon her first visit, when the question was discussed, in a low voice, whether the prescription should be "a hemlock sweat, or a dose of calomel and jallop." These were her invariable prescriptions, both for old and young, as well as for all diseases. The scale of occult science (to me at least), preponderated in favor of calomel and jallop; and holding in remembrance the nauseating taste, I have never been able to be reconciled to the appearance of a green bag, for from one of this kind the dose was taken. As a member of the bar, I never carried one. I could not abide it.

Dr. Morse continued on for several years in the double capacity of the healing art, and vending liquor by the gill and half-gill. In these times liquor was bought by the measure ; the bottle was never set before the customer, to drink according to his pleasure. In fact the old custom of selling by the gill and half-gill was not abrogated till within the last forty years. A bold landlord was he, who first introduced the habit of placing a full decanter before his customer.

After the decease of Mrs. Morse, Dr. Moreland, an old gentleman, resided a couple of years or so, in the town. This was probably about the years 1814 and 1815. He left, and was succeeded by Dr. Ebenezer Chamberlin, in the year 1816. He was born in

21

Swanzey, Cheshire county, New Hampshire, December first, 1790, and was the practising physician of the town, from the time of his immigration to his death, which occurred April twelfth, 1866.

An effort upon my part to give a biographical sketch of the doctor, I fear, will be abortive; and yet, probably, no one has more of the material at hand with which to do it.

He was a man of good common sense; but his propensity to turn everything which he touched into ridicule, was a governing passion. As a physician, he was careful and prudent; and his long practice, united with his observation of the numerous cases which fell into his hands, made him ordinarily proficient. He might be classed as a very respectable physician: he made no pretensions to surgery. A redeeming feature of the man was his perfect willingness to listen to the counsel and advice of a consulting brother: a somewhat rare virtue with the craft generally.

He was an eccentric man, and the fund of his anecdote was inexhaustible. The greater part of his abundant stock, and always on hand ready for delivery, will not bear repetition. He was not remarkably choice in his selections. He was an original, and I have never met with an individual who so thoroughly blended sense and nonsense together; and yet there was a vein of cleverness throughout his conversation. Before you reached the point of condemning an out-of-place expression, he would convulse you with laughter with an unexpected hit, the embodiment of wit and sarcasm.

As he was for fifty years the town physician, and known to everybody, great and small in it, it will not, I hope, be amiss to write out a few personalities of this unusual character.

It was during the time that Charles C. Curtis kept the public school in the old Academy, that a Saturday afternoon would be occasionally assigned for what was called a "manners school." On these occasions the friends and patrons of the school would be invited to participate: there would be lectures on proper and becoming behavior—suggestions as to polite conduct, and now and then there would be short dramatic entertainments and colloquies—all having in view the lesson of civility and gentlemanly and womanly deportment.

To give an impression of the clown, he must needs be exhibited. And this part was always assigned to the doctor. Without him the *role* would have been incomplete, and he acted it out to life.

His grimaces, and blunders, and vulgar attitudes, actions and expressions, were life-like models, and the then, young doctor would bring down the hearty applause of the house.

His observation of men and things was scrutinizing, and his conclusions were correct, but he had an odd way of illustration.

Having in a measure lost the run of affairs in my

native town, meeting the doctor, I inquired of him how matters were progressing there? "Progressing," he replied, "I will tell you how things are progressing. Only a few years ago, Calvin Wadhams, Benjamin Reynolds and Joseph Wright wore boots on Sundays; and now only think of it, the Rumseys wear boots every day in the week!"

A few years after he came to the town, he became religious and joined one of the churches. I was upon the bank of the stream at his immersion. He had a dispute with the minister (Elder Rogers, I think it was), while in the water, about the necessary depth where the sacrament should be performed. It was finally compromised at "a depth of water reaching the lowest button on his vest." At the conclusion of the ceremony, as he came dripping out of the stream, with a strong shake of the shoulders, he repeated in a loud voice, "This is glory enough for one day."

I am obliged to say, however, that he did not make a shining light in the church.

To illustrate this ruling passion which he had of the ludicrous, when upon his death bed, he was asked the question, "how he felt with the approach of death so near at hand?" He replied, "that he was entirely contented. That since his sickness began, and which would probably be his last, he had carefully reviewed the whole subject of the past, and carefully contemplating the future, the result of his conclusion was, that he had lived over forty years of his life in Shawnee, and had passed through the long time manfully, and he was now prepared for the worst; but did not anticipate, that under any state of circumstances, he could be placed in a more unfavorable position!"

But while the doctor had a rough exterior, and would make enemies by the severity of his criticisms and remarks, he was a kind-hearted, generous man, and the last one in the world to entertain or cause a feeling of malevolence. At the cost, however, of relaxing the bonds of friendship, he could not refrain from the perpetration of a joke. His gibes, however, were entirely harmless, and with those who knew him well, they were always forgiven.

He was commissioner of the county for three years, and held for a long time the commission of Justice of the Peace. He never possessed the faculty of accumulating property, and the consequence was that he died poor; but there was no citizen of Plymouth who did not feel that in Dr. Chamberlin's death, there passed from the stage a man of generous impulses, and one who would not knowingly do a wrong.

Dr. Charles E. Gaylord, father of the worthy gentleman of that name, still residing in the town, and in the enjoyment of a liberal fortune, the result of his own careful industry, can hardly be classed among the physicians of the town.

Dr. Gaylord was an eminent physician. He was the son of one of the original "Forty" who first planted the advanced standard of civilization on the wilderness frontier, in 1768. And there were none of that gallant and persevering band who suffered more in the toils, and exposures, and battles, than this family. Three of them were in Captain Ransom's company, in the Revolutionary war, and another fell in the Wyoming massacre.

The father of Dr. Gaylord gave him a liberal course of study, and he graduated at an early day, in one of the medical colleges of Connecticut. He settled in Huntington, in this county, where he spent a long life in a laborious practice. He had an excellent reputation as a physician and surgeon. In the latter part of his life he came to Plymouth, and resided with his son to the time of his death, which was on the fourth day of February, 1839. While resident in Plymouth, he would occasionally be called on, in cases of consultation. He did not, however, pretend to practice to any extent in Plymouth. I remember him well, but at a time when he had become debilitated by the infirmities of age. He was a man very highly respected for his social virtues, and lived to a good old age.

Dr. Charles E. Gaylord was one of the ablest physicians of the territory of old Westmoreland.

It was common to see the physicians of the adjoining towns, in Plymouth, upon professional calls, forty years since. Doctors Baldwin, Whitney, Crary, Covels—father and son; Atkins, Chrissey, J. J. Wright, Miner, Jones, all distinguished men: and all

RESIDENCE OF HENDERSON GAYLORD.

save Dr. Wright, who is now the oldest surgeon in commission of the United States army, have paid the great, last debt of nature, and their names even have almost become forgotten.

CHAPTER XVII.

EARLY PREACHERS—ROGERS, LEWIS, LANE, PEARCE, PECK.

HAVING already spoken of Noah Wadhams and Benjamin Bidlack, the two pioneers of the gospel of the town, I come now to the consideration of the state of the church, the different creeds, and the men who respectively supported them, after the conclusion of the two wars through which our people had passed.

Before the erection of the old Academy, the second floor of which was dedicated exclusively to religious meetings, and a common place of worship for all religious sects, services were conducted in private dwellings, school-houses, and sometimes in barns. The old stone-house in the lower part of the town, now occupied by Mrs. French, but in early days by the Colemans and the Hodges, was a very frequent place of meeting. Tradition informs us that Mr. Bidlack and Anning Owen, preached in this house very frequently. Both of these men were preachers of the Methodist faith.   Noah Wadhams would hold his meetings at his own house on the back road, and in the school-house upon " the Commonfield."   He was a Congregationalist, and previous to 1800, this order of people was largely in the ascendant, in point of numbers.

Not far from this time, Elder Joel Rogers, brother to Jonah, who has been frequently mentioned in our reminiscences of the town, hoisted the Baptist flag, and continued for many years to act in the capacity of a preacher.   He was joined by Elder Griffin Lewis a few years later.

Mr. Lewis resided in that part of Plymouth now called Jackson.   These two men were at the head of the Baptist part of the population.   They were both excellent and exemplary men ; and while neither of them could claim any pretensions to what is called pulpit oratory, they nevertheless might be classed as solid, sensible men, and preached solid, sensible doctrines.

When I first knew them, they were both past middle age.   They were of the old school of divines, who were governed by the idea that the sanctity of their lives, their exemplary conduct, their weekly discourses, and the importance of their mission, furnished a sufficient guarantee of success.   Progress in church, however, as well as in state, was steadily weaving a web of a different texture.   The agitating policy which had upturned the foundations of a government, was not limited to temporal affairs alone.   The spirit of the country was becoming changed: old customs were giving place to new ones;—and in the spiritual field, if the multitude would not come to the sanctuary, for religious instruction, the doctrines of the church must be carried to the hearth-stone and domicile of the indifferent and the heedless.

The Revolutionary ideas brought into the field a new class of competitors. Under the banner of Methodism, they were literally scouring the highways and by-ways, the lanes and alleys, and *forcing* the doctrines of the cross upon men who might have heard of the Christian religion, but to whom its necessities were a sealed book. This system of persevering labor and untiring energy was a controlling element of the primitive Methodists, and the old system of managing and conducting spiritual affairs must needs yield to the new order of things, in the hands of young and determined men.

The matter may be pretty well illustrated by the comparison of the speed of the old stage-coach with the locomotive—Napoleon with the Bourbons and the old dynasties of Europe.

The Methodist clergy were generally young, athletic and vigorous men. They had the power of endurance. They devoted their whole time to their calling, week days as well as Sundays. They travelled upon horseback in sunshine and storm; their clothing, which was not much, to be sure, they carried in their portmanteaus; and if they could not get enough food to allay their appetites where night overtook them, they went hungry.   Like the crusader of the Thirteenth Century, with staff in hand, his eyes fixed on the Holy Sepulchre, and his mind chafed to fury at the wrongs of the infidel Saracen; on they went, over bog and mire, over mountains accessible by a bridle-path only, and over streams without bridges; through snows and hurricanes, despising all obstacles and disregarding all perils, so that they planted their flag upon the embattled walls of the enemy's castle.

They were types literally of the Apostles, and whose acts they strove to imitate; and therefore they moved on, having "no scrip, no bread, no money in their purse."   Devoted and self-sacrificing, they would do a thousand times more severe labor for a yearly compensation of fifty dollars, than men like Beecher and Frothingham, of the present day, with a salary of twenty thousand.   With a firm grasp on the handles of their big subsoil, spiritual plow, they plunged through roots and stumps and rocks, through quicksands and hard-pan.   They prepared and sowed the field, and laughed and rejoiced at its product of an "hundred-fold."

With the manifestation of all this zeal and determined progress, there would be, of course, now and then an act of indiscretion.

At a quarterly meeting, held in the old Academy, somewhere about fifty years ago, one of the preachers declared from the pulpit, "that on the death of a Plymouth sinner, Satan would hold a grand jubilee, and throw wide open the gates of his dominion, and exclaim, at the top of his voice, 'clear the way, rejoice now, brethren, for here comes one of my beloved subjects from Shawnee.'"

I shall not repeat the name of the author of this threat; he was a venerable man, and in years after he died full of honors, and left a name of renown throughout the valley. To this language some of the people took umbrage; but they were mostly of the class who were down upon the men who were daily thinning the ranks of their wayward associates. The liberal, sensible part of the community. concluded that religious zeal was entitled to a clever margin; and like sensible men came down to the stubborn fact, that there was no more severity of punishment for a "Shawnee sinner" than for a sinner of any other locality. The doggerel rhymes, therefore, which the expression provoked, and which were designed to slap the Methodist church full in the face, did not long survive; and a twelvemonth cleared up the murky spiritual atmosphere.

The activity and energy displayed by this class of men, formed and fashioned anew the habits and disposition of the people. The man driven to his house from felling the forest trees, preparatory for his new ground crop, by severe cold, or heat, or storm, peering through his window at the Methodist minister, in his white hat and blue surtout coat, galloping ahead upon his horse, would conclude that he also was alike able to resist the elements, and would resume his labor. In this way men became accustomed to walk faster, talk faster, decide quicker, and work harder; and many has been the rough field whose ledges, inequalities and declivities would not have been reclaimed and cultivated for years but for the go-ahead example of the man in the white hat and blue surtout. His zeal gave a new impulse in temporal, as well as spiritual matters.

Under these influences the old Congregational establishment soon gave way. It could no more stand up against them, than the French squares at Waterloo, could resist the dashing charges of the Scotch Highlanders. The Baptists contested the ground, and while they maintained a respectable position in point of numbers, they were nevertheless far behind the Methodists. Several years later the Christian church attained a foothold in the town, which it still maintains, and has a very respectable congregation. The Baptist church finally became nearly extinguished, until more recently renewed by the Welsh immigration into the town.

Of the earlier Methodist preachers, some of them were of decided talents. Without disparagement to others, I name particularly George Lane, Marmaduke Pearce, and Dr. George Peck, with each of whom I was well acquainted, and who were on the

REV. GEORGE LANE.

Plymouth circuit before I removed from the town to Wilkes-Barré, which was in 1824.

Mr. Lane was assigned to what was known as the Wyoming circuit, in the year 1809. This included Plymouth. Gideon Draper, a man of whom the people of early times spoke in the highest praise, and who was reputed as an orator of unusual power, was associated with him as presiding elder.

Mr. Lane was a stout, thick-set, firmly-built man, of medium height, blue eyes, and fair complexion. He possessed a well-disciplined mind; his ideas were expressed in forcible language, and when warmed up with the excitement produced by his subject, he would deeply enlist the feelings of his audience. His method and manner were both agreeable and pleasant, and his argument was always the result of careful thought and, apparently, laborious research. His mind was thoroughly disciplined, and he possessed many of the elements of genuine oratory. He married a daughter of Elisha Harvey, and as has already been stated, was engaged in mercantile pursuits in Plymouth and Wilkes-Barré. The occupation, however, did not comport with his ideas of his duty, and after a few years he abandoned it and returned to his church, in the service of which he ended his days. He ever maintained a high standing among his people, and for many years was entrusted with the management of their large " Book Concern," located in New York; a position not merely of responsibility, in a financial point of view, but also requiring literary qualifications.

As Mr. Lane was many years a resident of our town, and married there, he may be considered a Plymouth man. He died in Wilkes-Barré, in the year 1858. Two of his sons survive him—Harvey B. Lane, a merchant of New York, and Charles A Lane, a citizen of Wilkes-Barré.

Marmaduke Pearce, father of the author of the "Annals of Luzerne," and the present postmaster of the city of Wilkes-Barré, came on to the Plymouth circuit in 1815. He was continued in the capacity of presiding elder and preacher, on that circuit, for some eight or ten years. He was an immense man, physically; about six feet in height, and weighing, in ordinary health, three hundred pounds. He had a well-developed head, fair complexion, and gray eyes. He was born in Chester county, in this state, August eighteenth, 1776—his father's farm and residence being upon the famous Paoli battle-ground, of revolutionary fame. A brother of Mr. Pearce—Cromwell—was Colonel of the sixteenth U. S. Infantry in the war of 1812, and was in some of the engagements on the Canadian frontier.

As a preacher, Mr. Pearce was the embodiment of sound common sense. Reason and logic were the weapons which he employed. His sermons did not generally exceed thirty minutes, but in that period, by reason of his unusual powers of condensation, he would say as much as most men in double that time. He seldom became excited, but in a cool and deliberate manner, would hold his audience at his will; because his sermons were the product of a strong intellect, abounding in the illustrations of practical life, plain and sound, but devoid of what is commonly understood, as oratorical flourish. He died at Berwick, Columbia county, Pa., in 1852, in his seventy-sixth year.

Dr. George Peck, a venerable man, still living, and still in the service of his church, in which he has been an exemplary ornament and shining light for more than half a century, made his debut in the old Academy of Plymouth, in 1818. I say debut, but probably this may not have been the theatre of his first efforts, but however, not far from the first. He was frequently after that assigned to the Wyoming circuit, in the capacity of presiding elder and preacher, and having married his wife in Kingston, an adjoining town, we may almost claim him as a Plymouth man. He preached there, at different times, through a term of several years.

I have a distinct and vivid recollection of the man from the commencement of his ministry in Plymouth. Of a tall and commanding figure, a countenance showing a high order of intelligence, a clear and distinct utterance, a fine flow of language, with a capacity of analysis, he, of course, would not only attract, but entertain an audience. The announcement of his name, though then comparatively a youth, would always bring out the people.

His style, at this remote period, was of the fervid and nervous order of oratory. His sermons were excellent specimens of this class. I have not heard him of late years; probably age and long practice have toned him down.

I remember now, though more than fifty years ago, with their cares and anxieties intervening, the substance of a sermon I heard him deliver in the old Academy. The text involved the relation between parent and child; and the impression made upon my mind, is still fresh and unimpaired. From memory alone I am able to repeat the text.

I would like to say more of Dr. Peck, and speak of him as he deserves; but it is of the memory of those who have gone that I am writing, and not of the living.

The biography of the living is out of place; for opinions are restrained, and besides, our motive may be the subject of criticism.

At a later period, the Rev. Cyrus Gildersleeve, pastor of the Presbyterian church, Wilkes-Barré, and Doctor James May, of the Episcopal church of the same place, preached occasionally in Plymouth. This extended over a period of probably ten years, commencing about 1824.

CHAPTER XVIII.

OLD FAMILIES.—THE BIDLACKS.

AMONG the earliest of the Plymouth settlers, though not of the first, was Captain James Bidlack. He came from Windham, Connecticut, with his family, in 1777, and built for himself a log house on Garrison Hill. At this time all the residences were clustered in a group at this place, and until after the ice-flood of 1784, there were no buildings elsewhere within the certified lines of the old township, unless on the east side of Ross Hill. Captain Bidlack had three sons—James, Benjamin and Shubal. James, as has already been stated, commanded the company made up of men from lower Wilkes-Barré, and was stationed upon Colonel Zebulon Butler's right wing at the battle of Wyoming, and being wounded, was captured and inhumanly tortured in the burning flames of Fort Wintermoot. The life of Benjamin was an eventful one.

After the house of Captain Bidlack was swept away in the great flood, he erected a small log house on a lot adjoining the Wright homestead farm, where he resided for several years, and at the time of his death. During the time he lived on Garrison Hill, March twenty-first, 1779, on returning home from Wilkes-Barré, he was captured by the Indians, not far from his house. He and the elder Jonah Rogers

were on horseback.   Upon the attack of the Indians,
they put spurs to their horses, and Rogers made his
escape; but the saddle-girth of the captain giving
way, he was thrown from his horse and taken prisoner.

The Indians took him to Canada.   In some way
he obtained his release, and in the following autumn
we find him at the town meeting.   Whether his release was effected by an exchange, or by other means,
we are not informed.   Subsequent to this period, there
is no further mention of the name of Captain Bidlack, nor am I able to ascertain when he died.   He
was a man past middle life when he came to the
valley.

His son Benjamin became one of the prominent
and leading men of the township of Westmoreland.
He enlisted at the commencement of the Revolutionary
war, and served throughout the contest.   His name
does not appear upon the rolls of Durkee's or Ransom's companies.   He probably was among the volunteers of Wisner or Strong;—these men were recruiting in Westmoreland before the two independent
companies were raised.   He was at Boston when
Washington took charge of the patriot army to op-
pose General Gage.   He was at Trenton on the taking of the Hessians; he was at Yorktown on the occasion of the surrender of Cornwallis, and was in
Washington's camp, at Newburg, when the army
was disbanded.

During the Pennamite and Yankee conflict, he was arrested and lodged in the Sunbury jail. He escaped from his prison, under laughable circumstances.

He was a remarkably good singer. The camp is a good school to develop this faculty. I had occasion, frequently, to visit our military encampments during the late rebellion, and it seemed as though almost every soldier had acquired the capacity of song singing, and very many of them became very clever in this particular.

Mr. Bidlack, in the later years of his life, would dwell with a great deal of satisfaction upon the vocal music of the men of the Revolutionary army. He had assisted in erecting the "Temple of Liberty" at Newburg, and the singing which he had there listened to, and in which he had joined, lingered upon his memory. The great battle had been fought and won, and many of the soldiers' songs were commemorative of this event. There was reason for the deep impression it seems to have made upon him. In speaking to a friend of the songs in the "Temple of Liberty," he remarked: "I never heard such singing in my life. Some of the officers from New England were trained singers, and many of the men could sing well, and they made the temple ring with sweet and powerful melody."

In his confinement at the Sunbury jail, his songs led the people to collect about the grated window of his cell. And in the evening, men, women and children would gather there to listen to the Yankee's songs. They finally prevailed upon the jailer to let the man out, who had afforded them so much pleasure, that they might see him.

And thus many a pleasant evening was spent in mirth, song and laughter. Upon one of these occasions, in singing a song called "The Swaggering Man," he told his audience that to give them a proper appreciation of the character he was representing, they must give him a cane, and make room for him, as he could not do his subject justice otherwise. They furnished him a cane, and cried out, "Give him room, make way, let him have a fair chance." The prisoner, after taking a drink, and passing backwards and forwards several times, acting out the character of a drunken man, to the infinite amusement of his audience, and suiting the action to the word, when he came to the chorus, "Here goes the old swaggering man," he bounded from them like a wild deer. Pursuit was in vain, "the swaggering man" was too fleet of foot and strong of limb for the pack at his heels. They could not overtake the quarry; and the dawn of day found him thirty miles from his prison door; and before sunset, he rejoined his family in his log house in Plymouth. For a more particular account of this incident, I refer the reader to Dr. Peck's History.

At this period of his life, Mr. Bidlack seems to

have been addicted to habits of intemperance. The army is a poor school for temperance. Many, very many grains of allowance are to be made for the poor soldier, amid the hardships and exposures of the camp. This vice, however, he had the courage and decision to cast off, after he had assumed the ranks of civil life. He reformed, became a religious man, joined the Methodist church, and devoted the remainder of his days to preaching the Gospel. For the last ten years of his life, he was placed upon the "superannuated list," but so long as he was able to travel the circuit, he labored zealously in the cause.

He was present at the remarkable discussion among the officers of the army, in Newburg, in 1783, previous to the disbanding of the troops. It was an occasion of unusual excitement. The officers and men had received their pay in Continental bills: they were worthless. They were about to be discharged and sent to their homes in poverty. Congress had no money nor credit. The situation became one of fear and alarm. The celebrated anonymous letters, said to have been written by General Armstrong, were circulated in the camp. These fanned the flame of discord, and but for the firm stand taken by Washington, the probabilities are, that the glorious fruits of the rebellion would have been destroyed. The conduct of this great captain and noble patriot was never reflected in brighter colors, than upon this memorable occasion. The name alone of Washington caused

the veteran soldier to lay down his arms; his veneration for his great leader made him submit to want
and destitution, and forego the righteous claims he
had upon his country for his severe labor. These letters were drawn with exceeding ability, and appealing
to the men to take care of themselves before their
arms were taken from them, and they disbanded, and
sent hungry and naked to their unprovided homes
and helpless families.

In their debates the officers spoke in their uni-
forms, with their swords by their sides. On one occasion one of them, laying his hand upon the hilt of
his sword, demanded with great vehemence: " Gentlemen, are you prepared to give up these swords, which
have procured freedom for the country, and for yourselves glory and renown ? Can you retire to your farms
or shops, and ingloriously abandon the profession of
arms ? Will you not rather spill your heart's blood
in defence of rights which have been so dearly bought
in the camp and upon the field of battle ?"

But the genius of Washington was equal to the
crisis. It was his noble example and boundless influence that quieted the storm, and subdued the fearful
and threatening commotion.

The arguments pro and con which were made in
this celebrated council, Mr. Bidlack had treasured up
in his memory, and when the old man would repeat
them, in his declining days, as he was very frequently
in the habit of doing, he would become animated, and

often eloquently emphasizing his periods, by bringing his staff down upon the ground with force. He would generally wind up his rehearsal with a benediction on Washington. And never was mortal man worshipped with more sincerity than he by his soldiers.

I was intimately acquainted with a large number of these venerable patriots. I attended their meeting, in the court-house in Wilkes-Barré, in 1832, where they were invited for the purpose of preparing their pension applications. I made out several of them. A pension application without the name of Washington embodied in it, they would look upon with suspicion. Time and time again I have introduced the name in their papers merely as a gratification to them. They were never tired of speaking of "Our Washington," as they endearingly called him; and they would give him the whole credit of achieving American Independence, reserving none whatever to themselves.

A large number of these old veterans met in Wilkes-Barré on a fourth of July, probably about 1830. There may have been some thirty of them. The Rev. Benjamin Bidlack was their orator. The old gentleman was then straight and erect, and moved off at the head of his column with a firm step and martial bearing. They marched after the drum and fife to the old meeting-house upon the square, a large crowd following after.

The occasion seemed to have invigorated their

venerable orator. He made a powerful impression upon his compatriots in arms, as well as upon the dense mass of spectators. He was a tall man, six feet in height; he had a bass voice, though well modulated, and his delivery was graceful, and his manner earnest. The prevailing feature of this speech was that the Providence of God marked every feature of the eventful struggle of the Revolution, and that Washington was his viceroy on earth, and the instrument of his will.

His description of the cannonading of the British fortifications at Yorktown was well drawn, and delivered with great effect.

"For fourteen days and nights," said he, "there was one continual thunder and blaze. At night it was so light that you could see to pick up a pin. A white flag was raised from the British breastworks, and the firing ceased. Cornwallis proposed to leave the ground with the honors of war, with colors flying, and to embark his army on the English ships in the nearest harbor. 'No,' was the answer, and the parley closed. 'Now,' said Washington, 'give it to them hotter than ever,' and sure enough the storm of the battle raged more terribly than ever. They soon came to terms, and the heart of the war was broken."

Language like this, from the mouth of one of the actors in the terrible scene, and addressed with all the fervor and power of youth, to the scarred and hoary veterans before him, many of them too who had taken a part in the decisive victory, went with a thrill to the very centre of the heart!

When the old patriot, with hands and eyes elevated to Heaven, and in his deep, sonorous, and pathetic voice, invoked the blessings of God upon the spirit of Washington, and upon the band of noble veterans, covered with honorable scars, and bent with years of hard service, assembled before him; big tears coursed down the deep furrows of his broad and manly face, and they wept like children. There was not a dry eye upon the thousand up-turned faces there present.

The old man's utterance failed him to pronounce a benediction, and he and his revolutionary comrades separated in silence and tears.

A feeling of conscious pride flitted over my mind at the conclusion of that day's business, that old Shawnee had won the garland of honors in the person of one of her pioneers. Eloquence and patriotism had clasped hands, and the people wept for joy.

Mr. Bidlack removed from Plymouth to Kingston, where he closed his days. He died on the twenty-seventh of November, 1845, in the eighty-seventh year of his age. During the last few years of his life he had become imbecile in mind, and died from the effects of a cancer upon his nose.

By his second marriage he had one son, Benjamin A., who was a representative from this district both in the State and National Legislatures. He was also appointed, under Polk's administration, to the mission at Bogota, Central America, where he died in 1847.

Shubal, the remaining one of the three sons of Captain James Bidlack, settled in Salem, after the family separated in Plymouth. Some of his descendants still reside there. Dr. Peck, in speaking of the Bidlacks, says: "They were a family of patriots—were all tall, large-boned, powerful men, and good soldiers."

I have already referred to the incident of the Bidlack mansion having been swept away by the great flood, with Benjamin in it. The name in Plymouth has become extinct, but seventy years ago it was prominent, and stood out in bold relief; it was a part of the historical feature of many a well-fought battlefield in the great revolutionary struggle.

CHAPTER XIX.

OLD FAMILIES, CONTINUED—REYNOLDS—NESBITTS—
WADHAMS—DAVENPORTS—VAN-LOONS—PRINGLES—
TURNERS—ATHERTONS—CASES—LAMEROUX.

I SHALL conclude my historical sketches with a short biographical notice of a few of the early settlers, who were not so closely connected with the trials, sufferings, and exposures, as those who have been already alluded to. Some of them came to the

valley at a very early period of its settlement, and returned to Connecticut, where they remained until
the troubles terminated; others emigrated to the
town several years afterwards. But inasmuch as
some of them shared in many of the hardships, and
others were of the principal families of the town,
though making their home there at a later period, it
is proper that they be noticed.

The Reynolds family may be classed among the
pioneers of the town. David, the ancestor, came
from Litchfield, Connecticut, under the auspices of
the Susquehanna Company, not long after the first
immigration to the town. He was one of the forty
adventurers assigned by the company for Plymouth,
though he did not reach the valley till the year 1770.
This would make the commencement of his residence
two years later than the arrival of the first settlers.
His father—William—came out with him, with the
view of seeing his son located in his new home, and
was in the habit of occasionally visiting his son, and
died while on one of these visits to him, and was
buried in the graveyard upon his son's premises.

David selected the farm now owned by the family,
and upon which stands the Nottingham coal-breaker.
He erected a log house a few rods east of the shaft.
Soon after the commencement of the Pennamite and
Yankee war, his house, with his other buildings, were
destroyed by fire—the work of Indians or his Pennamite enemies. He fled with his family to the fort

at Wilkes-Barré, and a short time after, made his way back to Litchfield. A very fortunate thing for him, probably, as it may have saved him from the fate of his friends and neighbors at the Wyoming massacre.

At the close of the Revolutionary war, he again returned to his possessions. But he still found war raging in the valley. This was about 1784. His stay was short—as he, with the other settlers under the Connecticut claim, were driven from the valley by the order and decree of Patterson, the civil magistrate, (?) under the Pennsylvania authorities, stationed at Wilkes-Barré. During this exodus, one of his children was born in the wilderness, between the Susquehanna and the Delaware. David did not return with the fugitives; he continued on his journey to his father's, in Litchfield.

When the domestic broils had become in a measure quieted, he came back, erected a house on the same site now occupied by the family mansion, where he remained to the time of his death, which occurred on the eighth of July, 1816.

I have a distinct recollection of the old man, though I was but eight years of age when he died. In the last few years of his life, he became totally blind. From this misfortune he never recovered.

The only members of David's family, within my recollection, were Benjamin and Joseph. There were others. Joseph resided for many years, and died, in that part of Plymouth now Jackson. Benjamin remained upon the homestead farm during his long and industrious life. He died in 1854, in the seventy-fourth year of his age. As he was one of the representative and substantial men of Plymouth for a half century or more, it is appropriate that I should notice him more particularly. He was a stout, square-built man, five feet eight or ten inches in height, light brown hair, and dark eyes. Inclined to corpulency, but very active. He had a pleasant and agreeable manner, and a character for much benevolence.

Fifty years ago, when political excitement ran high, he and Noah Wadhams and Stephen Van Loon were the active political men of the town. They were of the Jefferson school in politics, and strongly attached to that side of the question. But while they strongly adhered to their opinions, and were thoroughly convinced of their correctness, neither of them permitted their party opinions to affect their social relations.

Stephen Van Loon was elected sheriff in 1816, soon after the war, and when political affairs were conducted with much feeling. The boys even, of those days, wore the black and tri-colored cockades as the badges of the Federal and Republican parties.

Mr. Reynolds was also elected sheriff of the county in 1831. I had just been admitted to the bar, and though a mere novitiate in the law, he did me the kindness to name me as his legal adviser.

This was an introduction to the business of the profession ; it created, upon my part, an attachment to the man which ended only in his death.

He was a man of great industry; up with the sun and astir with his men upon the farm, he did not know what it was to be idle. He was a pleasant and agreeable man in his intercourse with his neighbors, and remarkably kind and indulgent to those dependent upon him. He reared a large and highly respectable family, and gave all his children a good common school education. It may be said that Benjamin Reynolds was one of "the solid men" of old Plymouth. His name was connected with three of the early mercantile firms of the town. He never gave the store any part of his time. The premises were too contracted and cramped for him. His ambition and pleasure were upon the farm, with an open sky above him.

He was for many years a justice of the peace for the town. In those days the justices were appointed by the Governor, and the very best men were selected. They were appointed for life, or during good behavior. It was in the times of the old constitution, and in the days when the office of justice of the peace was honored, and the incumbent respected. The men holding the commissions of justice, at the period of which I am writing, were as much, or more respected by the people, than the men of the present day who occupy the Common Pleas bench; nor do I speak in deroga-

WILLIAM J. REYNOLDS.

tion of the character of any of our judges. The days when Thomas Dyer, Roswell Wells, Matthias Hollenback, Nathan Beach, Noah Wadhams, Abiel Fellows, Elisha S. Potter, Lawrence Meyers, John Marcy, and men of that stamp were the keepers of the peace of the county, the men who formed the type and character of the times in which they lived. When, therefore, Benjamin Reynolds was appointed a justice for life, or during good behavior, it was not a mere compliment, it meant something; it was a mark of distinction.

His sons were all thorough business men. One of them, Honorable William C. Reynolds, amassed a large fortune. He was a successful merchant, elected to the General Assembly, and at one time one of the associate judges of the county. The success of Judge Reynolds is but an illustration of what can be accomplished by a life of industry and perseverance, guided by a sound mind and discerning judgment. He was the architect of his own fortune. He began business with comparatively small means, but as an offset to this, he was untiring in his efforts, and devoted all his time to his business. A merchant for the greater part of his life, and in which occupation he succeeded well; but his foresight and high character of intellect led him to make the investment of his spare funds in coal lands; and the increase of the value of these lands was the foundation of a large estate.

Judge Reynolds and myself were intimate in early

life. We went to school together, in the old Academy, in the winter months; and were plow-boys in the summer, upon Shawnee Flats.

Our fathers' lands adjoined; and many were the conversations we had, while we would be eating our frugal meal, at noon, under a tree shade, as to our future hopes and expectations in life.

In these discussions we came to the conclusion that some other occupation would be more advantageous to us both. He talked up the store, and I the bar. And while we carried on this juvenile dialogue, there was before us the apparently insurmountable obstacle of the means to buy his stock of goods, and to procure the necessary legal education, on my part. And well do I remember his manly argument, though more than half a century has elapsed: " THE WILL IS HALF THE BATTLE, AND DETERMINED PERSEVERANCE, WITH UPRIGHT, TEMPERATE, MORAL DEPORTMENT, THE OTHER HALF."

Apples of gold are contained in this noble sentence. And it is somewhat strange that time found him in his counting-house, and myself at the bar. The subject of our colloquy, as plow-boys, became a reality. And his " upright, temperate, moral deportment, and determined perseverance," not merely laid the foundation, but erected the superstructure of his fortune.

He was a man of fine social qualities, and the most kind and indulgent of fathers.

The photographic likeness of him herein inserted, is perfect and life-like. To my own mind, a more correct delineation of features was never transferred to canvas.

To me, this is a source of much satisfaction; for when I look upon it, there comes back the agreeable events of long past years; and the consoling reflection, that the intimacy of our childhood was only separated by death; and that nothing in the long interim occurred to mar or interrupt the friendship of many, many succeeding years. He died in Wilkes-Barré, where he resided at the time, some three years ago.

Colonel J. Fuller Reynolds, another, and a man of probity and excellent business qualifications, still resides upon the old family homestead. Another one, Abraham H., is a prominent business man of Kingston.

NESBITTS.

The Nesbitt family were among the first settlers. James Nesbitt, the ancestor, immigrated from Connecticut in 1769, and was one of the "Forty." His name appears on the list of settlers of the valley, made out by Colonel Zebulon Butler, on the twenty-fourth July, 1769; and also upon a list prepared by Colonel Butler, of the persons in the Fort at Wilkes-Barré, on the twelfth April, 1770. Both of these enrolments are still preserved, and are in the hands of Steuben Jenkins, Esquire.

23

He made his "pitch" (the phrase used in those days to indicate permanent location and settlement) at the foot of Ant Hill, where he resided with his family during the remainder of his life; and which was also the residence of his two sons, Abraham and James, during their respective lives after him.

He returned to Connecticut in 1774, on account of the Pennamite and Yankee troubles, but came back to Plymouth in 1777. From this period he remained on his farm to the time of his decease, July second, 1792. He was, therefore, a resident of the town at the time of the Wyoming massacre. He was in the Wyoming battle, and one of the survivors of Captain Whittlesey's company.

The proprietors of Shawnee flats, at the commencement of the Revolution, leased their lands to an association of the settlers, on condition that they would maintain their possessions, and keep the block house upon Garrison Hill in repair. Among the persons who thus became lessees, is the name of James Nesbitt. Mr. Miner represents the person as Abraham Nesbitt. This is undoubtedly an error, as he was at that time a boy only. The associates of Mr. Nesbitt in this enterprise were, Major Prince Alden, Alexander and Joseph Jameson, Jonah Rogers, the elder, Samuel Ayres, Samuel Ransom, and others. The two Jameson, were at this time residents of Hanover; but the troublesome times brought the people together for self-preservation. The Jamesons were never permanent residents of Plymouth. Major Prince Alden was a citizen of the town, but for a year or two only. He was a Hanover man, and the owner of the very valuable homestead farm of the late Colonel Washington Lee.

The name of James Nesbitt appears in the proceedings of several of the early town meetings. He was an officer at a meeting held December sixth, 1779.

On the death of the old gentleman, he divided his homestead farm between his two sons, Abraham and James; the latter taking the part of it north of the back road, and the former that part between the back road and the river. These brothers resided many years upon their patrimonial estate. Each of them reared large families, and were among the representative men of the town. Abraham died January second, 1847, and James, August sixteenth, 1837.

James Nesbitt, Jr., a son of Abraham, was elected sheriff of the county, upon the expiration of the official term of Mr. Reynolds, and was also elected to the General Assembly of the State, after retiring from the sheriffalty. He was a man of unusual business qualifications, and left a large estate to his son Abraham, now a resident of Kingston, and his daughter, late the wife of Samuel Hoyt, Esquire, of the same place. He resided many years on the eastern slope of Ross Hill. His dwelling stands near the railroad bridge that spans the Susquehanna at that placc. The largest part of this now very valuable estate, he inherited in right of his wife, who was the daughter of Philip Shupp, owner of Shupp's mill of early days. The farm is still owned by his son and son-in-law. It is an evidence of their sagacity and good judgment to have held on to this estate, as the coal which underlies its surface has now become exceedingly valuable.

I must relate an incident connected with the purchase of a part of this property, for the purpose of showing the astonishing increase of the value of land, on account of coal developments, and to which I was a witness.

A part of the estate of the late James Barnes, who resided many years on the north-eastern slope of Ross Hill, was exposed to public sale—some thirty or forty acres of woodland, adjoining the Nesbitt farm. He was a competing bidder for the land at the sale. This was probably in 1832 or 1833. As he bid "seven and a half dollars" an acre, I stepped up to him and remarked, that I thought him wild in bidding seven dollars and a half per acre for uncultivated woodland. He replied, "that the land adjoined him, and that he could make pasturage of it; that he was aware that he was offering more than its value, and should not bid any farther." The auctioneer failing to get another bid, struck it down to Mr. Nesbitt, and he thus became the owner of it, and, as I thought, against his inclination.

THE WADHAMS HOUSE.

The same land to-day, I presume, could not be bought at a thousand dollars an acre. Its intrinsic value exceeds two thousand.

After the expiration of his term, as sheriff, Mr. Nesbitt remained in Wilkes-Barré, and entered into mercantile pursuits. He died in that town some thirty years since.

WADHAMS.

The Reverend Noah Wadhams, a clergyman of the Congregational church, and the progenitor of the Plymouth family, was one of the original "forty" of the first immigrants. He came from Litchfield, Connecticut, in the year 1769. He had previously been first pastor at the church at New Preston, in that county—installed in the year 1775. A portion of this immigration came the year previous, but the main body of them came in the year 1769. Mr. Wadhams was the shepherd of the small flock, which took up their residence in the wilderness, made more forbidding because of the savage people who were in possession of the valley.

Our Puritan ancestors were thoroughly imbued with the idea that religion and progress were inseparable; that an enterprise which did not have a sprinkling of the church about it could not succeed. A very safe rule, perhaps, and the observance of which might well be followed upon the part of their descendants, even down to the third generation. When,

therefore, an expedition was fitted out by the Susquehanna Company, with a view of founding a Yankee
town, upon any part of the company's chartered territory, the providing of a pastor was considered of as
much importance as that of a physician, or a person
skilled in any of the mechanical branches. Without
a clergyman, the expedition would be incomplete.
And that this personage might not be an incumbrance
upon an infant colony, the company made provision
for his support and maintenance.

Thus, at a meeting of the company, held in 1768,
I find among other things the following entry:—" The
standing committee was directed to procure a pastor,
to accompany the second colony, called the ' first forty,' for carrying on religious worship and services according to the best of his ability, in a wilderness
country."

The proceedings further make provision, " that he
shall receive one whole share, or right in the purchase,
and such other encouragements as others are entitled
to have and enjoy." This share amounted to some
three hundred acres, besides the perquisites, which
sometimes accompanied the grant. The company
further required the colonial adventurers to provide
their pastor, when they located upon the promised
land, " with sustenance according to the best of their
ability."

It will be seen, therefore, that there was a condition precedent attached to every Yankee grant, to sup-

port and maintain a religious pastor. And this the immigrants faithfully executed, as we find in all the divisions and allotments of land among them, that a certain part was set off for education and religion. This was done by the people of all the "seventeen" towns.

As early as 1762, when John Jenkins and his band of bold and fearless associates entered the valley and located at Mill Creek, the Rev. William Marsh accompanied them as pastor. In the autumn of 1763, Mr. Marsh was one of the number, of which mention has already been made, who were slain by the Indians.

The Rev. George Beckwith, Jr., from Lynn, Massachusetts, came to Wyoming in 1769, as the successor of Mr. Marsh; he remained a year or two, and was succeeded by the Rev. Jacob Johnson, of Groton, Connecticut. Mr. Johnson was the pastor of the Wilkes-Barré "forty" from 1773 to the time of his death, in 1795—for nearly a quarter of a century. Mr. Johnson was a man of strong mind, though possessed of some eccentricities of character. It is said that he prepared his grave with his own hands, a year or two preceding his death, on the rocky eminence on Bowman's Hill, at the termination of Franklin street, in Wilkes-Barré. And upon this rocky promontory still repose the bones of the old Puritan leader, along with those of his wife—their's being the only graves of the locality. Some of the descendants of Mr.

Johnson were men of mark in later years.   Ovid F. Johnson, an eminent lawyer, and at one time Attorney-General of the State, was a grandson.

Rev. Andrew Gray was the pastor of the Hanover "forty." He continued for many years in that capacity in Hanover. It was under his administration that the old church was erected on the Hill, a short distance below the Colonel Inman homestead.

When, therefore, preparation was being made to start the Plymouth colony, on their journey to the wilderness, it became a necessary part of the programme to select a pastor.

The Rev. Noah Wadhams was chosen for the purpose, and he accepted. He was at this time, 1769, forty-three years of age, and had a family of small children. Leaving his family at home, he embarked with his flock amid the perils which lay before them, on the distant shores of the Susquehanna. The spirit of adventure was a ruling passion with our ancestors, and it has by no means become extinct with their descendants.

Mr. Wadhams was born in Middletown, Connecticut, on the seventeenth of May, 1726. He was a graduate of the college of New Jersey. His diploma, bearing date the twenty-fifth of September, 1754, is now in the custody of his great-grandson, Calvin Wadhams, Esq., counsellor-at-law, of Wilkes-Barré; and what is a most singular coincidence, this same great-grandson graduated at the same university, just one hundred years after his paternal ancestor.

The old diploma is a venerable looking paper. It bears the name of Aaron Burr, father of the celebrated man of Revolutionary fame, as president of the college. There are also attached the signatures of the trustees of the college, Jacob Green, William E. Smith, Richard Treat, John Braynard and John Pierson. The document is the surviving witness of three generations, past and gone: a testament also of the times of George III., and when the present state of New Jersey was one of the colonies of his realm.

Mr. Wadhams continued his pastoral relations, interrupted by an occasional visit to his family, in Litchfield, until the year succeeding the Wyoming massacre, when he removed them to Plymouth. From this time to the period of his death, on the twenty-second of May, 1806, he faithfully pursued his religious duties; preaching in Plymouth, and in other parts of the valley. He was a man of very considerable talents, having received a liberal education, as already stated, and as a mark of merit, he had also conferred upon him, by Yale College, in 1764, the degree of master of arts.

He left four sons, Ingersoll, Calvin, Noah, and Moses. They were all too young to have taken any part in the early and angry strifes of the valley. I find all their names, however, upon the assessment list of the township, returned in 1796. Moses died of the yellow fever in 1803.

Calvin and Noah were for many years prominent business men of the town. The success of the former was remarkable. At the time of his death, in 1845, Calvin Wadhams was the man of the largest wealth in the township; and probably there was not more than one other citizen of the county, who possessed more property than he.

He was a stout, athletic man, as I remember him, about five feet eight inches in height, dark blue eyes, and a florid complexion. He possessed an agreeable presence, and always had a kind expression upon his lips. I knew him well and intimately, and I don't remember of ever seeing him angry, or even excited. He was strictly temperate, very industrious, and lived in a plain and economical manner.

He possessed a sound judgment, and no man knew better the value of real estate. All these qualifications, united with good health and a strong constitution, he could not but succeed. He made up his mind to become rich, and he succeeded. But in his progress towards the accomplishment of this purpose, his business relations with the world immediately about him, and connected with the theatre of his operations, were not marked by acts of oppression; nor did he avail himself of the opportunity of enforcing the collection of his debts, and becoming the owner of the property of his debtors at forced judicial sales.

He was, in addition to his occupation of farmer, what would be called, in these times, a private banker. He was in the habit of loaning money, and it seemed to afford him more satisfaction to lend to the poor than the rich. A plausible story, upon the part of a man of small means, was pretty generally successful, and such people would procure the loan of money from Calvin Wadhams, when it would have been out of the question to have succeeded elsewhere.

Accommodating such people, as a matter of course, he would be annoyed when the day of payment came; and to resort to execution was the last remedy he employed. To avoid this, he would extend the time, and receive almost any thing under the name of property in payment. I question if he ever sold out the house or home of any one who had become indebted to him. In this particular, his conduct was remarkably praiseworthy.

But his chief occupation, and the one from which he derived the most satisfaction, was that of a farmer. He was a practical farmer too, for he put his own hand to the plow; and in the later years of his life, when the infirmities of age had overtaken him, you might see him in the field superintending the gathering of his harvest. When he became unable to walk there, he would ride there in his carriage. It had been his custom so many years to superintend the work going on upon his farm, that he could not contentedly relinquish it.

He was kind and indulgent to the men in his employment, and he would sell them corn upon credit, when they might have gone further and with less success.

Living in a frugal way, and with his mind constantly upon his business, he accumulated a large estate. His old homestead farm—and being but a part of the estate which he left at his death—was recently sold, by his family, for seven hundred thousand dollars.

As to his habits of frugality and industry, he was a genuine type of the men of the generation immediately preceding us. Labor, temperance, and economy, in his judgment, proved the true standard of manhood, and that made up the rule of his long and prosperous life.

He was a religious man, and strongly devoted to the church of his faith. Born and educated as a Congregationalist, he left the creed of his ancestors, and embraced the Wesleyan doctrines. Having done this, he remained firm and steadfast in that creed to the end of his life. His home was ever open to the brethren of the Methodist church. At a quarterly meeting of these people in Plymouth, he would entertain as many as fifty of them at a time. Nor was his hospitality confined to the people of his own religious sect—it was broad and general, and his home was open to all. He died at a ripe age, and in the full enjoyment of all his faculties.

But one of his children survived him—the late

W. A. P. H. M^c...A.W

Samuel Wadhams, Esq., who inherited the larger part of his father's estate.

He inherited too, the business qualifications and the even temper and kind disposition of his father. Stepping into the occupation of so large an estate, he exhibited great skill and judgment in its management, and made valuable additions to it. Samuel Wadhams was a remarkably methodical man in his business affairs. He understood the detail, and knew well how to manage and control. He was probably more cautious than he might have been, in view of the accumulation of property. But he had that other and probably more useful qualification, prudence.

He came to his conclusions with moderation, and they were generally right. Those who succeeded him will not have occasion to reflect upon his memory, for a lack of genuine good sense, as to the mode and manner of managing the large estate, the most of which he inherited. He was cautious in entering the great field of speculation which lay before him; he hesitated at the contraction of debt; he seemed to have been governed by the idea, that as his fortune was ample, there was no need upon his part of putting any of that fortune in jeopardy, by grasping with cupidity for that which might, and still might not, be as advantageous as the theories of speculation pointed out. And there is not, in this view of the case, any reason to question the propriety of his conclusions.

He had enough. Possessing the cautious and methodical characteristics of his father, he turned over the large estate, with the accumulations it had received, through his careful management, to his children; which makes each of them an ample fortune. He died on the fifteenth of December, 1868, in his sixty-third year. He died as he had lived, a man of unblemished integrity; upright in his dealings, and a worthy Christian member of society.

He left three sons—Elijah C., Calvin, and Moses, and one daughter, who is the wife of Hon. L. D. Shoemaker, the representative in Congress from this district, at this time.

The faces of three members of this family, representing three generations, accompany the short biographical sketches I have attempted to draw of them.

Noah, the third son of the pioneer, was one of the early Justices of the Peace of the county. He was a graduate of the famous law school of early days, at Litchfield, under the management of Judge Reeve. He was admitted to the bar of Luzerne county, not far from 1800 ; but the profession did not seem to have afforded him any attractions, and he settled down upon his patrimonial estate in Plymouth, where he spent the remainder of his life. He was an industrious, upright man. As a justice of the peace, his decisions seldom found their way to the appellate court. His knowledge of the law, assisted by his good common sense, enabled him so to decide, be-

tween the parties before him, that they seldom appealed.

As an evidence of the way in which the early people of the town economized their time, the regulations of Esquire Wadhams' court will afford an excellent illustration. Saturday afternoons were his return days, as well as the times fixed for the trial of the cases before him. This gave the magistrate an opportunity to do a half-day's labor before the opening of the court, and if an unusual amount of business was on hand, and it became necessary to extend the session into the night, it was so much gained. But the adjournment of an unfinished case went over to the succeeding Saturday. This was the general rule; there may have been exceptions to it. Noah Wadhams was a frank, outspoken man, and one not intimately acquainted with him, might have thought him rude and severely harsh, in his manner. But he was remarkably sensitive; and while his outward deportment carried the semblance of a brusque and haughty appearance, the heart and disposition of the man were as docile as a child's. The defendant upon whom he would pronounce the judgment of the law, with the appearance of not merely cold indifference, but boisterous anger, would find in him the most accessible person to become his bail, even for stay of execution. His eyes and tongue were but a poor exponent of the emotions of his heart.

Probably a purer man, or one who strove harder

to do even and exact justice, in his official capacity, never received or acted under a commission of the peace. He was a model magistrate, and for many long years did he enjoy the confidence and respect of his neighbors.

He was as positive a man in his politics, which were of the Jefferson school, as his brother Calvin was in his, which were Washingtonian. No two men were ever more diametrically opposed to each other than these two brothers, in their political principles. One a radical Democrat, the other a radical Federalist.

Noah Wadhams died in 1846, in the seventy-sixth year of his age. His farm was situated between the river and the back road, and extended from the Lackawanna and Bloomsburg railroad depot to the small stream heretofore referred to, and on which now stand some of the most expensive and best buildings of the borough. There are now, none of his family left in Plymouth.

DAVENPORTS.

The Davenports, a very numerous family of the present day in Plymouth, were among the early settlers of the town, and one of them was of the original "Forty." I am not able to ascertain the length of time he remained in Plymouth after his immigration.

The name of Danford is on the original list. The surname is so obliterated that I cannot decipher a letter of it. It was undoubtedly Robert, however, father of Thomas, who came a few years afterwards. The name of Davenport and Danford are the same. The family were known by the latter name many years since my recollection; and it is so written in the old deeds of conveyance. The family is of low Dutch origin, and this may account for the different manner of spelling the name.

The name of Conrad Davenport is upon the dead list of the Wyoming battle. I think this man was a resident of Newport, and a member of Captain Stewart's company, and probably of that family of Davenports still residing in Union township, but who are not related to the Plymouth family.

The Danford whose name appears upon the roll of the Susquehanna immigrant company, and to whom was allotted some of the lands still in possession of the family, came out, most likely, as an explorer; and, on his return, giving a favorable account of the new country, his son Thomas succeeded his father in the Plymouth possessions. Robert does not seem to have returned to the valley. It is also pretty well settled that he was a member of Captain Whittlesey's company in the battle, and a survivor of that terrible disaster. Such is the tradition of the family at the present time, and most likely a correct one.

Thomas Davenport, the ancestor of the now resident family, came from Esopus, on the Hudson, state

24

of New York, in the year 1794. His name is registered on the assessor's list of 1796, and he was then
the owner of a large landed estate. His name does
not appear on the enrolments of the people of the
town before this period. He died in the year 1812,
leaving a large family—six sons and four daughters.
His sons were Thomas, John, Robert, Samuel, Daniel and Stephen.

A considerable part of the old homestead farm is
still owned by the descendants. In early days the
four Davenport houses, with their long stoops extending the length of the entire front of each, presented a
unique appearance, compared with the other buildings
of the pioneers. The latter followed Yankee models,
built after the Litchfield houses of Connecticut.
The former were after models of the people of Sir
Hendrick Hudson. This row extended from the
" Swing-gate " to the mountain road, near the Nottingham colliery. The residence of the ancestor was
situated about half way between the two points
named.

Two of these ancient buildings still stand; but
they have lost the old ornament of the front stoop,
and they do not have the cheerful appearance they
possessed forty years ago.

From the death of the old gentleman down to the
year 1820, the entire estate remained in common, notwithstanding three of the sons had residences of their
own, and three of the daughters were married and re-

siding away from the paternal mansion; still, for the period of eight years, the property remained in common. A somewhat strange state of affairs, compared with the present times—for now the earth has scarcely time to settle down upon the lid of the ancestral coffin, before the process goes out for carving up and dividing the ancestral estate.

The Davenports, for the period of time named, labored in the same field; fed, we may say, from the same board—as the crib and granary contained the same common stock of grain—and they were, in fact, a commune of themselves. The whole machinery moved without a jar; there was perfect accord. When they would meet together of an evening, after the day's labor, upon the old homestead stoop, it used to be the remark of others, that " Congress had assembled." And here were discussed, not those intriguing and subtle questions which now occupy the time of a somewhat degenerate body of men, known by the same name, but the more useful and necessary and solid questions of life, such as how such a field should be tilled? What should be the character of the succeeding day's employment? Which of them should swing the cradle, and which rake and bind? How much of the crop should be thrashed and sent to Easton, and how much put into bins for the year's supply? Solid, sensible, and man-like discussions. And in this way the Davenport congress managed their affairs. Secret schemes, involving the means of living, independent of industry and hard labor, had no place upon their "private calendar."

And so they went on through years of prosperity, their names appearing neither on the criminal, or civil dockets of the courts, of the county, as litigants. The family for two generations, within the knowledge of the writer, have been upright, industrious, and active business men. Of the six sons of old Thomas Davenport, Stephen, late County Commissioner, and now a resident of Huntington, is the only survivor.

Daniel, as has already been stated, became seriously involved in the coal trade, at an early day, and lost most of his estate. He was a man of integrity, of frank and pleasant deportment, and very popular with the people of the town. His misfortunes in the coal business enlisted the sympathies of the citizens deeply, and these troubles were undoubtedly the cause of his premature death.

He was a representative man of his day; and he gave employment to, and fed large numbers of laboring men, for those times, and of them all, no one ever had cause for complaint in his dealings and intercourse with them. I refer back to this generous and kind-hearted man with feelings of lively emotion. He was but three or four years my senior; we were intimate for many years. We occupied the same bench in Thomas Patterson's school, in the Old Academy; and when I came to the bar, he was one of my first and best clients. These reasons make me cling with great regard to his memory. He left a large family at his death, as did also Thomas, John and Robert. In the division of the estate of their father, each received a competency.

Jacob Gould and John Pringle, both highly respectable men, married daughters of the old gentleman. Mrs. Pringle is living; she and Stephen are the only survivors of the family of ten.

The Davenports were among the substantial business men of the town for a great many years. They were of that class which, above all others, are entitled to public consideration, because they were devoted to their own affairs, and were not in the habit of meddling with those of others. They faithfully maintained their credit, and their lives were marked with strict economy, industry and fair dealing. The six sons were all farmers, and they literally were governed by the sentiment contained in the couplet of our great American philosopher, Benjamin Franklin, that—

> "He that by the plough would thrive,
> Himself must either hold or drive."

VAN LOONS.

The family of Van Loons also immigrated from Esopus in the year 1794. There were three brothers — Abraham, Mathias and Nicholas. As the name indicates, they were of low Dutch origin. I find them all on the assessment list of 1796. They came to Plymouth after the valley troubles had ceased to exist. They were a family of hard workers, and were among the active business men of the town. Abraham, or as he was generally called, Brom, had a large family of children. His residence stood on the south side of the Nottingham shaft, at the corner of the Main and Mountain roads.

Stephen, his eldest son, was elected high sheriff of the county in the year 1816. He was captain of the militia of the town in 1814, and mustered the men of his company into the United States service, who were drafted from it. He was a man of very considerable energy, and during the war of 1812 was a very noted politician of the town. Being of the democratic party, he was rewarded by it, with the office of sheriff, as a compensation for his political services. He discharged the duties of the office faithfully. He died February 1840 or 1841.

Samuel Van Loon is a son of Stephen, a man well known in the county. He was also elected to the same office in 1859. He was the last of the five sheriffs of the county selected from Plymouth men. It is somewhat remarkable that the township of Plymouth should have held this office a third of the time, from 1816 to 1859. The county being large in territory, and the population numerous, Plymouth had more than her share of sheriffs. The order in which they were elected is as follows: Stephen Van Loon, Benjamin Reynolds, James Nesbitt, Caleb Atherton and Samuel Van Loon.

Another feature marks the case, which is well worth recording—these gentlemen were all of them descendants of the first settlers of the town. The grandfathers of three of them were of the original "Forty." The ancestors of the two Van Loons came but a few years later.

John, another son of Abraham, was a man of keen and sarcastic wit. How many times I have listened, with others, to the stories of John Van Loon, while the men of the harvest field were laying under the shade of the big cherry-tree, on my father's farm, on Shawnee Flats, taking the "hour's nooning." Like Shakspeare's Yorick, "he was a fellow of infinite mirth." He would for a half hour keep the company in uproarious laughter.

At the risk of being charged with a departure from the dignified theme of history, I must relate a specimen of his numerous stories, though I do not vouch for the truth of it!

He was a pilot of the Susquehanna, and made the navigating of arks a part of his employment.

At the foot of the Halifax mountain, this side of Harrisburg, an old man by the name of Hoaklander kept a way-side inn. The ark and raftsmen were accustomed to stop at this tavern. The house stood at the base of a very high hill and with a steep ascent.

As Van Loon related the story: "Hoaklander had a one horse sled, which he used in transporting his fire-wood from this mountain side. The harness had buckskin traces. On a thawing spring day in March he ascended the hill with his one horse sled, put on his load of wood, and started homeward, leading his horse. On arriving at his house at the bottom of the hill, he found his sled missing; in a great fury he jerked off the harness, and threw it over a stump by the way-side, and put his horse in the stable, vexed beyond endurance at the result of his work.

The weather changed at night, and it became suddenly very cold; the effect of this was. to retract the stretched buckskin traces. The old man was awakened by a rumbling noise during the night, like distant thunder. The sound continued; he jumped from his bed and went to his door, when lo! in the moonlight he saw his sled load of wood precipitately descending the mountain pitch; and to his astonishment it came up to his door with a rush."

Daddy Hoaklander and his buckskin traces would well bear an annual repetition.

John removed with his family to the State of Ohio, where he died some twenty-five years ago.

Jeremiah, another brother, removed to the same State a few years before John.

Acquainted with two generations of this family, it affords me much satisfaction to speak of them all as men of probity, industry, and congenial social dispositions. A streak of mirthful humor was a prevailing characteristic with most of them.

PRINGLES.

This family were among the early settlers. There were two brothers—Samuel and James. I find the name of Samuel on the assessment list in 1796. He owned the farm upon which is located the Gaylord coal shaft and breaker. James resided in what is now called Jackson. Samuel raised a large family. His eldest son, Thomas, married a daughter of Elisha Harvey. He removed some forty years since to Kingston, where he died. His sons are now among the best and most enterprising business men of that township. Thomas Pringle was a most exemplary and upright citizen; a prominent member for a good number of years in the Methodist church, and his house, to the day of his death, was a temporary home for the circuit preachers of that religious order.

Samuel, the ancestor, died many years since; he also was a man of good standing, and a worthy and upright citizen. The old stone farm-house and pleasant surroundings made an inviting spot in old times; but heaps of culm and stacks of machinery have defaced its former appearance; and it is very doubtful that if the spirit of the old farmer, of early days, were to return there now, whether he could recognize the locality.

TURNERS.

John Turner, the first settler in the town of the family of that name, immigrated at an early day; but he was not of the first colony. He came to Plymouth about the year 1780. His son, the late John Turner, informed me that his father removed to the town, from near Hacketstown, Warren county, New Jersey; but I find in an obituary notice of this gentleman, published soon after his death, which occurred on the third day of July last (1871), and apparently prepared with care, that the family residence originally is fixed at Bushkill, Northampton county, Pa. I think, however, that the family were originally from the State of New Jersey.

The first settler died of an epidemic, which was remarkably malignant and destructive of life in Plymouth, in the year 1803, and known as the " Fall Fever; " but in reality a type of yellow fever. A brother of his also died the same season of the same disease. Four sons survived him—Emanuel, Daniel, John and Jonah. Emanuel settled in Huntington; Daniel in Kingston, both in this county; Jonah at Hope, Warren county, New Jersey, and John remained upon the homestead farm in Plymouth.

It is of John, who was born in the town in 1787, and died there as above stated, and resided there during his whole life, of whom I shall more particularly speak.

He was a tall, stout man, with remarkably fair complexion, and blue eyes, and possessing an agreeable presence. Like nearly all of the early residents of the town, he pursued the occupation of a farmer, though in later years of his life, he opened a store, and connected this branch of business with coal operations. Still his chief occupation, and the one best suited to his tastes and inclinations, was that of a farmer.

He was a man of abstemious habits, and his whole life was marked by untiring industry. He was literally a man of domestic habits; always upon his plantation, and always engaged. He had no idle moments. Uniform in his politics, and firm in his party principles, which were of the Jefferson school, he never however s ught office; and with the exception of holding the commission of postmaster of the town a few years, and acting in the capacity of municipal appointments, his whole life was that of a private citizen.

He was a strong advocate of education, and was mainly the cause of introducing the teaching of the dead languages into the Plymouth school. I speak in this particular from my own knowledge, as upon his directions I made an engagement with both Mr. Patterson and Mr. Nyce, graduates of Dickinson College, Pennsylvania, as teachers in the Old Academy. These gentlemen were principals of the school, the one succeeding the other in the years 1828-1830. I think, too, that Mr. Turner sustained a much larger proportion of the expenses of the school, during these years, than his legal share. He was determined that the teaching of the languages should be made a part of the school exercises; and after much difficulty and pretty serious opposition, he succeeded in carrying his point.   This enabled him to give his children a good education, and he availed himself of the opportunity. Two of his sons became thorough business men.

Samuel G. Turner, his second son, was a man of much energy, and pursuing the occupation of merchant and coal dealer, gathered up a very handsome estate.   He might be classed, at his decease, among the men of wealth of the county, at a time too when men were measured by a more liberal standard than in the days of his father.

He represented the county in both branches of the State Legislature, and with much credit and ability. He was the father of the mine ventilating bill, and is deserving of much praise for his active exertions in preparing and passing this law.   He possessed more than an ordinary degree of intelligence, and his judgment in real estate was very superior.

He removed to Wilkes-Barré some six years since, and remained there till his death, which occurred in the early part of January, 1873.   Samuel G. Turner may be ranked among the most successful men, in a business way, of the town or of the county. He died in the prime of life, and at a period when his prospects of a successful future were very brilliant.   Living somewhat as a gentleman of leisure, he devoted much of his time to political affairs, and in his capacity of legislator, there attaches not the least suspicion of a want of fidelity. This testimony, in the times in which we are writing, is eminently deserving of notice.

Frank Turner, following the example of his father, has taken a very active part in promoting the character and efficiency of the common schools of the town.

As was the custom in early days for all to labor, Mr. Turner devoted himself assiduously to his occupation : early and late, during the period of seed time and harvest, he might be seen in the field, and doing his full share of the work on hand—the first on "the Flats," in the morning, and the last to leave at night. Careful, prudent and judicious, the accumulation of much more than competency was the result. These habits he kept up until age and decrepitude forbid their continuance. During the few years preceding his death, his sight and hearing became very much impaired, and from necessity, he lived in a secluded manner.

He was the last of a class of hardy and industrious men, who for a long period of years gave tone and high standing to old Plymouth, as a place where labor was dignified in the character of the men who performed it.

I conclude this notice with a quotation from an obituary, from the pen of my brother, C. E. Wright, Esquire, upon the death of Mr. Turner. The remarks are truthful and well expressed:

"There was much in the life and character of John Turner to excite admiration, and furnish a model for imitation. He was frugal, industrious, studious and constant. In his life, when in the enjoyment of health, there was little of waste time. He had a discriminating mind, and the habit of constant thought.

"As you beheld him, you were assured the machinery of the mind was never at rest. He read much, and digested what he read. In his demeanor he was always dignified and grave. The low buffooneries of the world he looked on with contempt. He would have graced the highest walks of social or civil state, had fortune cast him upon them.

"In his political opinions he was changeless. From the first to the last he was a Democrat—not a noisy brawler, but quiet and fixed. No one could ever force on him a demand for office. He had his business line of life laid down, and from it he never swerved.

"Mr. Turner's taste seemed to be for the intellectual. The halls of public debate had a great charm for him. A man of research, he delighted in any exposition of art, science, literature or governmental policy. Hence the advocate, the lecturer, the professor, or divine, found in him a patient, attentive, and discriminating auditor. Sharing, in a good degree, his confidence and friendship while in life, I am happy to afford his memory the tribute of my humble pen."

ATHERTONS.

The Athertons were among the first settlers of the valley. Caleb, the ancestor of the Plymouth branch, heads the list of Captain Ransom's company. The other brothers, who immigrated from Connecticut, were among the first settlers of Kingston. Jabez was among the slain upon the Wyoming battle-field, and came to the valley with John Jenkins, as early as 1763.

Members of this family, therefore, were subjected to as severe trials as often befall the lot of man.

The name in Plymouth has become extinct, with that of Whittlesey, Alden, Bidlack, Pike, Rogers, Allen, Heath, Roberts, and many more; tradition in a few years to come, will hardly preserve them. But the times have been when these names were familiar with the entire population of the town. It is my desire, and that alone which challenges my pen to preserve and perpetuate, so far as possible, the names and memories of these men of a preceding age, and to give an idea to succeeding generations who they were, how they behaved, what they endured, and what they accomplished.

While I am unable to speak positively, I think that Caleb Atherton was of the first "forty." Nor can I ascertain whether he was in the Wyoming battle, or when, or where he died.

His son Moses, who succeeded his father in the occupation and ownership of the family estate, was born and died in Plymouth. I find his name on the enrolment of 1796; so that his birth must have been very soon after the occupation of the town by white men—assuming that the name of no person was placed upon this list under twenty-one years of age.

His residence was a few rods south of the Academy, and adjoining the Turner farm. The present two-story frame house, upon the site of the first building, was erected within my recollection—probably fifty-five years ago. The old barn on the opposite side of the way, and which was old fifty years ago, still stands in defiance of the angry elements with which it has been in yearly conflict for a hundred years.

Moses Atherton was a man, in stature, under the medium size; he presented a peculiar appearance from the manner in which he always wore his hat; it was always drawn down half-way over one ear, and elevated an inch above the other. Being a short man, it became necessary in his conversation to elevate the side of his head the least covered by his hat, which tended to tilt it still further over, which added to the singularity of his presence. He was always ready, and would seek the opportunity for a religious controversy. A convert to the doctrines of universal salvation, he went armed with all the panoply of that liberal sect. Every passage of the Old and New Testament which could be made available for the support of this doctrine, was at his tongue's end. Therefore, upon all occasions of a gathering of the people—at town meetings, militia trainings, elections, or assemblages of any kind—Mr. Atherton would be present, ready, willing and anxious to take up the cudgels of universal faith. And in whatever part of the crowd you would see the little man, with hat on one side, one ear concealed by its crown, and the other exposed to daylight, surrounded by a knot of listeners, you could be assured that universal salvation was the theme. He never tired in argument: his subject was inexhaustible.

He was a man of industrious habits; he had a large family of children, and his four sons became highly respectable men of the town. His oldest, Truman, resided many years at Huntsville, in what is now Jackson township, and was the owner of the flouring and lumber mills there. He was a representative of the county in the General Assembly of the State for two years, and a most worthy and excellent citizen. He is still living, at an advanced age, in Huron county, Ohio, where he removed some ten years ago.

Caleb, the second son, was elected High Sheriff of the county in 1838. He has been dead several years. Adnah, another son, is a resident farmer of Wyoming county; and Stephen, the youngest son, is a lumber dealer in Lancaster county, Pennsylvania.

It was my design to have extended these old family sketches further, but my readers may well conclude that they have been carried too far already.

There was a class of pioneers, however (whose names, at least, I must not omit), who scaled the northern wall of the valley, the Shawnee mountain, and settled down on its western slope, literally in the wilderness. A class of hardy adventurers to whom the rocks and forest trees, and the less productive soil, were no obstacles. At the head of them were Thomas Case, Thomas and John Lameroux and Jesse Brown, James Pringle, Eden Ruggles, and Joshua and Bennajah Fuller, all of whom commenced their improvements there before 1800.

25

In fact, from these families sprang a very large number of the people now resident in Jackson. Thomas Case had a family of eight sons, all of whom grew to manhood, and Thomas Lameroux six. What a power to reclaim the forest, and tame down the wilderness, in two families only! They faithfully accomplished the work. The vast extent and character of the stone wall upon the farms of these two old settlers, were a matter of marvel in early days. The work was all done by their own family forces, and well done; and the miles of it to-day, stretching out over their plantations, are a monument of the toil and industry which were bestowed a half century since.

I remember well, when a young man, how one of the sons of these families would be pointed out, as an object of especial regard, for having laid so many feet of stone wall in a day; and one of the others as having dressed so many pounds of flax in a day.

How much nobler an object of praise than the delicate white hand of modern youth, bedizened with rings, or the nicety and precision with which the hair of the head can be divided.

So far as it related to mutual acts of kindness, a parallel may be drawn between these people of the north-western slope of the mountain and their neighbors below, with the ancient Gael, or Scottish Highlander, and the Saxon of the plains.

They would come down and help, at the harvest on Shawnee Flats, receiving corn in exchange for their labor, and would drive down their cattle for pasturage, when the big "Swing Gate" was thrown back upon its hinges, after the crops were gathered, as a kind of general invitation to all, to enter the inviting field with their flocks and herds.

These hardy and industrious people were a true type of the times in which they lived. Labor to them was inviting and honorable; and it was a subject of boast with them, that their farms supplied them with all the necessary wants of life, and that they and their children cultivated them with their own hands.

Simple and plain days, of a race of men now gone, and their descendants scattered over the broad land. Ah! and the bones of many of them bestrew the battle-fields of the late internecine war.

How well I remember these old patriarchs, dressed in their holiday suit of homespun, coming down to the election polls in the valley, fifty years ago, with staff in hand, to deposit their ballots! Not noisy or boisterous, but sober, dignified, and thoughtful men. Their arguments were interchanged in candor, and their politics discussed in mild, inoffensive language.

The polls closed, they returned to their mountain homes, and whatever the result of the election may have been, they yielded with grace to the will of the majority. An effort made to cast an illegal vote, branded with disgrace the name of the man who had the hardihood or daring to give countenance to the act.

CHAPTER XX.

MY reminiscences of Plymouth men, end with a biographical notice of my father. I throw myself upon the indulgence of my readers, in paying a short tribute of paternal regard to one of the kindest of parents, as well as the best of men. I am well aware that it is somewhat out of place, for the son to be the biographer of the father, but as this one has passed from the mortal stage, and that one is in the last act in the drama of life, he will at least feel less sensitive to criticism, than he might under other circumstances.

I am fully aware, too, of the force and power of family pride, as well as family prejudice, and shall therefore make an honest effort to confine myself to a truthful statement of facts. If I exceed this, there will be one consolation left, that mine will not have been the first instance of a departure from the truth. But those few who are now living, and who knew the man, I am pretty certain will not charge me with coloring too highly the portrait I am drawing. Those who did not know him, if they are in doubt and feel inclined to pursue the subject, must seek the traditionary evidence of the town, and compare the result of such inquiry with the narrative presented.

He was a resident of the town for more than half

JOSEPH WRIGHT.

a century, and during that long period, was intimately connected with its municipal government, and was one of its representative men. As the annual assessor and auditor of the public accounts, he served probably a much longer term than any other citizen in it. Being remarkably correct in figures, and writing a most excellent hand, these burdens, for this reason, were the more frequently imposed on him. Such qualifications were not so common in the early history of the town as they are now. The annual settlement and auditing of the municipal accounts most generally passed under his inspection. In later years, Henderson Gaylord took upon himself a share of this duty, and for a period of more than thirty years, these two men performed, or supervised, this responsible duty.

The discharge of public services did not pay so well forty years ago as now. It was no sinecure then. At the annual town meeting, the question would be, " Will you accept the office? " Present customs shape it somewhat differently: " Will you please to give me the office ? " A sense of public duty and obligation under the old usages, assumed the imposition. I fear very much that the emoluments of the office have a good deal to do with it now. But then the cost of living now is more, rents are higher, and there does not seem to be employment for all the good people! Then the deputy is to be paid out of the fees and perquisites; whereas, under the old and simple process of our ancestors, the principal was willing to do the work with or without pay! Changes will come; changes have come! Taxes, too, will increase; taxes have increased ! Have they reached the maximum ? And who shall answer this question ?

The old records of the town from 1807 to 1855, will probably show the name of Joseph Wright, in connection with the administration of its municipal affairs for at least half that period of time. I think, also, that there is no person either who will allege that the duties in this position were not faithfully, honestly and correctly discharged.

Having thus been so long a resident of Plymouth, and so closely associated with its prosperity and growth, I feel that the people of the town will consider the memory of the man as much their property as that of his family. Making his home there at a later period, and after the close of the early disasters of the settlement, there will not be of course that interest in his personal biography as with many of those who preceded him.

The family, consisting of seven brothers, came from England in 1681, with William Penn's colony of Quaker immigrants. John Wright, one of the number, in a short time after the landing, commenced a residence in the eastern part of Burlington county, New Jersey, and was the first settler at Wrightstown, being the founder in fact of the village, or little town of that name.

He held a commission of justice of the peace and captain of the militia, under the royal seal of Charles II. A diary kept by this pioneer is still in the possession of the family. Among other things therein recorded, it appears that "he subscribed and paid £3 towards building the brick meeting-house." This building is still standing, after a lapse of almost two hundred years, and was probably the first meeting-house erected in that State. It appears also that he " made the first barrel of cider in the State of New Jersey." The circumstances attending the jubilee over this " first barrel of cider," I must insert. It was an event in the history of the new country.

"He invited all his neighbors to partake; they very willingly attended. Duke Fort was appointed tapster; and a merrier assemblage never took place in the neighborhood of Penny Hill, for so Wrightstown was then called."

Among the curiosities contained in this old diary I add the following : " The soil is very productive, and the earth yields very bountifully; but then the farmer has poor encouragement, considering that those terrible pests, the wild geese and wild turkeys, destroy almost entirely one's crops."

The frontiersman of Minnesota and Dacotah may be to-day noting down the same text, to be the wonder of the people two hundred years hence.

At Wrightstown, on the second day of May, 1785, the subject of this notice was born; and of the fourth

generation of the family in America.   His father,
Caleb Wright, removed with his family to the "Susquehanna country" in the year 1795.

He purchased and settled upon a farm in Union
township, two miles above Shickshinny, where he remained till the year 1811, and then returned to New
Jersey.   During this time Joseph had married, and
commenced a small retail store in Plymouth—already
mentioned.   He alone of the family remained here.

Joseph Wright was the second merchant of old
Plymouth.   His ancestors for two hundred years before him having belonged to the "Society of Friends,"
he steadily adhered to the faith of that religious order of people to the hour of his death.   Notwithstanding he had been expelled from the Society, because he had married outside of the church limits,
and in direct violation of its discipline, he ever considered himself as one of the order, however, and bound
by its formulas and creed.   He would say, "that in
matter of substance he had lived up to the faith of
his fathers; but that in two matters of form only,
viz.: his marriage, and submitting to the military
draft of 1812, he had wandered a trifle, but that this
was by no means a matter of regret."   And probably
these were the only two instances in which he had
failed, during a long and eventful life, of fulfilling the
requirements of his creed.   And yet it is somewhat
difficult to reconcile his professed religious obligations,
in view of his conduct in entering the service in the

war of 1812. His argument was, "my people enjoin peace, and so do I, unless the enemy is upon the border, and then there should be no peace till he be expelled; nor can I relieve my conscience by sending a substitute in my place, for I would thus only be doing indirectly what the country demands directly of all her citizens. I must, therefore, lay aside the Quaker coat, and shoulder the musket, if the requisition of the draft falls to my lot."

It did; and in 1814 we find him in Captain Halleck's company of Pennsylvania militia, on the march for the defense of Baltimore, which was besieged by British guns. Patriotism had triumphed over religious fealty; the tri-colored cockade usurped the broad brim.

The regiment, however, was countermanded in its march, and he, with the others, was discharged; but for the small service he lived to receive the government bounty in a land warrant of one hundred and forty acres of the public domain—an acknowledgment upon the part of the government of which he was exceedingly proud. And who shall say that vanity, under such circumstances, is not tolerable?

The occupation of a merchant does not seem to have been congenial to him. He pursued it but a short time, and abandoned it, for, to him, the more active and agreeable employment on the farm. And into the business he went with all his energy and indomitable will.

Endowed by nature with an iron constitution, and possessing a frame-work begirt with stalwart thews and sinews, he was prepared to resist ordinary obstacles, and his mind was made up to fight out the great battle of life in a heroic and resolute manner. The marshals of the First Consul, fighting under the eye of their great captain, never entered the field with a more determined purpose to win than did he. And with this fixed and unchangeable determination, you might see him at all hours and seasons, and in all kinds of weather, steadily pursuing his occupation. Entirely temperate in his habits, and eminently moral in all his relations of life, and having a well balanced mind, and much more than ordinary intellect, success was certain.

The early Plymouth men, almost, I may say, without exception, seem to have had a hankering for a share of the broad acres of the great field. Their wealth and social consequence seem to have been measured by the number of acres they could acquire of it. As the wealth and position of the nomadic chiefs of the hills of Judea were estimated according to the number of cattle of their grazing herds, so were these men as to the number of acres they owned of the "Shawnee Flats."

Sharing therefore this feeling of ambition, if not to a greater extent than most of his neighbors, at least to an equal degree with any of them, he deserted the shop, and entered the field of labor, literally, without the least mental reservation. His aim was the acquisition of land; and had he followed out this idea alone, he would have died a man of very large wealth. In the place of leaving for his children thirty or forty thousand dollars, it might have been ten times multiplied.

He was a model farmer; no man understood its theory and practice better. He knew when to sow, and when to reap; how to crop, and the mode and manner of agriculture, from the most important to the smallest details. And his rapid success was an evidence that he thoroughly understood the business. And, as Byron said of George III.:

" A better farmer ne'er brushed dew from lawn."

He possessed a solid judgment, and he came to his conclusions after deep thought and deliberate reflection. He read much in his intervals from his daily toil. Josephus, Rollin, Hume and Ramsay were his standards as to ancient and modern history. Shakspeare, Sir Walter Scott and Burns were his poets. He could almost entirely repeat the "Lady of the Lake," and " Marmion." And the "Cotter's Saturday Night" was his ideal of the master.

Thus reading, and reflecting upon what he had read, there was presented to him an obstacle in his pathway to a liberal fortune. He stopped to consider it, and relaxed his efforts for the addition of acres, and turned his thoughts upon the education of his children.

"Knowledge, if properly applied," he would say, "is of more importance than gold or silver. A stock in trade of education needs no policy of insurance; it cannot be burned by fire; it cannot be encumbered with debts and sold under the auctioneer's hammer; and therefore my sons may choose, at the proper age, whether they will pursue my occupation, or acquire a learned profession."

Adopting, therefore, this idea, and treating it as a fixed fact, he set himself about the work of its accomplishment. To do it, however, must necessarily dispel the hope of becoming rich; the money, therefore, annually laid aside to buy more acres, must now be applied to other purposes. "Boys," he would say (and by the way this was the manner in which he would address us when we were gray-headed men), "boys, it is my purpose, if my life be spared, to give each of you an opportunity of fitting yourselves for the pursuit of a learned profession. While I am entirely satisfied with my own lot in life, I cannot but feel that if I had had a better education, I should have been a happier man. Though as to this, I may be mistaken; for I entertain a greater respect for a first-rate farmer or mechanic, than I do for a second or third-rate professional man. Knowing, therefore, that I am a first-rate farmer, my position is one that I am proud of; and as such, the community respect me. Had I held an indifferent standing in any of the professions, with my ambition, I should not have the same feeling of pride that I now enjoy. Therefore, it is probable that it is all for the best. You must understand, however, that you must thoroughly learn my trade first. For this I have two reasons. In the first place, you will leave me with a fully developed frame, with sinews and muscles matured, and you will thus be prepared for the rough shock of the world, whether in the camp or civil life. All this may be done now, but not after you have reached the years of manhood. In the second place, if you shall not have the talents and ability to sustain yourselves in a learned pursuit, you will have the knowledge of my trade to fall back upon as a reserve, and so be enabled to make a living with the lessons of industry I shall teach you. Bear in mind, too, if you choose a profession, to strive and be at the head of it, or do not make the effort at all. You will, therefore, continue to labor daily in the field by my side, in seed time and harvest; attending the school, at home, during the winter months, till you severally reach the age of eighteen years; by that time you will have matured your physical power, and also have learned my trade; and I hope will also have obtained sufficient knowledge and judgment to decide for yourselves as to your future course. And as you shall then determine, the responsibility must rest with you, not me."

Here is the reasoning of a philosopher, and could not have been improved with the possession of the learning and wisdom of all the schools. Plain common sense, accompanied with a sound discretion, · seldom to be found in a man who had been blessed with so few opportunities in early life.

Acting, therefore, under this advice, myself and two younger brothers, in arriving each at the age of eighteen years, with a pretty good knowledge of the rudiments of learning, acquired during the winter months, in the old Academy, under the tuition of Jonah Rogers, Thomas Patterson, Charles C. Curtis, and Thomas Sweet, as well as a pretty good development of body and frame from the field lessons on Shawnee Flats, went through a classical course of study, and severally became members of the Luzerne county bar. With what degree of success, however, it does not become me to speak. My readers, however, will pardon me in saying of my younger brother, Harrison, now deceased some fifteen years, that a more profound lawyer and jurist, or an abler or more eloquent advocate, never practised law in the courts of the county of Luzerne. He died in the meridian of life, and with the most brilliant prospects of an eminent professional career before him.

While my father professed to belong to the old Federal school in politics, and was a regular reader of the United States Gazette, so long as Mr. Chandler continued to edit that paper, he did not have anything to do, ordinarily, with party affairs. He would generally make his own selections from both party tickets at the polls, and seldom voted what is called a "straight ticket." He was, however, a great admirer of Henry Clay, and whenever the name of this great statesman came before the people, then his energies knew no bounds. In fact all of the old party men of the Federal, or in later days the Whig school, were wonderfully attached to Mr. Clay. They would make any reasonable sacrifice for his advancement, and I have seen many of his old friends and supporters shed tears over his defeat. He was literally the idol of his party, and a more noble and gallant political leader never occupied the commanding position of party ranks. The unkindest remark I ever had from my father, came from him in consequence of some strictures I had made upon Mr. Clay, in a speech, advocating Mr. Polk's election, in 1844. He remarked to me, "that he blushed to be the father of a son who had not the independence of character to sustain such a man as Henry Clay, in preference to a man of the talents and statesmanship of James K. Polk! That no personal benefit could arise to me, if he should by scheming strategy and deception mislead the public mind, and secure the election; of which, in his judgment, there was not the remotest chance."

This language was expressed with much energy and deep feeling, and months elapsed before the impression wore away from the old gentleman's mind. Mr. Polk, however, was elected, and as events turned out, there was a strange reality in the prophecy; for notwithstanding I had been the presiding officer of the boisterous and stormy convention which gave him the nomination at Baltimore, and participated in all the preliminary movements which terminated in his nomination and subsequent success, I was unable to control the appointment of a ten-dollar postmaster, in this district, during his administration of the government.

Meeting, therefore, with this rebuff, after the important relations between him and myself, I must confess that my mind would go back to the expressions made by my father. For I never did know, and do not now know, the cause of Mr. Polk's turning a deaf ear to every suggestion I made to him on the subject of local patronage. A third of a century has however elapsed, and it is now a matter of exceedingly small moment.

My father had a wonderful passion for the drama, and particularly in the representation of the plays of Henry IV., and the Merry Wives of Windsor, in the character of Falstaff. The humor of these plays seemed to have filled full the cup of his enjoyment. In his early days he was in the habit of visiting Philadelphia two or three times a year to purchase the goods for his store. He would attend faithfully to the work of the day, but would always go to the theatre at night, if any play was posted that pleased him. I have heard him say "that if he were in Philadelphia with but two dollars in his pocket, he would spend one of them at the theatre."

This, in fact, was about the only thing in which he was extravagant, and the expenditure of a dollar for any thing else not absolutely necessary, very seldom occurred.

Hospitable in his house, moderately indulgent only to his children, economical in his apparel, though always dressed neatly and becomingly, when not engaged in labor, he may be classed as a man of the strictest economy, and governed by the most rigid rules of frugality; not parsimonious, but prudent and close in his management. To all this, however, he made one grand exception in the expenditures, for a man considering his means and habits of life, in the education of his sons. In this he was liberal to a fault. The ruling and absorbing passion of his early life to become rich, became merged in the nobler and more exalted sentiment of education, and in that moving idea he was most generously seconded by my mother. On that topic they acted in perfect accord, as well as to the full and perfect accomplishment of their purpose. Through years of toil and personal privations they accomplished the object nearest their hearts. And it affords me much satisfaction to record the fact, that neither of them ever expressed a regret for these sacrifices they assumed.

26

Although sectarian in his Quaker creed, the spirit of universal toleration in matters of religion never more eminently shone out in the character of any man. His doors were always open to the visiting clergy, and they were profusely entertained with the best his house afforded. To those of them who were poor and needy, he was liberal. They did not go away without carrying with them some evidence of his generosity.

He was temperate in all things—in his tastes, in his language, and all his habits. I never saw him under the slightest influence of liquor ; nor did I ever hear a profane or irreverent expression escape from his lips.

During the last few years of his life, though in very easy, if not to say affluent circumstances, he would not permit himself to be idle. If he did not take a farming implement in his hands, he would nevertheless spend most of the day in the field, and if a necessity arose, would cheerfully give his aid and assistance.

In the fulfilment of his engagements he was exact, and up to the hour. No man ever had more horror of debt. In the settlement of his estate, and it was a large one, the whole amount of his indebtedness, of his own contracting, did not amount to ten dollars. He avoided the law; and would incur the loss of a small debt sooner than prosecute the claim. He would say to his debtors who had disappointed him, "you have deceived me, but I shall take care that you do not have another opportunity." In his business transactions of half a century, and they were large, I know that an action of law was never instituted against him; nor do I remember of an encumbrance of judgment or mortgage entered against him, or of a suit brought by him. He bought and he paid—and he never bought till he had the means to pay.

He was literally a peace-maker among his neighbors. Frequently called upon to act as umpire in neighborhood disputes and difficulties, he would most generally reconcile the conflicting opinions of the parties who sought his advice and counsel. Understanding the whims, caprices, and peculiarities of the people before him, and knowing how to humor and when to use argument, his strong and well-adjusted mind generally terminated the controversy. I have seen neighbors thus before him, who would refuse to speak to each other civilly when they came, shake hands before they left, and go away apparently the best of friends. He would frequently bring these people in his presence by strategy, and after he had healed up the open wound of dispute, and reconciled them to each other, he would tell them how they had been brought face to face, and for what purpose; and then they would all laugh, and after emptying a mug of cider, all part in merry glee. His judgment fee would generally be "a big apple!" I have seen the parties litigant, on more than one occasion, in the way of carrying out the joke, come afterward and make a formal tender of "the big apple," and demand "a receipt in full of the taxable cost of the case."

The Danes have a law, that is in force in their West India possessions, and probably also with the home government, that no suitor shall be permitted to bring his case into coutr, till he has first made an effort to settle the matter of dispute with his adversary, before a mutual friend or umpire. Might we not improve our own jurisprudence by engrafting this Danish law upon a limb of our legal tree?

And so, in a few paragraphs, I have sketched the outlines merely of a moral, industrious, upright, and exemplary man :

"For even his failings lean'd to virtue's side."

The last acts of his life were in keeping with his previous conduct. But a few days before his death, and when it was manifest that the end was near at hand, some one at his bedside inquired if he would have a minister, in view of religious services? He said, "No; I am not aware that I ever did a human creature a wrong, and I have, therefore, no confession to make; and as to the future, I have an abiding and firm faith in the creed of my fathers. Death has no terrors to me. I rather consider him my friend." And under this state of mind he entered the spirit world.

The expressions are fresh in my memory, and so

they will be while it exists; and I have thought a thousand times how happy a man I should be, if it were in my power, to truthfully utter such a sentiment. in my own case.

He died on the fourteenth day of August, 1855, in his seventy-first year. His remains rest in the Hollenback Cemetery, in the city of Wilkes-Barré.

THE END.